Advance Praise

"No one did more to bring an end to America's cruel and unjust war in Vietnam than the patriotic GIs and veterans who turned against it. This extraordinary history of their struggle should inspire all of us who seek to end the ongoing and interrelated threats of war, nuclear doomsday, and environmental catastrophe."
—**Daniel Ellsberg**, author of *Secrets:*
A Memoir of Vietnam and the Pentagon Papers

"An extraordinary collection of first-hand accounts and unforgettable photos from the rank-and-file soldiers and GI organizers who spearheaded one of the most important yet often overlooked peace movements in U.S. history. Finally, the amazing story is told of how resistance to the Vietnam War from inside the military helped force an end to that tragic imperial conflict."
—**Juan González**, Richard D. Heffner Professor of Communications and Public Policy, Rutgers University, and co-host of *Democracy Now*

"The popular protest and resistance to the U.S. war in Vietnam that developed, most dramatically and effectively, among the soldiers who refused to take part in a criminal war, played a leading role in revealing its horrors. This powerful record of their struggles and achievements is a most welcome contribution, with critical lessons for the future."
—**Noam Chomsky**, author of *At War with Asia*

"*Waging Peace* is an essential reminder of the collaboration between U.S. soldiers and civilians to oppose the Vietnam War. The essays highlight the diversity of the anti-war movement and the war's far-reaching impact on American and Vietnamese lives. It is required reading for anyone seeking to understand the complexities of what it means to be patriotic in a time of war."
—**Heather Marie Stur**, author, *Beyond Combat:*
Women and Gender in the Vietnam War Era

"This collection of first-person accounts and essays on the GI peace movement is long over-due and much-needed. Active duty military men and women, as well as vets from all branches of the armed forces, marched against the War, reported war crimes or refused deployment to Vietnam, risking court martial and sometimes their lives. "For decades after the war, a sort of conspiracy of silence or forgetfulness seemed to erase the significance of these events in helping to end the war," Ron Carver writes. Yet the GI movement was crucial to bringing peace to Vietnam, as this book convincingly shows."
—**Sophie Quinn-Judge**, Fellow, Center for Vietnamese Philosophy, Culture, and Society, Temple University; author of *Ho Chi Minh: The Missing Years*

"To be in a military unit and oppose a war that had the blessing of one American president after another took extraordinary courage—the kind that was displayed by only a few in the Congress and, sad to say, by not many more in the media. The men and women who spoke out, often at great cost, during the immoral and unnecessary war in Vietnam are voices that need to be heard again and again, as they are in *Waging Peace in Vietnam*."

—**Seymour Hersh**, Pulitzer Prize recipient for his journalism exposing the Vietnam War tragedy at the hamlet of My Lai

"*Waging Peace in Vietnam* presents unassailable evidence of the power and reach of the anti-war movement among GIs and veterans during the American War in Vietnam. Its publication could not be more timely. In our age of endless wars, political repression, nuclear peril and environmental crisis, this history of individual moral courage and collective solidarity could serve as a primer for the resistance, a guide to the actions of ordinary citizens— soldiers, veterans, and civilians—that decisively put an end to the war. This book will inform and hearten people of conscience and enliven our sense of what is possible."

—**Carolyn Forché**, author of *What You Have Heard is True: A Memoir of Witness*

Waging Peace in Vietnam

Join the Revolt! was the slogan on a popular poster for the GI Movement (photographer unknown).

Waging Peace in Vietnam

U.S. SOLDIERS AND VETERANS WHO OPPOSED THE WAR

Edited by

Ron Carver, David Cortright, and Barbara Doherty

New Village Press • New York

Published in the United States
by New Village Press
bookorders@newvillagepress.net
www.newvillagepress.org

New Village Press is a public-benefit, nonprofit publisher

Distributed by New York University Press

Paperback ISBN: 978-1-61332-106-5
Hardcover ISBN: 978-1-61332-107-2
EBook ISBN: 978-1-61332-108-9
EBook Institutional ISBN:
978-1-61332-109-6

Publication Date: September 2019

First Edition

Library of Congress
Cataloging-in-Publication Data
Available online at http://catalog.loc.gov

Front cover photo: Image from the Join the Revolt poster for the GI Movement (see frontispiece for the full poster). Photographer unknown.

Back cover poster: Photograph by Richard Avedon. Designed by Marvin Israel. Copyright Darien House, Inc.

Cover design: Lynne Elizabeth

Interior design and composition: Leigh McLellan Design

Excerpts of oral history interviews by Willa Seidenberg and William Short appeared in *A Matter of Conscience*, published by the Addison Gallery of American Art, Andover, MA, 1992.

Chapter 2: Andy Stapp, 1991; Curt Stocker and Tom Roberts, 1990; Lamont Steptoe, 1991; Skip Delano, 1988; Terry Irvin, 1990.

Chapter 4: Dave Blalock, 1988.

Chapter 5: Dave Cline, 1988.

Chapter 6: Dennis Stout, 1989.

Chapter 7: Gerry Condon, 1990; Mike Wong, 1990.

Chapter 8: Clarence Fitch, 1988; Greg Payton, 1988; Keith Mather, 1990

Chapter 9: "Fragging" from *Dien Cai Dau* ©1988 by Yusef Komunyakaa. Published by Wesleyan University Press. Used with permission.

Chapter 10: Carl Dix, 1991; John Tuma, 1987; William Short, 1991

Chapter 11: Charlie Clements, 1988.

Chapter 14: "Taking Portraits and Oral Histories" is an excerpt from *A Matter of Conscience*, used with permission of Willa Seidenberg and William Short.

Chapter 3: Excerpt from *My Life So Far*, by Jane Fonda (New York: Random House, 2005); used with permission of Displaced Films.

Chapter 5: "Protest" was originally published in *Earth Songs: New & Selected Poems*, by Jan Barry (Bloomington, IN: iUniverse, 2003); used with permission of Jan Barry.

Chapter 6: "Making the Children Behave" is reprinted from *Thank You for Your Service: Collected Poems*, by W. D. Ehrhart (Jefferson, NC: McFarland & Company, 2019); used with permission of W. D. Ehrhart.

Chapter 7: "Letter to My Brother From Onondaga County Jail" originally appeared in the journal *Deadly Writers Patrol* (Spring 2018), copyright Gerald McCarthy; used with permission of Gerald McCarthy.

Chapter 9: "Witness in Chains" was originally published in *Dusty Road*, by Lamont B. Steptoe (Camden, NJ: Whirlwind Press, 1995); used with permission of Lamont B. Steptoe.

Chapter 13: "Song of Napalm" was originally published in *Song of Napalm*, by Bruce Weigl, (New York: Grove/Atlantic, 1988); used with permission of Bruce Weigl.

To the millions on both sides,

killed, maimed, and morally

injured by the bullets, bombs,

and chemical weapons

unleashed during our war in

Vietnam. And for people of

conscience now and into the

future who have the courage

to stand against unjust war.

Contents

A Time Line of the Vietnam-Era GI Antiwar Movement

1964   **August.** False claims of North Vietnamese attacks in the Gulf of Tonkin lead to U.S. air strikes and an escalating air war over the coming years that becomes the heaviest bombing campaign in the history of warfare, with more than seven million tons of bombs and ordnance used against Vietnam, Cambodia, and Laos.

1965   Major escalation of U.S. ground troops begins.

   January. Lt. Richard Steinke becomes the first U.S. serviceman to refuse to fight after arriving in Vietnam. In November of that year, Lt. Henry Howe of Fort Bliss, Texas, attends antiwar protest in El Paso and is sentenced to two years of hard labor.

1966   **June.** Pfc. James Johnson and Pvts. Dennis Mora and David Samas—the Fort Hood Three—publicly refuse orders to deploy to Vietnam.

   October. Capt. Howard Levy, MD, refuses orders to train Green Beret combatants at Fort Jackson, South Carolina.

1967   **December.** Andy Stapp and others at Fort Sill, Oklahoma, form the American Servicemen's Union and organize chapters at dozens of military installations and ships.

   Late 1967. *Vietnam GI*, one of the first known GI antiwar newspapers, begins publication. Hundreds of other GI papers appear throughout the military over the next five years.

1968   U.S. troop strength in Vietnam exceeds 500,000. Over the next two years the intensity of combat and casualties among front-line ground units reach levels equivalent to the heaviest combat in U.S. military history.

   January. The first GI antiwar coffeehouse, the UFO, opens near Fort Jackson.

   Summer. Veterans and civilian activists launch the "Summer of Support" project to establish coffeehouses around other military bases. Over the next three years more than two dozen GI antiwar coffeehouses open at Army, Navy, and Marine Corps bases in the U.S. and overseas.

   July. Major racial rebellion occurs at the Fort Bragg stockade in North Carolina.

   August. Soldiers at the Army's overcrowded Long Binh Jail in Vietnam rebel, burning parts of the prison and occupying a section for more than a month.

   October. Navy nurse Lt. Susan Schnall leads GI antiwar march in San Francisco.

   In an incident described by military lawyers as "mutiny," twenty-seven inmates at the Presidio stockade in San Francisco hold a sit-down strike and refuse to report for duty following the fatal shooting of an unarmed fellow prisoner.

1969   **July.** Nixon announces beginning of troop withdrawals.

   Major racial uprising occurs at Camp Lejeune, North Carolina.

   August. A *New York Daily News* headline reads SIR, MY MEN REFUSE TO GO, describing an incident of mass mutiny by an Army unit of the 196th Infantry, one of many examples of combat refusal and avoidance in Vietnam.

October. Soldiers at military bases in the U.S. and in some units in Vietnam join millions of Americans in locally based Vietnam Moratorium protest events.

November. A full-page ad calling for an end to the war, signed by 1,365 active-duty service members, appears in *The New York Times*. Hundreds of active duty soldiers join hundreds of thousands of protesters in the massive November 15 antiwar march in Washington.

1970   Antiwar protest and resistance spread to the Navy as the tempo of naval air operations intensifies along with the scale of U.S. bombing in Southeast Asia.

May. The shooting deaths of two students at Jackson State University in Mississippi and of four students at Kent State University in Ohio touch off a massive wave of antiwar resistance across the country.

Soldiers rally for peace simultaneously at more than a dozen military bases in the first "Armed Farces Day" event.

July. Nearly one thousand mostly black soldiers gather in Heidelberg, Germany, for a "Call for Justice" rally protesting the war and racial oppression.

1971   Antiwar dissent increases in the Air Force as underground newspapers appear at dozens of air bases in the U.S., Europe, and Asia.

The official desertion rate of soldiers going on unauthorized leave for thirty days or more reaches 7 percent of the Army, the equivalent of seventy thousand men.

January. Nixon announces the beginning of the transition to an all-volunteer force.

April. Statements on the floor of the U.S. Senate express concern about fragging as reports multiply of violent soldier attacks against superiors in Vietnam.

May. The second annual "Armed Farces Day" is marked by antiwar protests at dozens of Army, Navy, and Air Force bases.

November. More than a thousand civilians gather at Alameda Naval Air Station to protest the sailing of the USS *Coral Sea* aircraft carrier, as thirty-five sailors stay behind.

1972   **May.** Racial clashes involving hundreds of airmen touch off the largest mass rebellion in Air Force history at Travis AFB in California.

July. Two aircraft carriers, the USS *Ranger* and the USS *Forrestal*, are put out of action by sabotage.

October. A large-scale racial rebellion erupts aboard the USS *Kitty Hawk* while on duty at Yankee Station off the coast of Vietnam.

November. Sailors aboard the USS *Constellation* protesting racial conditions are returned to shore and off-loaded at San Diego. A few days later more than a hundred sailors raise clenched fists at a dockside rally and refuse to board as the ship departs, an incident *Time* magazine calls a mass mutiny.

December. Nixon unleashes massive bombing attacks against Hanoi, Haiphong, and other cities in North Vietnam. Some B-52 pilots refuse to fly and join a lawsuit against the bombing filed by Congresswoman Elizabeth Holtzman (D-NY).

1973   **January.** Paris Peace Accord ending the war is signed.

March. POWs return and the last U.S. ground troops leave South Vietnam.

June. Congress cuts off funding for any further U.S. military action "in or over or off the shores" of Vietnam, Cambodia, and Laos, which takes effect in August 1973.

FINAL ★★★★

DAILY NEWS

NEW YORK'S PICTURE NEWSPAPER ®

8¢

10¢ OUTSIDE L.I. AND SUBURBS

Vol. 51. No. 53   Copr. 1969 News Syndicate Co. Inc.   New York, N.Y. 10017, Tuesday, August 26, 1969★   WEATHER: Mostly sunny, breezy, warm.

'SIR, MY MEN REFUSE TO GO!'

Weary Viet GIs Defy Order

Story on Page 2

NEWS photo by Ed Clarity

Airing His Views? Cable splicer Anthony Ciccone comes out of his manhole just in time to catch a couple of mini-skirted cuties pass at Ann St. and Broadway yesterday. Ciccone was coming up for a breather as the 94-degree heat at 2:20 p.m. made life miserable for most of us. Mini-happy returns, Tony. —*Other pictures in centerfold*

Dissent and Resistance Within the Military During the Vietnam War

David Cortright

One of the least-known but most important chapters in the history of the Vietnam antiwar movement was the rebellion of troops within the military. In June 1971, the prestigious military publication *Armed Forces Journal* published an article, "The Collapse of the Armed Forces," which stated: "The morale, discipline and battle worthiness of the U.S. armed forces are, with a few salient exceptions, lower and worse than at any time in this century and possibly in the history of the United States."[1] A year later, the eminent military sociologist Morris Janowitz seconded that analysis, declaring, "The military establishment, and especially its ground forces, are experiencing a profound crisis in legitimacy due to the impact of Vietnam, internal racial tension, corruption, extensive drug abuse, loss of command and operational effectiveness, and widespread antimilitary sentiment."[2] In virtually every corner of the military, the burden of fighting an unpopular and unwinnable war led to dissent, social disruption, and institutional decay.

Opposition to the war within the military can be classified into two broad categories: dissent and resistance. The dissenters were part of what became known as the GI movement: soldiers publishing "underground" newspapers, signing antiwar petitions, attending protest rallies, and engaging in various forms of public speech to demand an end to the war. The resisters were those who defied military authority, disobeyed orders, went absent without leave, committed acts of sabotage, refused combat, and in some cases violently attacked their own officers and sergeants.[3]

In 1970, the Army hired social science researchers to survey soldiers at several military bases and determine the extent of antiwar opposition. One quarter of the soldiers interviewed admitted to engaging in acts of antiwar dissent, defined as participating in a protest, going to an antiwar coffeehouse, or reading a GI antiwar newspaper. The researchers also asked soldiers about acts of disobedience, such as disobeying orders, insubordination, or sabotage. Here again they found one quarter of interviewees admitting to such acts.[4]

Similar conclusions were reached by historian Richard Moser, who conducted an assessment of the scale of the GI dissent and resistance for his book *The New Winter Soldiers*. After reviewing a number of studies and surveys of soldiers and veterans conducted during the war years, Moser offered the "conservative estimate" of approximately 25 percent of low-ranking service members participating in antiwar activity. These figures are roughly equivalent to the proportion of activists among students at the peak of the antiwar movement.[5] In the rural and conservative communities adjacent to large military bases, the proportion of antiwar activists among soldiers was higher than the antiwar proportion in the local youth population.

Dissent

Antiwar groups emerged within the enlisted ranks and among junior officers throughout the military during those years. They appeared first in the Army and Marine Corps in 1968 and spread to the Navy and Air Force in 1970. The major expression of antiwar sentiment in the ranks was the GI press, the underground newspapers that were published by service members on nearly every major U.S. military base and on many ships throughout the military. In my research for *Soldiers in Revolt,* I identified more than 250 separate GI newspapers and estimated the total number at approximately 300.

Antiwar protests and acts of resistance occurred at or near many military bases in those years. These included demonstrations and vigils and the circulation of antiwar petitions. The most famous petition appeared as a full-page ad in *The New York Times* the week before the historic Moratorium Mobilization in Washington, D.C., on November 15, 1969.

As the GI movement spread, civilian supporters and recent veterans helped the movement by creating GI coffeehouses outside major military bases. At these places, antiwar soldiers could escape military life and exchange ideas freely. The coffeehouses featured free coffee, live music, counterculture posters and newspapers, and antiwar literature and artwork. They also served as centers of political education and antiwar organizing.

Resistance in the Army

One of the most common and significant forms of GI resistance was absence without leave. Absentee and desertion rates during the Vietnam War soared to record levels. The desertion rate in the Army increased 400 percent between 1966 and 1971.[6] In 1971, the AWOL rate in the Army (those absent from duty for fewer than thirty days) was 17 percent, affecting one of every six soldiers. The official desertion rate (those absent for more than thirty days) was 7 percent. This meant that more than seventy thousand Army soldiers deserted that year, the equivalent of several divisions. Desertion rates also rose in the Marine Corps, reaching 6.5 percent in 1972. Vietnam-era desertion rates were three times those of the Korean War.[7] The massive wave of AWOL and desertion during the war deprived the military of about one million person-years of service.[8] As Moser wrote, this widespread unauthorized absence of troops "forcibly curtailed military capabilities and contributed to the aura of chaos that hung over the armed forces by the early 1970s."[9]

It is important to note that these soldiers did not desert under fire. Almost all desertions occurred on bases in the United States or in Germany or Korea. The desertion rate among troops in Vietnam was lower than elsewhere and was especially low within combat units.[10] This was not because of any enthusiasm for the war but, rather, due to the absence of routes of escape.

Incidents of organized dissent within Vietnam itself were relatively rare, but acts of direct resistance were pervasive and tore at the very fabric of military capability. By 1970, the Army and Marine Corps in Vietnam were experiencing what I call the "quasi-mutiny": widespread defiance, intentional incompetence, and other forms of noncooperation that effectively crippled the military's operational capacity.[11] Historian Richard Moser called this the "grunts' ceasefire": acts of resistance by a significant minority of troops that undermined the military's ability to wage war.[12]

According to former Army combat commander Shelby Stanton, thirty-five incidents of combat refusal occurred in the Army's First Cavalry Division during 1970.[13] Stanton found this information by examining the internal unit archives of the division. Some of the incidents involved entire units. This was an extraordinarily high number: an average of three combat refusals per month in just one division. If we extrapolate the experience of the First Cavalry to the other six Army divisions in Vietnam at the time, we arrive at a total of more than two hundred combat refusals. The Marine Corps probably experienced a similar number of incidents. Whatever the exact number, it is likely that hundreds of mutinous events occurred in the latter years of the war. When commanders sent their units into the field, they could not be certain that the troops would follow orders. In the face of such widespread resistance and noncooperation in the ranks, U.S. combat effectiveness melted away.

Acts of direct resistance were pervasive and tore at the very fabric of military capability.

Resistance in the Navy and Air Force

Protest and resistance in the Navy were most pronounced aboard the giant aircraft carriers that were the backbone of the Navy's assault against Vietnam. Throughout the war, three carriers were normally on duty at Yankee Station, in the Gulf of Tonkin, conducting air strikes and bombing runs. When the air war intensified in 1972, as many as six carriers, half of the Navy's fleet, were assigned to bombing operations. This led to a significant wave of dissent and sabotage on several major carriers.

By 1971, acts of sabotage by crew members against their own ships became a serious problem in the Navy. Figures supplied to the House Internal Security Committee investigation of subversion within the military listed 488 acts of "damage or attempted damage" in the Navy during fiscal year 1971, including 191 incidents of sabotage, 135 arson attacks, and 162 episodes of "wrongful destruction."[14] The House Armed Services Subcommittee investigating disciplinary problems in the Navy disclosed "an alarming frequency of successful acts of sabotage and apparent sabotage on a wide variety of ships and stations."[15]

Antiwar opposition in the Air Force intensified in December 1972 as the Nixon administration unleashed a massive B-52 bombardment of Hanoi and Haiphong. The extensive Vietnamese air defense forces in the two cities shot down dozens of the bombers and accompanying fighter-bombers, resulting in the deaths of more than one hundred crew members and the capture of forty-four prisoners of war.[16] Some B-52 bomber pilots began to question their mission, and several refused to fly further missions on moral grounds. Two of the pilots joined Congresswoman Elizabeth Holtzman of New York in filing a lawsuit to challenge the constitutionality of the continued bombing of Cambodia.[17]

Bombing continued for a few months after the signing of the Paris Peace Accord in January 1973, but the Air Force announced a reduction in the number of missions in May 1973 because of Pentagon worries about a "deepening morale crisis" among B-52 pilots and crews, according to a *Washington Post* report.[18] The Air Force was saved from the deepening crisis when Congress voted to prohibit any further U.S. air or ground operations in Vietnam, and bombing operations finally came to a halt that August.

Conclusion

It is arguable that by 1970 U.S. ground troops in Vietnam had ceased to function as an effective fighting force. The disintegration of military morale was a factor in the Nixon administration's decision to accelerate troop withdrawals.[19] Senior officers, from Chief of Staff William Westmoreland on down, were arguing for a faster pullout.[20] One of the strongest advocates for rapid withdrawal was Secretary of Defense Melvin Laird, who reportedly returned from an inspection tour of Vietnam in early 1971 "shocked and distressed" by morale problems and in favor of faster force reductions.[21] Laird recognized, his biographer wrote, that the war was "destroying the U.S. military." The "often unwilling" soldiers who fought the war were increasingly "demoralized by jungle warfare, dissipated by readily available drugs [and] torn by racism on the job." Faced with this crisis in the ranks, "Laird saw his mission as no less than the salvation of the U.S. military."[22] The only way to accomplish this was to pull out the troops and end the war.

Revisionist historians argue that the military was winning the war in Vietnam and that it was a "stab in the back" by politicians and the media that caused U.S. defeat. This ignores the fact that many within the military opposed the war and were increasingly unwilling to fight. Antiwar dissent and resistance were pervasive by the latter years of the war and were eroding the military's will and ability to engage in further combat. To save the Army, it became necessary to withdraw troops and end the war. The dissent and defiance of troops played a decisive role in limiting the U.S. ability to continue the war and forced an end to the fighting.

Early Resisters

An American in Paris: An Appreciation for a Nascent Movement

Linda J. Yarr

Paris, 1969: At the height of the war, my Vietnamese friend Thông gave me a book with an inscription: "Long live the Friendship, the Solidarity and the brotherhood of the Great American People and the Vietnamese People." Those words were emblematic of the oft-expressed policy of the Democratic Republic of Vietnam (DRV) and its southern arm, the National Liberation Front of South Vietnam (NLF). Throughout the conflict the Vietnamese have dubbed the "American War," their public pronouncements maintained a clear distinction between the United States government, which was waging an unjust war, and the American people, who might be persuaded to see the war as nothing more than imperial overreach or misguided fealty to a Cold War ideology.

Four years earlier, as a French major in college, in 1965, I was eager to set off for France after graduation. Mixing with students of all nationalities, it was not long before I was confronted by the question, "What are you Americans doing in Vietnam, anyway?" Implicit from the French was the sentiment, "We tried to hold Vietnam and failed; what makes you think you could do better?" Students from Algeria, Chile, and Senegal schooled me in the anticolonial, or anti-neocolonial, struggles of their compatriots and expressed solidarity with Vietnamese people who were fighting for their own independence. They saw this American student as a representative and beneficiary of U.S. policies.

To be honest, I didn't have a clue about Vietnam. I was absorbed by the writing of Hugo, Flaubert, and Balzac. But the Vietnamese students I met were different. They were the sons and daughters of parents who lived in South Vietnam but had gravitated to student associations in France that actively supported different sides in the conflict: the Democratic Republic of Vietnam in the north, the Republic of Vietnam (RVN) in the south below the seventeenth parallel, or the collection of nonaligned peace groups known as the

Third Force. Curious to learn more about what was happening in Vietnam, I invited some of the Vietnamese students to a dialogue with American students residing in the U.S. house on the international student campus, the Cité Universitaire. The event had to take place outside the campus because events dealing with politics were not allowed at the student residence. The Vietnamese students impressed me with their openness, candor, and willingness to answer questions calmly, despite what was obviously an emotional experience—reviewing the events of a war in their homeland.

The quest to learn more about Vietnam and my country's actions there led me to the Paris American Committee to Stop War, a group of American longtime expatriates, one of whom had been honored by the French government for her service to the Resistance during World War II. Joining protests, drafting petitions, and interacting with other peace activists in France, the group also crossed paths with activists who were dedicated to helping draft resisters and antiwar GIs based in Germany to travel to Sweden in search of a safe haven.

Two decades earlier, America's efforts to shape the government of Vietnam had begun with U.S. funding for France's post–World War II campaign to reassert colonial rule. It continued with the CIA's installation of Ngo Dinh Diem as the president of the new Republic of Vietnam in 1955. By 1965, domestic opposition to these policies began to coalesce when the Students for a Democratic Society (SDS) rallied in Washington, D.C., in April 1965. The rally was modest in size, but it was a harbinger of the larger movement that would follow.[1]

Once the Johnson administration began escalating deployment of ground troops and committing them to offensive action, America's peace groups began to build a mass peace movement, but they struggled to avoid being seen as unpatriotic or unconcerned with the safety and security of our own troops.

The early GI resisters offered an opportunity to support people in the military and gave an inspirational spark to the wider movement. Soon after Donald Duncan resigned as an Army officer in protest over the war, in September 1965, he began speaking before peace groups and in front of antiwar rallies across the country.[2] This was just five months after the SDS rally the previous spring.

In June 1966, JJ Johnson, David Samas, and Dennis Mora became the first three soldiers to publicly refuse to deploy to Vietnam. After they received their orders they went immediately to New York and approached Dave Dellinger, chairman of the Fifth Avenue Peace Parade Committee, for support and strategic advice. The Peace Parade Committee called a press conference and later mobilized peace groups throughout the country to support the "Fort Hood Three" and other resisters.[3]

Later, when Capt. Howard Levy refused to train Green Beret combatants in basic dermatology, the Peace Parade Committee called for his release on bail, while using his image in handcuffs to inspire tens of thousands of New Yorkers to march against the war.[4]

Lt. Richard B. Steinke

US Officer Refuses to Serve in Vietnam

A United States Special Forces army officer, Lieutenant Richard B. Steinke of Milwalkee, was convicted on June 25 by a court martial at Naha, Okinawa, of refusing to join a special forces counter-guerrilla unit in South Vietnam.

The following day, June 26, Steinke was sentenced to a discharge from the service and stripped of all pay and allowances. He also could have been sentenced to five years' imprisonment with hard labor, but was not.

The charges arose when Steinke refused to go to special forces camp Gia Vac in the north central part of Vietnam last January 31. Lieutenant Steinke said he refused to serve because he disagreed with United States policy in Vietnam and felt that the war there "is not worth one American life."

Various senior officers failed to sway the Lieutenant's announced decision not to go. He was examined by an army psychiatrist in Saigon, who said the Lieutenant was legally sane but experienced "difficulty getting adjusted." Steinke tried to resign his commission to avert court-martial.

Under cross-examination, Steinke's commanding officer said that 20 other soldiers in Steinke's political administration of combat areas course were also unenthusiastic about being transferred to teams in remote areas, but "all the other men obeyed the orders."

Included among the charges Steinke was convicted of was "wilful disobedience to expose himself to hostile elements and hazardous conditions."

Lt. Steinke is 27-years old and graduated in the top 10 per cent of the West Point class of 1962. He is married with a one-year-old daughter.

Firm rejects Vietnam War Contract

Opposition to the Vietnam war spread to the business community during the spring when a California electrical equipment manufacturer rejected a government contract awarded to his company to supply generator plants for the war effort.

F.J. Galland, president of the Galland-Viller Manufacturing Co. of Berkeley, announced that his firm would no longer supply any equipment for South Vietnam "until such time as we may become convinced that such action would aid in the peaceful development of that area." Galland, whose company was the low bidder on the contract for 1,500 watt generator plants, said he was aware of the penalties for rejecting such a contract but added: "An examination of conscience has led us to the conclusion that we can no longer participate in any way in furthering the war in Vietnam."

The government responded with threats to sue for damages against the firm. But Galland instructed his Saigon representative to remove Galland-Viller's name from all bid and procurement lists, and said: "To continue to profit as businessmen for assisting this war would place us in a completely unacceptable moral position in relation to our own standards .... We are firmly convinced that this war ... is not in the best interests of the Vietnamese people nor ultimately in the best interests of the US."

Project '65 at Comox

At 10 am on June 5 a group of 40 young people sat down before the gates of Comox Air Base in protest against the military policy of Canada.

The sit-down, blocking 5 of the 6 entrances, continued for 12 hours. The action was preceded by a rally in Victoria, B.C. addressed by Dr. Brock Chisholm, and a 140 mile peace walk from Victoria to the RCAF base.

A surprising 500 people attended a public meeting two days after the arrival of the walk in the Comox area.

Encouraged by the good public response, before and after the action, the participants organized a 6 hour combined teach-in and sit-down at the gates of the air base on July 18.

Work in the community is continuing and plans for a third action August 28 – 29 lasting from 32 to 48 hours are being made. The project is publishing its own news bulletin. For details write to: Comox Project 65, Gen. Del. Courtenay, B.C.

In January 1965, Lt. Richard Steinke became the first U.S. serviceman to refuse to fight after arriving in Vietnam. In November of that year, Lt. Henry Howe of Fort Bliss, Texas, attended an antiwar protest in El Paso and was sentenced to two years hard labor.

The war resistance within the U.S. military took many forms, as narrated in this volume—beginning with Duncan, Levy, and the Fort Hood Three's resistance. Around the country, producers of the underground press took great risks to disseminate news of dissent. Growing ranks of draft resisters, deserters, and veterans returned from the war to tell the truth about the actions of American soldiers in Vietnam. Opposition to the war from within the military gained momentum and was both supported by and helped to fuel the civilian peace movement.

I returned to a United States roiled by antiwar activism in which military symbols had pride of place, such as a rally with draft-card burning at Columbia University, where veterans discarded their medals.

Enrolled as a graduate student at Cornell University to study Vietnam more deeply, I joined the campus chapter of the Committee of Concerned Asian Scholars. CCAS was founded in 1968 to offer a critical perspective on mainstream studies of Asia, and began to publish articles and pamphlets and to hold teach-ins aimed at telling the truth about the war that was spreading from Vietnam to Laos and Cambodia. Its journal, the *Bulletin of Concerned Asian Scholars*, continues to this day as *Critical Asian Studies*.

War resisters within the military and veterans who had direct knowledge and experience of the war provided the peace movement with concrete evidence of both the cruelty and futility of the war effort. Civilian peace activists mobilized for mass protests, petitioned their Congressional representatives, wrote letters to editors of the local and national press, published research on Vietnam, Laos, and Cambodia to uncover the falsehoods uttered by military and political leaders to justify the war, and provided financial and moral assistance to war resisters. "Waging peace" within the military and by civil society was a richly textured movement that brought together many segments of American society, a fact that is little known in the United States but is amply recognized by the Vietnamese, even as many still suffer from the legacy of the war.

'The whole thing was a lie!'

Donald Duncan

One of the first axioms one learns about unconventional warfare is that no insurgent or guerrilla movement can endure without the support of the people. While doing research in my job as an area specialist, I found that, in province after province, the Viet Cong guerrillas had started as small teams. They were now in battalion and regimental strength. Before I left, the Viet Cong could put troops in the field in division strength in almost any province. Such

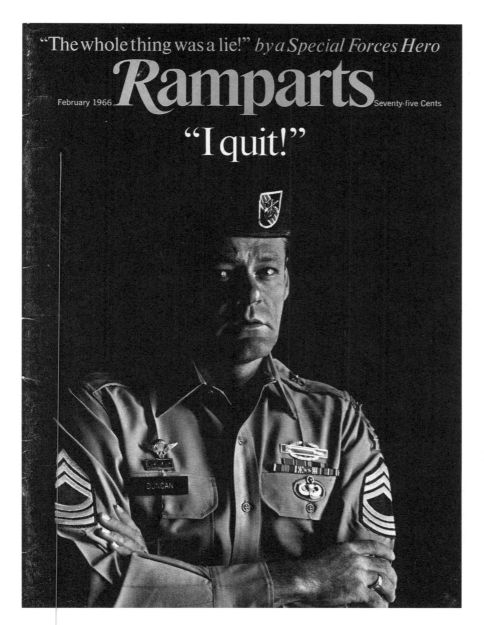

"The whole thing was a lie!" *by a Special Forces Hero*

Ramparts

February 1966   Seventy-five Cents

"I quit!"

A highly decorated Green Beret, Donald W. Duncan was one of the first American soldiers to publicly expose U.S. war crimes. Disgusted by the military's policy of using South Vietnamese troops to torture and murder captured liberation soldiers, Duncan refused a promotion and quit the Army. Duncan traveled across America, visiting GI coffeehouses and helping to build the GI antiwar movement. Source: *Ramparts*, February 1966.

growth is not only impossible without popular support; it actually requires an overwhelming mandate. . . .

The Viet Cong soldier believes in his cause. He believes he is fighting for national independence. He has faith in his leaders, whose obvious dedication is probably greater than his own. His officers live in the same huts and eat the same food. His [Saigon] government counterpart knows that his leaders are in their positions because of family, money, or reward for political favors. He knows his officers' primary concern is gaining wealth and favor. Their captains and majors eat in French restaurants and pay as much for one meal as they make in a week. . . . He has had so many promises made to him, only to be broken, that now he believes nothing from his government. . . .

The whole thing was a lie. We weren't preserving freedom in South Vietnam. There was no freedom to preserve. To voice opposition to the government meant jail or death. . . .

It's not democracy we brought to Vietnam—it's anticommunism. This is the only choice the people in the village have. This is why most of them have embraced the Viet Cong and shunned the alternative. The people remember that when they were fighting the French for their national independence it was the Americans who helped the French. It's the American anti-Communist bombs that kill their children. It's American anticommunism that has supported one dictator after another in Saigon. When anti-Communist napalm burns their children it matters little that an anti-Communist Special Forces medic comes later to apply bandages. . . .

You knew what they wanted you to do [with the prisoners]—get rid of them. I wouldn't do that, and when I got back to operation base a major told me, "You know we almost told you right over the phone to do them in." I said that I was glad he didn't, because it would have been embarrassing to refuse to do it. I knew goddamn well I wasn't going to kill them. In a fight it's one thing, but with guys with their hands bound, it's another. . . . The major said, "Oh, you wouldn't have had to do it; all you had to do was give them over to the Vietnamese [ARVN]." Of course, this is supposed to absolve you of any responsibility. This is the general attitude. It's really a left-handed morality. . . .

I had to wait until I was thirty-five years old, after spending ten years in the Army and eighteen months personally witnessing the stupidity of the war, before I could figure it out. . . . Those people protesting the war in Vietnam are not against our boys in Vietnam. On the contrary. What they are against is our boys *being* in Vietnam. They are not unpatriotic. Again, the opposite is true. They are opposed to people, our own and others, dying for a lie, thereby corrupting the very word democracy. . . .

In my final weeks in [Vietnam], I was putting out a very small information paper for Special Forces. On the last page of the first issue were the names of four men—all friends of mine—reported killed in an action on the same day. To those friends, I wrote this dedication: "We can best immortalize our fallen members by striving for an enlightened future where Man has found another solution to his problems rather than resorting to the futility and stupidity of war."

Excerpted from "The Whole Thing Was a Lie," by Donald Duncan, *Ramparts*, February 1966.

The Fort Hood Three

On June 30, 1966, three Army soldiers created a turning point in the broader antiwar movement when they announced that they were refusing orders to deploy to Vietnam. Pvts. David Samas and Dennis Mora and Pfc. James Johnson had made their decision after being stationed together in Georgia and later at Fort Hood, Texas. In mid-July, on their way to speak about their decision before an audience of eight hundred at a public event in New York City, the Fort Hood Three were whisked away by police to McGuire Air Force base, adjacent to Fort Dix, New Jersey. They were later court-martialed, and each served time at Fort Leavenworth federal prison. The actions of the Fort Hood Three helped to forge an enduring alliance between antiwar GIs and the civilian antiwar movement that encouraged thousands more GIs to join the resistance.

If a small nation can overcome, perhaps we can, too

JJ Johnson

No, Sir.

Those words, uttered more than a half century ago, prevented my complicity in a war of aggression that my comrades Dennis Mora, David Samas, and I branded as immoral, illegal, and unjust.

History records that the Fort Hood Three's refusal to deploy to Vietnam was significant because it was one of the first and because we three represented, to a certain degree, a cross section of the nation—one white, one Latino, and one African American. And because we announced beforehand our intentions to disobey and allied ourselves squarely with the antiwar movement, our actions represented a significant political protest.

But each soldier must grapple with his conscience individually. Indeed, before we were driven to McGuire Air Force Base, each of us was told that the others had already boarded the plane and were on their way to Vietnam. So, let me briefly explain how I came to my decision.

On draft day, December 6, 1965, my opinion about the war was not yet formed. I later befriended Dennis Mora, who had refused to step forward for the oath at the Army induction center. Fortunately, we were in the same unit for advanced training, where we formed a Vietnam study group. Dennis's movement connections proved invaluable, as was David Samas's perpetual sense of humor.

Before then, from the first day of reception at Fort Jackson, South Carolina, I understood that the treatment—or more correctly, abuse—of the GIs

BRING THE TROOPS HOME NOW
NEWSLETTER
VOL 1 NO 12   JULY 11, 1966   10c

RH
WLI
D909
v.1,12

IN THIS ISSUE:

- **Vietnam : Renewed Escalation**
- **Canada's Anti-War Movement**
- **GI's Fight Viet Duty**

In 1966, Dennis Mora, David Samas, and JJ Johnson (left to right) became known as the Fort Hood Three for their refusal to deploy to Vietnam.

was designed not to train us to promptly obey orders as essential preparation for combat. Instead, I was convinced that our mistreatment was more about crippling us intellectually, shutting down our reasoning so that we would be prepared to follow along blindly.

I began to view the recent rebellions in our nation's ghettos and the emergence of a counterculture in a different light. Civil liberties and civil rights were in the air and I was being ordered to march in lockstep in the opposite direction. My decision not to take part in our nation's aggression was aided enormously by a mighty support system. My mother, who had a sixth-grade education, did not hesitate to raise her voice on my behalf. My brother threw himself into the antiwar movement. My sisters stood unflinchingly by my side. My father, an active trade unionist and a self-avowed liberation theologian, also bravely joined the fight.

The antiwar movement, of course, lifted us up and amplified our voices. The three of us, rather than moderate our stance to gain more favorable treatment after our court-martial, drew from that support to grow stronger and more resolute. Muhammad Ali's induction refusal and Dr. King's decision to oppose the war further validated our stance. Ali drew the connection between Vietnam's national liberation struggle and black equality when he famously said, "Why should a black man go kill innocent yellow people? No Vietcong ever called me nigger."

What we had learned earlier in our study group was being whispered and then shouted throughout the armed forces. The embers of military resistance seemed to burst into flames. That mood was also evident at Leavenworth, where newsreels accompanied weekend movie screenings. When news of U.S. military setbacks in Vietnam were reported, Leavenworth prisoners jumped up and cheered. The newsreels were discontinued.

Another indicator of the raging opposition to the war was the rise of the prison population from about five hundred when the three of us entered in 1966 to more than fifteen hundred when we left about two years later.

A powerful factor in my refusal and ability to remain steadfast was the Vietnamese people. Of all the material that circulated in our study group, I was most impressed by the writings of Ho Chi Minh. I learned that his name means "he who enlightens." And that he did.

I also saw his example in the courage and leadership of his people. The three of us concluded that if a small nation without the wealth, firepower, and resources of the most powerful nation on the globe can overcome, perhaps we can, too.

I traveled to North Vietnam in 1969 as part of a peace delegation that accompanied U.S. POWs home. I found my Vietnamese brothers and sisters to be among the gentlest people I had ever met, as well as the fiercest fighters. I was moved by their warm embrace and undying solidarity.

Today, I continue to draw strength from their example. I do not pretend to have the answers to our common struggle for a world of peace, justice, equality, and environmental sustainability.

But through it all, I remain optimistic and continue to fight for a world in which Mother Earth's bounty will be shared by all. I quote Indian author and activist, Arundhati Roy: "Remember, we are many and they are few. Another world is not only possible, she is on her way. On a quiet day, I can hear her breathing."

On Dissent, Vietnam, and Fake History

Howard Levy

Years into the "War on Terror," the United States is still involved in Iraq, Afghanistan, and more than sixty other countries in a strategically wrong and unwinnable campaign. I oppose our policy now, as I did in the 1960s, when I was a doctor serving in the U.S Army. I felt compelled then to oppose another ill-advised and, as it turned out, unwinnable war.

My actions got me sentenced to prison, where I served twenty-six months. By the time I got out, the civilian movement against the war in Vietnam had exploded across the country, and tens of thousands of Vietnam veterans and

The court conviction of Dr. Howard Levy transformed him into a martyr, which helped increase the growth of both the GI antiwar movement and the broader peace movement.

DR. LEVY BEING LED FROM COURTROOM AFTER SENTENCING

Dr. Howard B. Levy was drafted into the U.S. Army in June, 1965. He refused to train Special Forces aidmen—medically-trained Green Berets—because, he said, they use medicine primarily for political and military, not medical, purposes. Dr. Levy refused to commit what he felt would be a violation of international laws—including the Nuremburg decisions and the Geneva Conventions of 1949—and of his medical ethics. This led to his court-martial, and on June 3, 1967, he was sentenced to three years at hard labor.

The verdict is now being appealed by Levy's lawyers, but the appeal could easily take the length of the sentence. Meanwhile Dr. Levy is in jail, and the army refuses to release him on bail. Public pressure may persuade the Army to grant bail to Dr. Levy until his appeals are completed.

Free Dr. Howard Levy, Capt., U.S. Army. Demand His Immediate Release on Bail!

No More Hiroshimas! End the War in Vietnam Now! Bring Our Boys Home Alive!

Join With Thousands of New Yorkers to Commemorate HIROSHIMA DAY, and to Protest Dr. Levy's Confinement! Demand That Dr. Howard B. Levy Be Released on Bail Pending Appeal!

Sponsored by: Fifth Avenue Vietnam Peace Parade Committee
Co-Sponsors: New York Medical Committee to End the War in Vietnam
Veterans and Reservists to End the War in Vietnam
Veterans for Peace in Vietnam
Vietnam Veterans Against the War
Student Mobilization Committee to End the War in Vietnam

Saturday, Aug. 5th
*ASSEMBLE: 12 Noon, Columbus Circle
WALK: Down Broadway
RALLY: 2 P.M. Bryant Pk. (42nd St. & 6th Ave.)

* Doctors and nurses please wear professional attire.

clip and send to: Fifth Avenue Vietnam Peace Parade Committee
17 East 17th Street, N. Y., N.Y. 10003
Phone: 255-1075
..... I enclose $..... to support Dr. Levy.
..... I want to help.
..... I want more information on Dr. Levy's case and on
the War in Vietnam. $ .50 enclosed to cover costs.
name .... phone ....
address .... zip ....

active troops had built the largest antiwar movement within the military in U.S. history.

I was a medical student in dermatology in 1961; at that time the military was drafting young doctors. I agreed to join but deferred my service until I could finish my residency in 1965. During that four-year wait the war in Vietnam escalated and so did my conviction that it was morally wrong. I vehemently opposed the war, but I still intended to honor my commitment and do my job.

When I finally entered the Army, I was stationed at Fort Jackson, in South Carolina. In my free time I joined a local voter registration drive in the town of Prosperity, an hour from the base.

My civil rights work, and my experiences inside the Army, showed me just how rampant racial injustice was, as black soldiers suffered disproportionately in combat and stateside. Also painfully clear was the toll the war and the draft were taking on working-class Americans, who were being sacrificed as cannon fodder to bolster President Lyndon Johnson's false narrative that the war was just, and could be won.

On base I was assigned to train Green Berets in simple dermatology treatments. It became clear to me that the Army was developing ploys like this to "win hearts and minds" in Vietnamese villages—while still burning them to the ground in search-and-destroy missions. This is an unethical, political use of medicine, because Green Berets are combat soldiers, not medics. Schemes like this threaten the loss of international codes of protection for all medical providers. Thus Doctors Without Borders and similar organizations have come under military attack in recent years when asked to do the bidding of the American military.

When I refused to continue instructing the Green Berets, the Army brought charges and I was convicted of disobeying an order, promoting disloyalty and disaffection among troops, and conduct unbecoming an officer and gentleman. My effort to put the war on trial failed when the military court said the truth is no defense.

I was convicted but not silenced. Even as the trial unfolded, as I walked the two hundred yards past the Fort Jackson barracks to the clapboard Army courthouse, I was greeted by soldiers, black and white, showing their support with raised fists and peace sign salutes.

My own case was an early one of that era, so it got a lot of attention. The Fort Jackson courtroom was filled with reporters from around the globe. The Army hoped that parading me in handcuffs would intimidate and silence GI dissent. But the tide of GI resistance was building and kept swelling, until it affected military strategy and helped end the ground war.

The real crime is that the Pentagon has commissioned academics to rewrite the history of the Vietnam War. The military lied then and you can bet will lie again in an attempt to eradicate the memory of the GI antiwar movement.

This is an unethical, political use of medicine.

Dr. Howard Levy was convicted for refusing to train Green Beret Special Forces combat soldiers in medical procedures the troops would use to pacify villagers in Vietnam.
Source: Everett Collection Historical/Alamy Stock Photo.

This book and the "Waging Peace" exhibit offer a long-overdue tribute honoring GI antiwar protestors, past and present. Among the source materials documenting the soldiers' revolt is a trove of documents from the Wisconsin Historical Society's GI Press Collection—a digitized compilation of hundreds of newspapers, written and distributed by active-duty GIs who opposed the Vietnam War.

Future historians choosing to ignore the GI movement will find their reputations in tatters.

Writing for Peace: The GI Press

A Vital Wing of the Larger GI Movement

Derek Seidman

The last half decade of the U.S. war in Vietnam saw an historic phenomenon: a wave of antiwar newspapers, circulated across the globe, published by and for the American GIs who were angry at having been drawn in to fight the war. These papers came to be known by a few terms: the GI underground press, the GI antiwar press, or simply the GI press. They were a vital wing of the larger GI movement against the Vietnam War.[1]

The GI press was made up of scores of antiwar newspapers that were oriented toward active-duty U.S. service members. The total number of the papers can never be known for sure, but credible estimates range from 144 to nearly 300.[2] In part, the GI press was inspired by the explosion of the 1960s alternative press—papers such as the *Berkeley Barb,* the *Los Angeles Free Press,* and *The Great Speckled Bird* in Atlanta.[3] The makers of the GI press sought to bring this new media into the military to reach U.S. soldiers—and, hopefully, to help those soldiers build a bridge to the antiwar movement.

The papers spoke the everyday language of the rank-and-file GI, and they served as a voice for draftees and enlistees who, under the constraints of military service, had little. They often carried irreverent titles that mocked the war and the military—*A Four Year Bummer, Kill for Peace,* and *Green Machine*, for example. Perhaps the most biting title in the GI press was *Fun Travel Adventure,* or *FTA,* which mocked one of the Army's recruitment slogans and riffed on a widespread, darker GI sentiment, "Fuck the Army."

Their pages were filled with critical news about the war, cartoons that lampooned the military leadership, updates about soldier protest, and information on where GIs could find legal help. Most of all, the GI press promoted a wider narrative for soldiers to connect with: one that opposed the war, lambasted the army brass, and offered identification with and participation in a worldwide movement of GI dissent as a response.

Newspapers Written by and for America's Soldiers

More than three hundred antiwar newspapers were published throughout the world by and for U.S. active-duty soldiers on military bases and ships from 1968 through 1972. These newspapers expressed the voices of hundreds of thousands of soldiers and junior officers who spoke out against the war and against injustices and racism within the military.

The GI underground press arose in 1967 and flourished for several years. The first paper was probably *Vietnam GI*, which was started by Jeff Sharlet, a Vietnam veteran. Sharlet wanted to reach soldiers and veterans with an antiwar perspective, written by their peers. The paper was an immediate smash hit with GIs, who responded with hundreds of letters. "What impresses most of the guys is that *Vietnam GI* is written to us," said one letter, "the first termers and lower rank enlisted men, not the lifers." [4] Another widely read and prominent early GI paper was *The Bond*, which became the paper of the American Servicemen's Union—a group of radical antiwar soldiers led by Pvt. Andy Stapp that wanted to unionize lower-ranking GIs.

Into the early 1970s, the GI press exploded, with dozens upon dozens of papers—some short-lived, some lasting for years—flourishing across the United States, Europe, and the Pacific Rim. One paper, the *Stuffed Puffin*, was even published in far-off Iceland.

The contents of the GI press spoke to the disenchanted soldier. The papers criticized the war and mocked the "lifers" who commanded GIs (the title of one fleeting paper out of Fort Leonard Wood was *The Pawn's Pawn*—one of many that railed against the class divide in the war and the army's authoritarian culture). Papers criticized racism in the military and U.S. society, and analyzed the racist and imperialist nature of the Vietnam War. Many contained hilarious features, such as a regular contest for "Pig of the Month" or "Lifer of the Month." In one case, the "winner," a despised officer nominated by the readers, was awarded a well-ripened set of pigs' feet. [5]

Active-duty GIs were central to the production and distribution of the GI antiwar press. Every paper had its own local context. Some were produced for a single base and some aimed at a global readership; some were more radical and hard-edged, while others relied on the language and visuals of the hippie counterculture. There were reports of the rare paper being produced in the lower decks of ships, and even in Vietnam. But typically, the papers were put together—columns penned, articles and letters collected, visuals laid out, and the whole thing usually mimeographed—by a combination of GIs, veterans, and antiwar civilians. The papers were aided financially by a network of civilian-backed fund-raising efforts. One prominent organization that raised hundreds of thousands of dollars for GI papers and coffeehouses was the United States Servicemen's Fund.

Once printed, the papers would be circulated on military posts and in surrounding towns, as well as in transport hubs like bus stations, and in GI antiwar coffeehouses where service members congregated. Soldiers across the United States, Europe, the Pacific, and Southeast Asia requested bundles of different papers, which they would distribute in mailrooms, mess halls, and barracks. This was a key way that GIs from all over the world were able to join the GI movement—by interacting with and spreading the contents of the GI press.

The news reports in the GI press also inspired soldiers to take action. Papers contained stories about antiwar protests across the country, some

A Crisis in Legitimacy

"The military establishment, and especially its ground forces, are experiencing a profound crisis in legitimacy due to the impact of Vietnam, internal racial tension, corruption, extensive drug abuse, loss of command and operational effectiveness, and widespread anti-military sentiment."

Morris Janowitz, "Volunteer Armed Forces and Military Purpose," *Foreign Affairs,* April 1972.

staged by soldiers specifically, others by the wider antiwar movement. The papers also promoted upcoming local and national protests, and covered causes célèbres—stories of the national and global heroes of the GI movement whose actions and arrests grabbed media headlines. By reporting on protests involving GIs at other bases, the papers also encouraged soldiers to create their own.

It's worth noting that troops who produced and circulated the GI press took serious risks. They could face harassment, punishment, and even time in the stockade if they were caught spreading material that was considered subversive. Skip Delano was stationed at Fort McClellan, Alabama, and was a key organizer in the GI organizing efforts there. Delano and others put out a paper called *Left Face*. He recounts elsewhere in this volume:

> *We'd have to spend a fair amount of time figuring out how to get the paper out, into hands of people on the base. You'd sneak around at night and you'd run in barracks and you'd throw it on the beds and you'd split and get the hell out of there. I can remember running out and jumping into the trunk of a car and laying in the trunk; the MPs would come and you would be hiding in the trunk of some cars and hoping you wouldn't get caught. Because if you got caught, you could get six months in the stockade, the potential punishment for distributing unauthorized literature, which the papers were characterized as.* [6]

Along with production and distribution, the very act of reading and writing for the GI press was a way that thousands of soldiers across the world could plug into a movement of global GI dissent. Letters to specific papers brimmed with readers' words of praise, stories of perceived injustices at their own bases, countercultural musings about love and peace (and sometimes drugs), and updates on their own GI organizing efforts. These letters are windows into an otherwise-lost world of Vietnam-era soldier dissent that had the GI press at its center.

For example, *The Ally*, a paper produced in Berkeley and circulated globally for years, with a print run in the thousands, received hundreds of letters in which GIs described their feelings about the war, the military, and their attempts to help build the GI movement. From Korea to the Philippines, from Long Binh to Da Nang, and from bases across every U.S. region, GIs sent letters describing local protests, paper-distribution efforts and run-ins with the brass, and offered critical riffs on the war and the military. [7]

Like many other papers, *The Ally* would print these letters in its pages (in a section called "Sound-Off!"—the paper's most popular feature). These printed letters showed readers that they were not alone in their thoughts— that GIs all over the world felt as they did. In this way, the GI press functioned as the "social media" of its day and, like the GI antiwar coffeehouses, was a core vehicle for the advancement of the wider GI movement.

By the early to mid-1970s, the GI press was in decline, though some papers would continue operations for years after the Vietnam War ended. In today's Internet age, the power of the GI press lives on—not so much in the print press that the GI movement used, but in blogs, social media accounts, and podcasts by antiwar military groups and individuals who draw inspiration from the history of soldier dissent during the Vietnam era.

The story of the GI underground press is a testament to the scope and dynamism of the historic wave of soldier dissent during the Vietnam War. Fortunately, through the digital GI Press Collection compiled by James Lewes and made available online by the Wisconsin Historical Society, scholars, journalists, activists, and others now have access to an extensive archive through which we can continue to explore the history of the GI movement.[8]

Curt Stocker and Tom Roberts, 1990.
Source: Photo by William Short.

'We even had a little darkroom in our room'

Curt Stocker and Tom Roberts

Tom: Curt and I had only known each other for one day in Vietnam and less than a day at Fort Carson, in Colorado Springs, when we decided to start a newspaper.

Curt: I had some copies of a battalion newspaper from Vietnam called *Dimension*, which, it turns out, Tom had started before I got there and that I had become editor of. And in the course of talking about the war and our experiences and what are we doing here and what are we going to do about it, we thought, Let's start a newspaper, because there isn't one here.

Tom: I think we were catalysts on each other.

Curt: I was intent upon showing up at Fort Carson and saying, 'I quit.'

Tom: Or being a conscientious objector.

Curt: Or making some kind of a major stink. I was pretty pissed about the whole thing and fresh off the boat. I was ready to go in there and do something very radical. I hadn't really quite figured out what yet.

Tom: And I said, "Well Curt, if you're going to become a CO, it's really pretty meaningless. We should do something else. I'm not sure who came up with the idea of actually doing a newspaper first, but it came up, and once it came up, I think we just hopped on that idea. We said, "Yeah, that's it, a newspaper. We know how to do it; we've done it."

Curt: So, we immediately got into it. It was August 9th we got the first issue out. The name just came to me, "*aboveground*." Someone was saying, "Hey, you're going to do an underground newspaper." And I said, "No, we're going to be totally aboveground." That's how the name came about.

FTA was published by GIs at Fort Knox, Kentucky. Source: GI Press Collection, Wisconsin Historical Society.

Tom: Within two days, I think, after we distributed it, they had us on the carpet. Military Intelligence. They summarily transferred us. We had been roommates and it was real easy for us to bat around ideas and put out the newspaper. In fact, we even had a little darkroom in our room.

Curt: We were industrious little investigative reporters; wrote some really good stories, actually, while we were there. We caught this general who was the commander of the post flying helicopters without a pilot's license. When we were ready to run that one, they sent the FBI around to see our printer down in Colorado Springs and basically threatened to shut him down. The printer wouldn't print it.

Tom: He goes, "Well, the Army came in here and the FBI and they wanted proofs and this 'n that and they wanted to see the thing and it was just too much of a hassle and we're just not going to do it." But there was a lot of press coverage about that incident and an editor and publisher of this paper in Littleton, Colorado, offered to print the newspaper for us. He said, "I disagree with what you guys are saying about the war, but I believe absolutely in your right to say it without interference from the FBI or from Military Intelligence."

Tom: And money became a concern. But for the third issue a woman that I ran into kept us going. Her husband had just been killed in Vietnam through friendly fire, and she donated enough money for one issue from the GI life insurance policy that she got. And the United States Servicemen's Fund was the single biggest contributor.

Curt: We did stuff in the paper with curfews and issues that affected soldiers. And we found out about this plan for military interdiction in civilian activities, like big demonstrations and Kent State. It was code-named "Garden Plot," and it had to do with Fort Carson soldiers being in a position of readiness to be dispatched anywhere.

Tom: We broke that story in *aboveground*, and at least a year later it made front-page news. We scooped it by a year.

Interviewed 1990 by Willa Seidenberg and William Short

'Since I had been in Vietnam, I had every right to comment on it'

Skip Delano

Skip Delano, 1988.
Source: Photo by William Short.

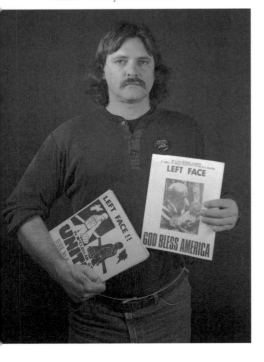

I joined the Army in February 1967. I got to Vietnam in May, and by August I was very clearly against the war and against the military, as well. I think for most soldiers, going to Vietnam and seeing the reality of the war, all this Mickey Mouse bullshit, as the whole army was, to actually be in the middle of a war where hundreds of people were being killed every day, it was just incomprehensible to most of us. I think most of us just immediately opposed that, and maybe our understanding of why we opposed it wasn't as sharp as it might have been, but just on a gut level. Having been raised like myself, a Presbyterian, and being active in the church in the area I grew up in, it just wasn't right, what was going on in Vietnam. While I was in Vietnam, I didn't see any way to take action against the war, so my own response was basically to withdraw from any kind of overt activity that promoted the war.

I came back very committed to fighting this whole machine that sent us there and kept us in Vietnam. I came back with six others who got assigned to Fort McClellan, Alabama—this is where I had taken my training to be a chemical repairman before going to Vietnam. We decided we wanted to try to take some action against the war and decided to put out a paper. I started

Last Harass was published by GIs for Peace at Fort Gordon, in Augusta, Georgia. Source: GI Press Collection, Wisconsin Historical Society.

going up to Atlanta, where there was very vibrant youth culture on the streets and an underground newspaper called *The Great Speckled Bird*. I got in touch with some people there who turned me on to somebody who could print the paper for us, and met a guy, another GI, who had some experience writing and working on a college paper.

Somehow it all just came together and we started putting out a paper, which we called *Left Face* because, I guess, though we were all pretty inexperienced with politics, it was real clear that our views were always to the left and that's where we were looking to—the Left. We'd have to spend a fair amount of time figuring out how to get the paper out, into the hands of people on the base. You'd sneak around at night and you'd run in barracks and you'd throw it on the beds and you'd split and get the hell out of there. I can remember running out and jumping into the trunk of a car and laying in the trunk; the MPs would come and you would be hiding in the trunk of some cars and hoping you wouldn't get caught. Because if you got caught, you could get six months in the stockade, the potential punishment for distributing unauthorized literature, which the papers were characterized as.

Immediately after we put out the first paper, in late October of '69, about thirty of us on the base signed a petition being circulated by the GI Press Service in support of a demonstration coming up on November 15th in Washington. As soon as it appeared in *The New York Times*, it was sort of like all hell broke loose on that base because people's names were on that ad. Everybody who signed it got called in by Military Intelligence and interrogated and harangued and people lost their security clearances and things like that. I thought and believed very much that since I had been in Vietnam, I had every right to comment on it to other people. In fact, I had a responsibility, and I took it seriously. I thought it was my democratic right to speak out, and I was really shocked to find out that wasn't reality or freedom in America.

Interviewed 1988 by Willa Seidenberg and William Short

'They hauled us off singing "America the Beautiful" '

Terry Irvin

GI Alliance and the GI-Airmen-Sailor Coalition had joined forces at Fort Lewis and McChord Air Base in Washington. In 1971, we decided a fun thing to do for the Fourth of July would be to pass out copies of the Declaration of Independence on base. Somebody found a copy of the Declaration of Independence and said, "Have you ever read this thing? This is really great stuff." And so we underlined things we wanted highlighted:

> *"certain unalienable Rights, among these Life, Liberty and the pursuit of Happiness . . . That whenever any Form of Government becomes destructive of these ends, it is the Right of the People to alter or to abolish it, and institute new Government . . . it is their right, it is their duty to throw off such Government, and to provide new Guards for their future security. . . . He has erected a multitude of New Offices, and sent hither swarms of Officers to harass our people and eat out their substance. He has combined with others to subject us to a jurisdiction foreign to our constitution. . . . For imposing Taxes on us without our Consent: For depriving us in many cases, of the benefit of Trial by Jury"*

Terry Irvin, 1990.
Source: Photo by William Short.

—which was a big complaint of ours. Military justice is almost as big an oxy-moron as military intelligence.

We went to the main PX on payday, when everybody would be there. There were probably a dozen GIs and three or four civilians. Word got out within twenty minutes and the MPs show up, swarms of them all over us. I was hauled off with my friend Henry Valenti and somehow we ended up having these leaflets with us. We were throwing them out of the window of the cop car as they hauled us off singing 'America the Beautiful.'

We were charged with distributing unauthorized literature on base. It hadn't been approved by the brass. We had tried and tried to get approval to

> Dear friends —
>
> Just a bit of news to let you in on what happens quite often here at Rig Headquarters (HHD, 18TH MP Bde), Long Binh On Memorial day of this year several of the "lower EM" decided to have a war protest parade in the company area. Since the folks at home have the privledge of parading in their hard hats and T shirts, then we felt i was appropriate to express our sentiments against the war in the same manner.
>
>   The results: 8 Art. 15's
>   The offense : Disturbing the "Peace".
>
> Can you dig that. We had a parade in VN and got "busted for "disturbing the peace". What can I say   — FTA !
>
>   Sp 4
>   getting short & getting OUT
>
> *Please withhold the name.

A soldier's letter from Vietnam to the GI underground paper *The Ally*: "Can You Dig That? We had a parade in Vietnam and got busted for disturbing the peace. What can I say—FTA." (FTA was a widely used expression by disgruntled GIs, meaning "Fuck the Army!")

distribute the *Lewis-McChord Free Press* on base and could not do it. Hell, they had skin magazines that were ten times more offensive than anything we put out, and they were everywhere. So why couldn't we put out our newspaper on base? I was the only guy who didn't take an Article 15; I decided I was going to fight this. I said I wanted to waive trial and elected to go to a general court-martial.

Now, in the meantime, the press is having a field day with this. We got on Walter Cronkite; we were his closing story on the *CBS Evening News,* this group of GIs that was arrested for passing out the Declaration of Independence on the Fourth of July at Fort Lewis. And the brass's response to this was that all the charges had been dropped and "just pay no attention to these

> January 3ʳᵈ, 1971
>
> Sir,
>
> We, the undersigned, are writing in request of editions of your paper. We would like as many copies over a hundred as possible. They will be distributed between two companies here in Chu Lai, South Viet Nam.
>
> We believe that "The Ally" is of tremendous value in the fight against "the pigs" in the military and are enclosing a $12⁰⁰ contribution. We will send more later.
>
> Keep up the good work!
>
> Steve R. Marston
>
> P.F.C. Frederick J. Horton

This letter was written to the staff of *The Ally* underground paper by GIs stationed in Vietnam: "We would like as many copies over a hundred as possible. They will be distributed between two companies (of soldiers) here in Chu Lai, South Vietnam."

people, we're not going to press charges." Yet I'm still up for general court-martial, facing three years in Leavenworth.

Finally, I went to see my lawyer, and he said, "Something very interesting has happened. They can't come up with any witnesses that said they saw you passing these things out. They have no proof against you." Now, like I said, we had these pamphlets with us in the police cars, in the jail cells; we're shoving them through the bars of the jail cell, passing them out to the MPs there in the Provost Marshall's Office. But they couldn't come up with a witness who said they'd seen me doing this? . . . So they dropped the charges.

Interviewed 1990 by Willa Seidenberg and William Short

the Ally

A NEWSPAPER FOR SERVICEMEN

INT. INSTITUUT
SOC. GESCHIEDENIS
AMSTERDAM

No. 10   October, 1968   FREE to GIs   Box 9276 Berkeley, Calif.

Brass helpless

GI's TO MARCH; THIS TIME FOR PEACE

A1C Michael Locks, 2Lt. Hugh Smith, and A1C John Bright at a press conference concerning the march. If they can openly organize and publicize this march, so can you. March with them or telegraph support.

IT IS ABSOLUTELY LEGAL FOR GIS WEARING CIVILIAN CLOTHES TO MARCH IN THE GIS AND VETS MARCH FOR PEACE ON OCTOBER 12.

IT IS YOUR RIGHT AND MORAL DUTY TO DEMONSTRATE.

ONLY THEN WILL THE PUBLIC KNOW OF THE SOLDIERS' CONCERN.

ONLY WE CAN END THIS WAR.

LET THE ONES WHO MUST DIE FOR PEACE, WAGE PEACE ALSO.

—Lt. Hugh Smith

It's LEGAL to march

"Members of the Armed Forces are entitled to march on October 12 if they wish to. This is a Constitutional right. If the Armed Services take any action against any active or inactive member of the Armed Forces the full weight of the 123-man Lawyers Selective Service Panel will be used in their behalf."

—Statement of San Francisco attorney Aubrey Grossman.

If you are prevented from marching or threatened with reprisal, call Ed Grogan, Esq. (415) TH 5-2825. He will assign a lawyer to your case. If you have a dime for the phone, you have enough money.

Lt. Smith and other active duty GIs and Bay Area veterans are giving servicemen an excellent opportunity to express their disapproval of being sent to fight an immoral, unjust, and unnecessary war in Southeast Asia. If every anti-war GI will utilize this chance, it will do more to end the war than all the diplomats with all their conferences and plans.

This march is being watched by the brass all the way up to the Secretary of Defense. It is going to end once and for all their baloney about how GIs are eager to go to Nam. This march has made the brass afraid of the GI. That is rare and that is something which no GI can allow to slip by unexploited.

Early in the year, some GIs at Ft. Jackson tried to hold a pray-in for peace at the post chapel. The MPs arrested them and it hurt the Army's "image" far worse than if the pray-in had taken place. The brass had to drop all charges. Now they know better than to arrest people who are engaged in perfectly legal protest.

The march is perfectly legal and the brass can't do a thing to stop GIs from organizing it or marching in it. They are trying to ship Smith to Formosa on September 30th. It remains to be seen if they will be successful. They gave A1C Michael Locks and A1C John Bright, two other organizers, orders to ship to Utah two weeks ago, but backed down after Locks and Bright sought a federal court injunction against the obviously punitive order. Lt. Smith's case is in the courts and it is unknown as we go to press if he will be shipped out or not. THE MARCH WILL TAKE PLACE REGARDLESS.

GIs in uniform and in civilian clothes will head the parade. They will be clearly identified as active duty servicemen by banners and by "GI for Peace" hats (for those in civilian clothes). GIs will be followed by reservists, veterans, and civilians, in that order.

If you are restricted to base or if you're too far away to join the march, you can still make it a success. Send a letter or telegram to GIs and Veterans March

(Continued on Back Page)

More GI's Resist

As election time approaches resistance increases. This seems to be the development, anyway. But none of the major presidential aspirantees offer any pledges for the GI — none intend to give him any when elected.

LBJ 12 STILL HANG ON

A dozen black GIs are still holding out and controlling one section of the Long Binh stockade. "No force or threat of force has been used against them," a spokesman said. "They are receiving food and water and can rejoin the other prisoners whenever they decide to cooperate."

FORT HOOD 43 MINUS 7

To date twelve of the forty-three black GIs who refused riot duty in Chicago have been court martialed. Seven have been convicted of "disobeying an order to report for reveille," and the others won acquittal. The harshest sentence was as follows: six months at hard labor, forfeiture of pay for six months, and reduction to the rank of Pvt.

Ever since the soldiers were first taken into custody the brass was very careful not to charge any with mutiny or desertion. Other members of the mass refusal were returned to the control of their commanding officers and received no punishment whatsoever.

AWOL ARMY OFFICERS NABBED IN SAN FRANCISCO

Two absent Army officers, Lt. James Anderson, and Lt. Robert Harris, both stationed at Fort Campbell, Kentucky, were recently apprehended in San Francisco, California, by MPs. The following punishments were given to them: Anderson, loss of two-thirds pay for three months; Harris, loss of two-thirds pay for six months, and six months confinement.

The commissioned GIs had been gone for three weeks and wanted to file as conscientious objectors to war requesting discharge. Lt. Anderson was permitted to file after returning to Ft. Campbell. They are being represented by attorney Whitworth Stokes Jr. of Nashville, Tennessee.

Another Letter from LBJ

Dear Editor,

Don't get me wrong about RA. I'm only two years, at least at first I had 2 years to go. I'm from Cleveland, Ohio. And I just got out of LBJ. It's a long story to tell you about how I got in. But I'm out now. Here is my story about LBJ.

I'm a Soul Brother and I left LBJ on the 4th of September with only 17 days to go. I'm not past my DRO's until September 14, they won't let me go home. I'll leave here December. LBJ is not a place where you can say you are in jail. Up in LBJ you go through many different changes. I had 4 months to do and if you are good they give you five days good time for every month.

This is true. At first I was up for a 212 which means out of the Army, but they said LBJ is best for me. We get up at 4:30 every morning. Chow is from 5 to 6 and at 7 we go out for work call with guard. It's two sides to LBJ. I call it a good side and a bad side. We have roll call three times a day and the only thing that is good about LBJ is when you get short. For chow it's like shit, one glass of milk,

It was like this on the night they burned LBJ down... I don't know the right time but I think it was about 12:30. At first I didn't know what was wrong, but everybody was up and running for help; it started from the bad side up to the Box. Oh yes, the Box is out of sight. It's like being in jail in jail; it's a trip. Everything was burning down. Mess hall and all the buildings where we sleep. They read your mail (outgoing and incoming). How can a GI win. I realize I did something wrong to get in jail. But I'm happy it burned down. This is one thing the Army is paying for. One captain died and about 10 others were killed in the fire.

Well, sir, I will write you more because I'm a jazz fan.

Long Binh

P.S. Long Binh is over; no more jail. Oh yes, most of the Soul Brothers are still together on the bad side; they won't leave. It's about 20 CIDs on this case but they will never find the real truth in it or how it began. Take my word on this because I don't know how it started myself. They have three in the box for killing.

VIETNAM DUTY UPHELD

Justice John M. Harlan refused to halt a Marine reservist's assignment to Vietnam pending a Supreme Court decision on whether to hear the Marine's suit challenging the legality of his call to active duty.

The appeal of Paul V. Winters was turned down even though two groups of reservists have won reprieves from Justice William O. Douglas in similar cases. "I

Continued Pg. 6

ATT'Y AUBREY GROSSMAN

EAST COAST MARCH

As the Ally goes to press, we have information of another GI march for October 12th.

The Servicemen's Peace & Freedom League is planning to march on the White House at the same time that West Coast GIs will be marching in San Francisco.

East Coast GIs should contact Gil Sierra, 1854 Wyoming St., N.W., Washington, D.C. 20009, or District of Columbia peace groups.

Inside this Ally...

U.S. elections: ALLY comments...p.2+3

A WAC speaks...p.8

SUPREME COURT and the MARCH...p.7

'I wanted to go in the Army— to organize it'

Andy Stapp

In 1965, four of us burned our draft cards and got booted out of Penn State. I remember feeling that the U.S. was committing war crimes and a draft card was like a South African pass card by the very fact they said you could get five years in jail for burning it . . . a piece of paper. I wanted to go in the Army—to organize it.

At some point in training, the Army figured out I had burned my draft card and was a left-wing radical. They thought I should have my own room, but they couldn't give a private his own room. That's only for officers. You just can't isolate somebody in the Army; it's all collective labor. So they put guys around me they thought were the most Army type. Well, they were just the first two guys won over. And together we had a lot of success in the barracks, putting up antiwar literature everywhere. So much so that the Army went after us to stop it.

They figured out all the literature was in this footlocker of mine. This lieutenant came in, took the lock off, and when I came out of the bathroom, he was going to order me to empty the locker. Well, another guy saw what happened, and he went and put his lock on it while the lieutenant's back was turned. And they got this sergeant—who was very antiwar; I knew him well—and this colonel says, "Chop open his locker." And right in front of the colonel, this sergeant looked over at me like, Should I chop it open; is it okay with you? And I say, Go ahead; it's all right. So I was court-martialed for that, disobeying a direct order to open the locker.

I got in touch with the Emergency Civil Liberties Committee. ECLC was set up in the 1950s because the ACLU wouldn't defend Communists. ECLC sent out a shotgun press release about the court-martial that went to every left-wing group in the country. So a whole bunch of radicals descended on Fort Sill, just to make the Army's life even more hellish.

The battalion I was in was ordered to Vietnam without me. I just got transferred to another unit. They transferred me a lot. I was court-martialed again and acquitted. So then the Army just said, "We'll charge him with treason—causing or attempting to cause insubordination, disloyalty, and refusal to duty among members of the armed forces." The trial was on the first day of the Tet Offensive. I remember picking up the paper and seeing that sixty towns were attacked.

It took about two months to really get the trial going. In the meantime, we began putting out a newspaper called *The Bond*. And during Christmas leave I came up to New York and met GIs from nine different bases, and we set up the American Servicemen's Union (ASU). We had ten demands: an

Andy Stapp, 1991.
Source: Photo by William Short.

Facing page: The Ally was published by service personnel and supporters in Berkeley, California. Source: GI Press Collection, Wisconsin Historical Society.

RAP! was published by antiwar soldiers stationed at Fort Benning, Georgia, and their civilian supporters. Source: GI Press Collection, Wisconsin Historical Society.

Gigline was published by GIs at Fort Bliss, in El Paso, Texas. Source: GI Press Collection, Wisconsin Historical Society.

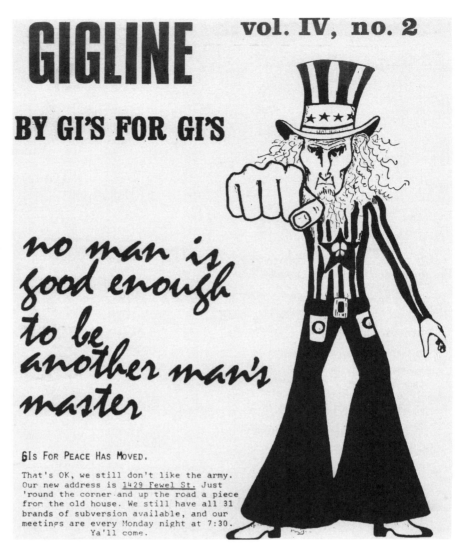

end of racism in the Army; the right to refuse illegal orders, like to go fight in Vietnam; rank-and-file control of court-martial boards; end of saluting and "sir"-ing of officers; no troops against antiwar demonstrators; right of free political association. Over a five-year period, the ASU had twenty thousand members, but not more than ten thousand at once. We had ASU chapters on about one hundred installations in the U.S. and about sixty ships.

Whatever the verdict was in my treason trial was secret, but it goes up higher to see if it's confirmed or not. And then I was discharged, with about two weeks left to go. This lieutenant drove me to the gate, and he said, "I am happy, Private, and I'll tell you why I'm happy—because I get to be the guy that tells General Brown that you're no longer in the Army." He was laughing and he said, "I want to tell you if you step one foot back on this base from this moment, you'll get six months in prison."

Interviewed 1991 by Willa Seidenberg and William Short

'Writing helped turn me from that violence'

Lamont Steptoe

The racist comments by the veterans who were training us in Officer Candidate School (OCS) — them saying the word *gook* and mocking Vietnam as a "live fire" problem — made me uncomfortable. An incredibly high percentage of Afro-Americans in the infantry were dying on the front lines. As these statistics about blacks in Vietnam began to roll in, I would talk to other black GIs returning from Vietnam. They would tell me stories about the unity of blacks in Vietnam, and all of this made me think.

I was called before a board of officers for my complaining about being treated a certain way by some of the cadre because I was black. The officers

Lamont Steptoe, 1991.
Source: Photo by William Short.

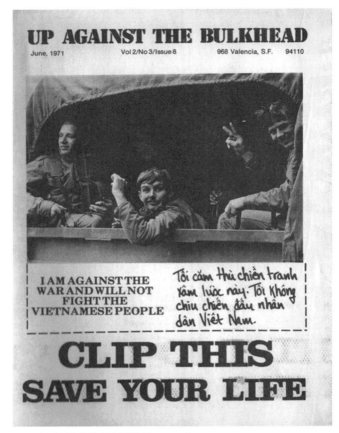

UP AGAINST THE BULKHEAD was written by war veterans and civilian supporters in San Francisco and distributed to thousands of military personnel on bases throughout Northern California. Thousands of copies were also mailed to soldiers in Vietnam. Source: GI Press Collection, Wisconsin Historical Society.

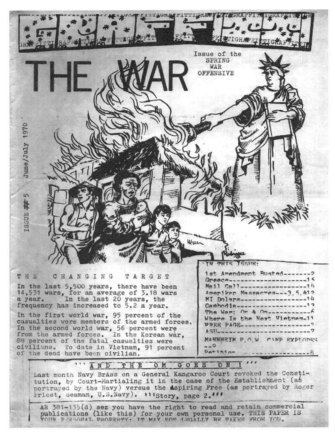

Graffitti was published by GIs in Heidelberg, Germany. Source: GI Press Collection, Wisconsin Historical Society.

were sitting there denying that there was any racism, despite me telling them over and over about instances where I felt I was treated differently than the white soldiers. Repeatedly all the white officers told me there was only one color in the military: olive drab.

I began to have a bad attitude. Sixteen of us resigned from OCS, all within two weeks, because we just didn't want to take it anymore. We were told that if we quit OCS, we would be punished. And they kept their word. If you fucked up in OCS, they sent you to a leg unit.

I got orders for a scout dog unit, which meant that I was going to walk point in Vietnam. I was freaked-out, terrified of dogs. There were very few blacks in scout dogs. I guess I was lucky, because they could have sent me straight to a military unit, to the front lines, where I would have spent 364 days in the field. But with a dog, the max time on a mission is seven days, because that dog's worth thirty thousand dollars and they care more about that dog than they do you. But it was a very dangerous job.

I'll never forget the look on a family's face when we searched a village one time and this lieutenant ordered me to kick in the door. On the other side was a family eating dinner. My dog jumped on the table and the family was terrified and shrank back against the wall. We ransacked the house and

The Whig was published by Air Force personnel at Clark Air Force Base in the Philippines. Source: GI Press Collection, Wisconsin Historical Society.

decided they had too much rice, so we took it. Things like that began to bother me and I began to be very angry toward the military and what we were doing.

I read the *Autobiography of Malcolm X* in Vietnam and it had a very strong effect on me. I wrote home and told my mother that I was going to become a Muslim after reading that book. It really gave me a sense of where I stood in relationship to the military, in relationship to America. I began to identify with the Vietnamese. The hooch girls would tell me, "You same— same us." I began to have this feeling for the Vietnamese people. I felt I was living this contradiction of being a black soldier in the land of another man of color and terrorizing him. I never allowed myself to call them gooks. Muhammad Ali said it so clear, " No Vietcong ever called me nigger."

On the anniversary of the assassination of Malcolm X, I convinced the other blacks in my unit to turn out with black armbands. It polarized the unit, because the white soldiers were taken aback. There were only a few of us blacks and [the white guys] thought we were friends. And we were in a sense, but they really didn't understand the politics of it as deeply as we did.

When I got back from Vietnam, I was very, very militant. But because I believed, and still do, that the pen is mightier than the sword and because I didn't want to just end up as a front-page lurid headline and break my mother's heart, writing helped turn me from that violence.

Interviewed 1991 by Willa Seidenberg and William Short

WITNESS IN CHAINS

I SAW

A BROTHER DRAGGED

BACK TO THE WAR

IN CHAINS

TWO WHITE MP'S

CRACKING HIS HEAD WITH STICKS

STOMPIN' HIS RIBS

WITH BRILLIANT BLACK BOOTS

CUSSIN' AND SWEARIN'

SWEATIN' LIKE THEY WAS

TUSSLIN' A HOG

I SAW

A BROTHER DRAGGED

BACK TO THE WAR

AT TAN SON NHUT AIRPORT

FIGHTIN' LIKE A HOOKED CARP

IT CROSSED MY MIND TO SHOOT

THE RED NECKED MILITARY POLICE

(A BLACK TURNCOAT EXCUTED AT DAWN)

IN ANOTHER LIFE

I SHOT THEM

Lamont B. Steptoe

Resistance HQ: GI Coffeehouses

3

Fueling Dissent

David Parsons

The individual and collective acts of resistance that became known as the GI movement coincided with the acceleration of American military action in Vietnam.

From the case of the Fort Hood Three—the 1966 arrest of three GIs for publicly declaring their opposition to the war and refusal to deploy—to the case of Dr. Howard Levy, an Army dermatologist who refused his assignment to provide medical training for Special Forces troops headed to Vietnam, by 1967 it was clear that antiwar sentiment was growing among American soldiers. The U.S Army, where the vast majority of draftees were being sent, was fast becoming the central site of an unprecedented uprising.[1]

The war was not the only issue aggravating American GIs. The military's pervasive racial discrimination, from unequal opportunities for promotion, to unfair housing practices, to persistent harassment and abuse, fueled increasing outrage among black GIs as the war progressed. The civil rights and black liberation movements had a profound influence on many black soldiers, who took part in widespread and diverse acts of resistance throughout the Vietnam era. Evasion, desertion, and insubordination rates among black GIs exploded in the war's later years. With an antiwar movement in the military capturing national headlines by 1968, black soldiers were often its vanguard.[2]

Antiwar soldiers and veterans had an electrifying effect on the imagination of civilian antiwar activists, some of whom saw great potential in a rebellion of America's armed forces and became interested in supporting and expanding the GI movement. Among them were Fred Gardner and Donna Mickleson, who opened the first GI coffeehouse in Columbia, South Carolina, outside of Fort Jackson, in fall 1967.[3] One of the Army's central training installations for soldiers headed to Vietnam, Fort Jackson had significant political, economic, and cultural influence in the city of Columbia. Gardner had been an Army reservist and understood the often-narrow range of

> **Coffeehouses became critical support institutions where active-duty soldiers, veterans, and civilian activists met to plan demonstrations and publish underground newspapers.**

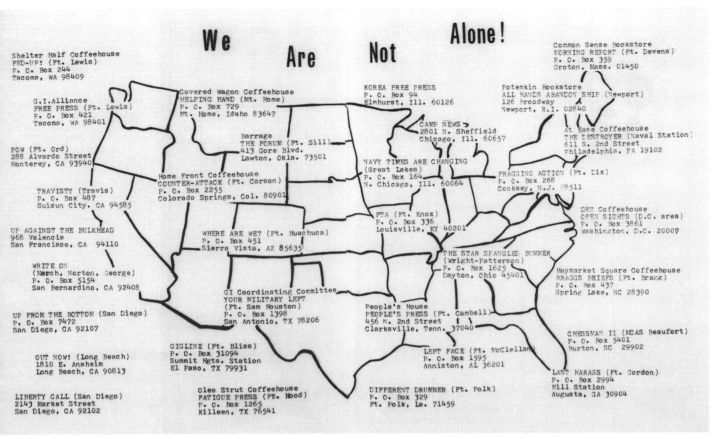

We Are Not Alone!

Shelter Half Coffeehouse
FED-UP! (Ft. Lewis)
P. O. Box 244
Tacoma, WA 98409

G.I. Alliance
FREE PRESS (Ft. Lewis)
P. O. Box 421
Tacoma, WA 98401

POW (Ft. Ord)
288 Alvarado Street
Monterey, CA 93940

TRAVISTY (Travis)
P. O. Box 487
Suisun City. CA 94585

UP AGAINST THE BULKHEAD
968 Valencia
San Francisco, CA 94110

WRITE ON
(March, Norton, George)
P. O. Box 5154
San Bernardino, CA 92408

UP FROM THE BOTTOM (San Diego)
P. O. Box 7472
San Diego, CA 92107

OUT NOW! (Long Beach)
1810 E. Anaheim
Long Beach, CA 90813

LIBERTY CALL (San Diego)
2143 Market Street
San Diego, CA 92102

Covered Wagon Coffeehouse
HELPING HAND (Mt. Home)
P. O. Box 729
Mt. Home, Idaho 83647

Barrage
THE FORUM (Ft. Sill)
413 Gore Blvd.
Lawton, Okla. 73501

Home Front Coffeehouse
COUNTER-ATTACK (Ft. Carson)
P. O. Box 2255
Colorado Springs, Col. 80901

WHERE ARE WE? (Ft. Huachuca)
P. O. Box 451
Sierra Vista, AZ 85635

GI Coordinating Committee
YOUR MILITARY LEFT
(Ft. Sam Houston)
P. O. Box 1398
San Antonio, TX 78206

GIGLINE (Ft. Bliss)
P. O. Box 31094
Summit Hgts. Station
El Paso, TX 79931

Oleo Strut Coffeehouse
FATIGUE PRESS (Ft. Hood)
P. O. Box 1265
Killeen, TX 76541

KOREA FREE PRESS
P. O. Box 94
Elmhurst, Ill. 60126

CAMP NEWS →
2801 N. Sheffield
Chicago, Ill. 60657

NAVY TIMES ARE CHANGING
(Great Lakes)
P. O. Box 164
N. Chicago, Ill. 60064

PTA (Ft. Knox)
P. O. Box 336
Louisville, KY 40201

THE STAR SPANGLED BUMMER
(Wright-Patterson)
P. O. Box 1625
Dayton, Ohio 45401

People's House
PEOPLE'S PRESS (Ft. Campbell)
456 N. 2nd Street
Clarksville, Tenn. 37040

LEFT FACE (Ft. McClellan)
P. O. Box 1595
Anniston, AL 36201

DIFFERENT DRUMMER (Ft. Polk)
P. O. Box 329
Ft. Polk, La. 71459

Common Sense Bookstore
MORNING REPORT (Ft. Devens)
P. O. Box 359
Groton, Mass. 01450

Potemkin Bookstore
ALL HANDS ABANDON SHIP (Newport)
126 Broadway
Newport, R.I. 02840

At Ease Coffeehouse
THE DESTROYER (Naval Station)
611 S. 2nd Street
Philadelphia, PA 19102

FRAGGING ACTION (Ft. Dix)
P. O. Box 268
Cooksey, N.J. 08511

DMZ Coffeehouse
OPEN SIGHTS (D.C. area)
P. O. Box 3861
Washington, D.C. 20007

Haymarket Square Coffeehouse
BRAGGS BRIEFS (Ft. Bragg)
P. O. Box 437
Spring Lake, NC 28390

CHESSMAN II (MCAS Beaufort)
P. O. Box 5401
Burton, SC 29902

LAST HARASS (Ft. Gordon)
P. O. Box 2994
Hill Station
Augusta, GA 30904

By 1971, there were thirty-two GI coffeehouses and support centers in the United States. This map was published by some of the GI newspapers.

options for soldiers looking to hang out off base in many military towns. He thought that a counterculture themed coffeehouse could provide a relaxing space for young GIs hoping to get away from the oppressive atmosphere that frequently surrounded them.

The UFO coffeehouse was an instant hit. Decorated with rock-and-roll posters donated from San Francisco promoter Bill Graham, it quickly became a popular gathering spot for local GIs—and a target of significant hostility from military officials, city authorities, and outraged citizens ("It's a sore spot in our craw," said one Columbia official). By the summer of 1968, the UFO had also caught the attention of major antiwar organizations like the National Mobilization Committee to End the War in Vietnam (or "Mobe" for short), who organized a "Summer of Support" to raise funds for more coffeehouse projects around the country.

Over the next several years, more than twenty-five GI coffeehouses opened near military bases in the United States and at a number of bases overseas. Coffeehouses evolved to become critical support institutions for the GI movement—places where active-duty soldiers, veterans, and civilian activists met to plan demonstrations, publish underground newspapers, and work to build the emerging peace movement within the U.S. military.

With their walls covered in psychedelic posters, staffed by long-haired radicals, and stationed in the heart of America's military towns, GI coffeehouses hit a nerve, to say the least. As anyone who participated in their everyday operation will testify, running a GI coffeehouse was never easy. In addition to the practical elements of running a small business, coffeehouse organizers faced deep antagonism and resentment from the communities in which they settled.

Without exception, every GI coffeehouse in the network was subjected to attacks from a variety of sources—investigated by the FBI and congressional committees, infiltrated by law enforcement, harassed by military authorities, and, in a number of startling cases, violently terrorized by local vigilantes. In 1970, at the Fort Dix coffeehouse project in Wrightstown, New Jersey, GIs and civilians were celebrating Valentine's Day when a live grenade flew in through an open door; it exploded, seriously injuring two Fort Dix soldiers and a civilian. Another popular coffeehouse, the Covered Wagon in Mountain Home, Idaho (near a major Air Force base), was a frequent target of harassment by reactionary local citizens, who ultimately burned the coffeehouse to the ground in November 1971.[4]

Despite this near-constant surveillance and intimidation, the GI coffeehouse network played a central role in some of the GI movement's most significant actions over the course of six years. When eight black GIs, all of them leaders of the group GIs United Against the War in Vietnam, were arrested in 1969 for holding an illegal demonstration at Fort Jackson, the UFO coffeehouse served as a local operations center, drumming up funds for lawyers and promoting the "Fort Jackson Eight" story to the national media. After GI and civilian activists created intense public pressure, officials quietly dropped all charges, signaling a shift in how the military would respond to soldiers expressing dissent.

The Oleo Strut coffeehouse in Killeen, Texas, was among the most widely known and longest-running GI coffeehouse projects. In 1968, in the weeks

The first GI coffeehouse, the UFO, opened in Columbia, South Carolina, near the Fort Jackson Army Base, in 1967. Fred Gardner and Donna Mickelson developed the idea of establishing coffeehouses outside of military bases to provide an alternative to the bars, brothels, and exploitative businesses that separate soldiers from their payday earnings. Source: Photo from *Win Magazine*, December 1, 1969. GI Periodicals, Swarthmore College Peace Collection.

Interior of the Fort Dix Coffeehouse in Wrightstown, New Jersey, before it was bombed and closed.

THE TIME HAS COME FOR A LONG-NEEDED

SHAKEDOWN

Vol. 1, No. 17   P.O. Box 68, Wrightstown, N.J.   March 6, 1970

This paper is written and published by a group of Ft. Dix GI's who in doing so have freed their minds from the involuntary servitude of the military machine. This is our "Ultimate Weapon."

FT. DIX COFFEE-HOUSE
bombed   .....   closed

I would like to start out telling you about one day of the life of a person who comes to the Coffee House in order to talk about his political views, and to be in a relaxing atmosphere, away from the green machine for awhile.

Getting back to the facts - at about 8:45 PM on the evening of February 14th the pigs came by and paid a visit to the Coffee House by rolling an incendiary Army OD type bomb into the place. The explosion caused only minor damage to the Coffee House. However, 4 people were injured, one seriously enough to have to be admitted to Walson Army Hospital.

After such an incident, I

As of last Friday the Ft. Dix Coffee-house was closed down, the people evicted from the building. To those of us who have been to the Coffee-house frequently, this was a terrible blow. The Coffee-house was a place to go for political education, political raps, or to get away from the green machine for a while. There we could feel comfortable among people that knew and sympathized with the problems of GI's.

The Coffee-house also provided civilian support for GI's and educated civilians about the oppressive life of GI's. The Coffee-house took on the defense of the Ft. Dix 38, GI's who were

paign around the Ft. Dix 38 brought public attention to the inhuman conditions in the stockade and the lack of justice in the military court system.

The Coffee-house also had a panel of lawyers who provided the GI's with legal counseling that they could not afford on their small (and insufficient) army pay. These lawyers gave the GI's legal advice and defended them at their court martials.

On November 16, 1969 in Washington, D.C., a group of about 500 GI's got together and formed a group called the Soldiers' Liberation Front. The group marched to the National Archives where the Constitution

BUT THE MOVEMENT GOES ON

stop and think to myself: Man, is this really my town, or what? I spent a year in Nam getting shot at. I come back here and people not only shoot at me, they throw bombs at me.

Just stop and look around at what I have. This is another Viet Nam right here. The bombing that took place at the Coffee House was just another physical example of the war going on right here.

charged with being responsible for a revolt in the Ft. Dix stockade June 5th. The Coffee-house not only helped provide legal assistance for them, but also built civilian and GI support for the men. As the climax of the campaign, on October 12, 1969, 7500 people march on Ft. Dix in defiance of the commanding general's orders. They were finally turned back by fixed bayonets and tear gas. The cam-

of the U.S. is kept and then to the Court of Military Appeals. The S.L.F. set up headquarters at the Coffee-house and had worked from there since then. On December 13 the S.L.F. marched on Wrightstown and let the people know that they were tired of the war and of being exploited by the jewelry stores and other businesses there.

But now we have lost our lease. The landlord did not evict us of his own free will. He was threatened by pigs who told him to get rid of us or his family would be hurt and his building destroyed. We are looking for another place to open a coffee-house in town, but right now the situation looks dim. We need moral and financial support from all who can give, and maybe we can get a new place.

In the meantime, we must prove that THOUGH THEY CAN CLOSE A COFFEE-HOUSE, THEY CAN NEVER STOP THE GI MOVEMENT. People should keep in touch with us through our P.O. Box #68, Wrightstown, N.J. 08562. Send news of what's happening in your company or articles and letters for SHAKEDOWN. SHAKEDOWN and other literature will keep coming out to keep us together.

The Coffee-house made it easy for us to meet and organize but its closing won't keep us from teaching our brothers and sisters what we know and building the movement of the people!

GIs wait for the start of a peace march and gather to read the latest issue of the *Fatigue Press* outside the Oleo Strut coffeehouse in Killeen, Texas. Killeen is the home of Fort Hood, the largest military base in the world in both size and number of soldiers. Source: Photo by Alan Pogue.

leading up to the Democratic National Convention in Chicago, local coffee-house staff and GIs mobilized to support the "Fort Hood 43" after a large group of black soldiers was arrested at a meeting to discuss their refusal to deploy for riot-control duty at the convention. One black veteran present at the meeting described its mood: "A lot of black GIs knew what the thing [Chicago] was going to be about and they weren't going to go and fight their own people." Army authorities were caught off guard by the publicity the coffeehouse brought to the case and began to examine their strategies for dealing with political expression among the ranks.

In May 1970, the Strut was featured in national media stories of actress Jane Fonda's high-profile visit to Killeen, during which she was briefly de-tained by authorities at Fort Hood, who arrested her for distributing antiwar literature outside the base's gates. After her release, she held an impromptu press conference at the coffeehouse, telling reporters, "I'm not here as a movie star—as a publicity stunt. I am a person who is fighting against the war and for GI rights. I went on Fort Hood because GIs aren't allowed to distribute literature there. I think it's appalling that men who are sent overseas to fight and die for their country are denied the constitutional rights which they are supposed to be defending."[5]

Though the GI coffeehouse network was short-lived, it left an indelible mark on the Vietnam era. While popular mythology often places the antiwar movement at odds with American troops, the history of GI coffeehouses, and the GI movement of which they were a part, paints a very different picture. Over the course of the war, thousands of military servicemen and women from every branch—active-duty GIs, veterans, nurses, and even ranking

Facing page: The GI coffeehouse outside Fort Dix, New Jersey, was bombed and forced to close in February 1970. U.S. Army Military Intelligence, in conjunction with the FBI, local police, and vigilantes, worked aggressively to shut down coffeehouses and arrest and harass the soldiers and civilians who promoted the GI peace movement.

officers—expressed their opposition to American policy in Vietnam. They joined forces with civilian antiwar organizations that, particularly after 1968, focused significant energy and resources on developing social and political bonds with American soldiers. Hoping to build the resistance that was already taking shape in the Army, activists at GI coffeehouses worked directly with servicemen and women on hundreds of political projects and demonstrations as they faced relentless legal and extralegal harassment.

The eruption of resistance and activism by U.S. troops during the Vietnam War was unprecedented in American history and became part of a significant crisis for the American military. Officials feared exactly the kind of alliance between civilians and soldiers that Fred Gardner and Donna Mickleson had in mind when they opened the first GI coffeehouse in 1967. The disruptions and challenges created by the GI movement were a significant factor in the government's decision to end the draft and switch to an "all-volunteer force" in the early 1970s.

Despite the extraordinary political and cultural impact that dissenting soldiers made throughout the Vietnam era, though, their voices have been nearly erased from history, replaced by a stereotypical image of loyal, patriotic soldiers antagonized and spat upon by ungrateful antiwar activists.[6] This distortion of history accompanies a larger cultural avoidance of what *actually happened* during the Vietnam War era. In the decades since the war's end, countless Hollywood movies, books, political speeches, and celebrated documentaries have worked to obscure the war's deep unpopularity among the ranks and the countless ways that American troops expressed their opposition. The history of GI coffeehouses disrupts this narrative by showing us places where that opposition most productively blossomed. By functioning as a central support system for the thousands of GIs who were turning against the war in Vietnam, coffeehouses helped bring the antiwar movement directly to the U.S. military's doorstep.

The Joy and Terror of Opening GI Coffeehouses

Judy Olasov

I was eighteen years old, starting my sophomore year at the University of South Carolina in the fall of 1967, when the UFO coffeehouse opened there to serve soldiers at Fort Jackson. Donna Mickelson painted a sign that looked like a Fillmore dance poster, declaring us to be the UFO, Unidentified Foreign Objects, like an alien spaceship.

We covered the walls with posters—Muhammad Ali, the championship boxer who refused to serve in the U.S. Army; a surfing movie; the actress Mar-

On Armed Forces Day in 1971, police arrested 128 Fort Hood soldiers who staged a peace march through nearby Killeen, Texas. Two weeks later, GIs from Fort Polk, Louisiana, and Fort Sill, Oklahoma, joined in solidarity with the Fort Hood GIs at a rally and concert featuring folksinger Pete Seeger held in an open field near the coffeehouse. Source: Photo by Alan Pogue.

Pete Seeger.
Source: Photo by Kevin Schaeffer.

ilyn Monroe; an atomic bomb mushroom cloud; Stokely Carmichael, the civil rights leader; a Toulouse-Lautrec art poster; a cannabis plant; John Lennon in *How I Won the War*; Lyndon Johnson holding up a hound dog by the ears.

This sort of restaurant was so culturally different from any other place in the conservative town of Columbia, we might as well have been dropped there from outer space. I immediately embraced the concept and became a regular. I was deeply affected by the Tet Offensive in late January 1968. Days later, the South Carolina state police gunned down a group of black students trying to integrate a bowling alley next to their campus.

One of the very important accomplishments of the UFO, and subsequently other coffeehouses, was that it integrated Columbia in two ways— soldiers and students, and blacks and whites. This was virtually unheard of in those days.

In March, I quit school and joined Fred Gardner in opening the second coffeehouse, at Fort Leonard Wood, in Waynesville, Missouri. The small town of Waynesville was a hostile environment. The only women in town who would talk to me were prostitutes. I was shot at once when I was driving to pick up pastries to bring back to our coffeehouse, which we called Mad Anthony's. We were under constant threat. By then I was nineteen years old and had never lived outside of South Carolina.

Antiwar movement people visited us from Chicago and other cities. Many would then open coffeehouses outside of other military bases. We were featured in several national publications, bringing increased attention to the GI antiwar movement.

After Missouri, I went on to work in San Francisco, then at the Shelter Half coffeehouse in Tacoma, Washington, near Fort Lewis and McChord Air Base. Eventually I moved back to San Francisco to support sailors who were organizing to stop their aircraft carriers from returning to Vietnam.

In late 1969, I decided to put my money where my mouth was and enlist in the Army to organize from the inside. I felt that was an important point to make. When I walked into the recruiting office, I was stunned to discover that women under twenty-one needed their parents' permission to enlist. I overcame that hurdle, but right before I was to report for duty, they told me that the Sixth Army Command had found me unsuitable for enlistment.

I am very proud of my work in the GI coffeehouse movement, and it pains me greatly that the U.S. government was somewhat successful in its propaganda campaign against us, telling lies such as 'antiwar protesters spit on GIs returning from Vietnam.' Our slogan was "Support Our Soldiers, Bring Them Home."

Actress Jane Fonda spent a week at the Oleo Strut coffeehouse in Killeen, Texas, in May 1970, helping with chores, listening to the soldiers' stories, and speaking at a peace rally in town. Source: Photo by Ron Carver.

'We were smuggled onto the base in the trunk of a soldier's car'

Jane Fonda

At the Home Front, a GI coffeehouse near Fort Carson in Colorado Springs, there were about thirty GIs and staff waiting, including a lawyer who had gotten the base commander to agree to meet with us to discuss a recent situation: A hundred soldiers had lined up in front of the medical dispensary flashing peace signs and saying they were sick—sick of the war. As a result, all of them had been put into the stockade, and it was rumored that they were being beaten. Given the potential media exposure that could result, it was hoped that my meeting the base commander would lead to the release of the soldier-protesters.

Surprisingly, the general took us on a tour of the stockade and let us talk to prisoners. If he hoped by this to show us that the GIs were being well treated, it backfired. We saw prisoners who seemed catatonic. One appeared to be schizophrenic. Some, who identified themselves as Black Panthers, said they had been beaten, and it appeared to be so. Perhaps the general had never been inside the stockade himself; perhaps he misjudged the effect it would have on me. In any case, the visit was abruptly called to an end and we were ushered out before I was able to determine which prisoners were the protesters.

I received word that a psychiatrist from a nearby military academy wanted to meet privately with me. I was taken to a motel where the young doctor talked to me about the training new recruits were being made to undergo, training he said was horrifying, turning the young men into "mechanical robots, devoid of humanity, ready to kill anything."

I had brought dozens of books to give to GIs I met along the way. They included copies of *The Village of Ben Suc*, the abridged version of Bertrand Russell's *Against the Crime of Silence: Proceedings of the International War Crimes Tribunal*, Robert Sherrill's *Military Justice Is to Justice as Military Music Is to Music*, and a collection of GI movement newspapers. Permission for me to reenter the base had been denied following the visit to the stockade, but several soldiers from the base offered to sneak us on. They wanted me to see an on-base coffeehouse the brass had created, complete with girlie shows, to keep the men from coming to the GI movement coffeehouse.

We were smuggled onto the base in the trunk of a soldier's car and managed to get to the on-base coffeehouse. It was a rather antiseptic room with a few pinup posters and a small stage, where we quickly distributed the books to the few soldiers who were there (no time to try to get to the stockade). I told them about the Home Front and why I had brought the books. But no sooner had I finished than several MPs arrived and escorted us off the base. Later some soldiers told me that the general didn't make more of a stink about it because he didn't want any media attention, since it was active-duty servicemen who had smuggled us in. I realized that the higher-ups feared word getting out as to the breadth and depth of soldiers' antiwar feelings.

'You're fired; you're evicted'

Ron Carver

Anniston, Alabama, population 31,000, was as Deep South and pro-war an Army town as you might find in America in 1970, when a group of civilians joined with Vietnam veteran Skip Delano to open a coffeehouse project there. In 1961, racist vigilantes had set a bus on fire while its freedom riders were

Anniston Coffeehouse Project Staff, 1971. Left to right: Vietnam veteran Dave Dorey, Paula Cohen, Doug LeFrenier, Louise Runyon, Wendy Forbush, and Ron Carver. Not pictured: Bob Levin and Vietnam veterans Skip Delano and Dave Blalock. Source: Photo by Ron Carver.

still inside. The police watched; no one was arrested. What more did we need to know about Anniston?

Fort McClellan was the advanced training base for chemical warfare (Agent Orange, Agent Blue, and napalm-B) and the basic training base for all who joined the Women's Army Corps (WACs).

As we were not able to rent a storefront downtown, we opened the coffeehouse in one of the small ranch houses we rented in the subdivision across from Fort McClellan's main gate. And then the repression began. Wendy lost her job at Pogo's restaurant, at the end of our street. A Military Intelligence officer had me fired from my job as a substitute teacher at the local high school, and, later, as a photographer for *The Anniston Star*. And then the local police threw Bob in jail for a week before they admitted that the crumbly stuff they'd found in his jacket pocket the day they raided our house was halvah candy, not cocaine.

One day our landlady, the wife of a staff sergeant stationed in Germany, ordered us to leave. Military Intelligence told her we were bomb-throwing anarchists; we were neither. She wasn't at home when we went to plead our case, but her kids let us in to wait for her. She was horrified when she arrived a short time later, but then laughed with relief, realizing her kids were unharmed and it was the Army, not us, who had misled her. So we worked out a plan. The United States Servicemen's Fund raised ten thousand dollars, a friend of ours bought the house, and the project continued as a thorn in the military's rear end—at a key Army installation. FTA.

Not-So-Friendly Fire

Tom Hurwitz

In the spring of 1970, the Green Machine organizing project moved from a rural location into a "movement house" in Oceanside, California: a stucco house on a nice but down-scale street. Now in an easy location for the Marines coming from the Camp Pendleton base by bus, we saw a real opportunity to recruit new members. The base was, de facto, very segregated. We had always had some contact among the black Marines, but it was limited. Now, we had a chance to reach a larger, more diverse constituency.

We printed a special addition of *Attitude Check*, our newspaper, with improved graphics and a dartboard target with the commandant of the Marine Corps at the center. In it, we invited the Marines to an open house, with Jane Fonda and members of the Black Panthers as guests. We worked like crazy to distribute the paper secretly to all corners of the base—and got back news that the brass was furious. It worked.

Hundreds of Marines showed up, including hundreds of black Marines. We got as many names as we could and invited guys to the next meeting. They came. The bravest and most interested regularly came to meetings. They camped at our house. We did political education. We listened to a lot of music and danced. We, the Marines, and the organizers, set up networks on the base to circulate the newspaper, books, and information.

We began to have an influence on Pendleton. For example, we would find out about racial provocations by the brass and noncommissioned officers (NCOs) on base. Marines who were part of the Movement for a Democratic Military (MDM) would then go and cool things out between white and black enlisted men. The MDM Marines recruited new members who stayed on base, not drawing attention to themselves, but organizing. For a month or so, things grew exponentially.

At the same time, the feds and the Marine Corps Criminal Investigation Division (CID) surveilled us constantly to monitor our organizing. In addition, the Republican Party was planning to hold its 1972 convention in San Diego. We heard rumors that the military was planning a crackdown before or during the convention. Martial law or a state of emergency was mentioned. We found out later that our phones were being tapped by five government agencies.

Then, cars belonging to movement groups, including the *Street Journal*, were firebombed in San Diego. A few movement houses were shot into, and a young woman was seriously wounded. What we did not know was that the notorious dirty trickster Donald Segretti had been sent by the Nixon Administration to San Diego County to create trouble for radicals and peace groups in advance of the convention. Now we know that he made contact with right-wing militia groups like the Secret Army Organization, made up of retired military types.

Our phones were being tapped by five government agencies.

Pfc. Jesse Woodard was wounded in 1970 when vigilantes fired automatic-weapon rounds through the window of the support center for antiwar Marines in Oceanside, California, near the Camp Pendleton Marine Base. Source: Photo by Ron Carver.

In mid-April, we were having our weekly meeting at the Oceanside movement house, with twenty or so of the most active Marines. The meeting broke up around 7:00 P.M. and some of us stood up; some stayed sitting on the floor, chatting. Suddenly, the venetian blinds on the front picture window were exploding with sparks. "Down," I was yelling. The Marines, with better gunfire reflexes than mine, of course, were already diving, or on the floor. I was hearing the gunshots now, a tommy gun, it turned out, slamming across the front of the house—and then silence.

"I'm hit, I'm hit!" Jesse Woodard, a private first class and one of the first of the new crop of MDM Marines, was lying, rocking back and forth, clutching his chest. I made sure he was being looked after by someone with corpsman training, and I crawled to open the front door. It was surreal. Inside, the house was in an uproar; outside, it was a normal, quiet Southern California night.

Teresa Cerda said that she saw cops on our corners as she left the house just minutes ahead of the shooting. From the middle of the block, I saw only empty street. I walked back in and called an ambulance and the cops. Then I looked at where I had been sitting. There was a bullet hole just eighteen inches over my head. If I had stood up and not chatted . . .

Petitioning to End the War

4

Standing Up to Be Counted

Francis Lenski

In May 2018, I returned to the University of Notre Dame to celebrate with some of my fellow classmates our fifty-year reunion. Although I anticipated that at the reunion I would probably reflect upon my collegiate life, I never expected I would also think about the seventeen months I spent in the United States Army during the Vietnam War. While I was at the reunion, my friend and fellow classmate David Cortright introduced me to the "Waging Peace in Vietnam" exhibit, which was displayed in the Great Hall of the Hesburgh Center for International Studies, home of the university's heralded Kroc Institute for International Peace Studies, where Dave is a director of several programs. What immediately caught my attention was the large poster replica of the petition against the war signed by 1,365 active-duty service members, including Dave and me, which appeared in a full-page ad in *The New York Times* on November 9, 1969.

In March 1969, I was drafted into the United States Army, having been yanked out of a Ph.D. program in history at the University of Chicago. After basic training, I was assigned to the Defense Language Institute Support Command (DLISC) at Fort Bliss, Texas, where I studied the Vietnamese language. Because of my inherent rebellious nature and in resistance to my military service, I did not learn very much Vietnamese, but I had the good fortune to become acquainted and friends with some of my Vietnamese instructors and their families. It did not take me long to confirm truths that many fellow Americans at that time seemed to ignore: that Vietnamese are indeed human beings; that Vietnamese children laugh and cry, as do American children; that Vietnamese mothers love their children as deeply as American mothers love theirs; that Vietnamese families desire peace; and that the people of Vietnam are as sensitive to pain and suffering as are any other people.

During my involuntary service at DLISC, I joined GIs for Peace (GIFP), an organization of military personnel with lofty aspirational goals: to promote peace; to end the Vietnam War, American militarism, and institutional racism; to support soldiers' constitutional rights and improve their social conditions; and to advocate for the betterment of the local community. In practice, however, the organization's many talented individuals were primarily dedicated to opposing the Vietnam War and advocating for its quick and just end, even though we were operating in a repressive environment. The main vehicle of our outreach to fellow soldiers and the greater El Paso community and beyond was our newspaper, *Gigline,* which began publication in 1969. After the first two leaders of GIFP were (punitively) transferred elsewhere, I became the chairperson of the group.

At some point in September or October 1969, it came to our attention that if the necessary signatures could be obtained, the national Vietnam Moratorium committee would fund a full-page ad in *The New York Times* of active-duty soldiers who opposed the war. Inasmuch as the nucleus of GIs for Peace was embedded in DLISC, that is where most of the discussions and action took place, as well as at the house that the organization rented in El Paso. Disregarding possible reprisals, such as punitive transfers to infantry school, several GIs for Peace members, whom the military authorities were already monitoring, readily and eagerly signed the petition. Others hesitated; still others kept their distance and initially wanted nothing to do with the petition.

As time passed, more and more of our fellow soldiers cast their lot with the early signatories. The process of discussion was quite open; we would pass the petition around in our language classrooms, in the barracks, and at our coffeehouse. Among some of us there was concern that what we were doing in distributing and signing the petition would have serious repercussions, but our opposition to the war was so adamant that we were willing to suffer the consequences. A few others were equally determined that they would not sign the petition. Eventually, almost everyone in our platoon signed the document. When the ad subsequently appeared in *The New York Times*, we proudly realized that Fort Bliss, although not the largest base, had the highest number of soldiers who signed the petition—142. We were elated to have made this public statement of our inveterate opposition to the war.

When we learned that the Judge Advocate General was investigating the legality of the petition, I sent a letter to President Nixon, stating in part: "I wish at this time to reaffirm my opposition to American involvement in Vietnamese internal affairs. Acting completely within my legal rights in signing a public statement against the war, I wish to state that I will not be intimidated, harassed, or silenced. I will continue to speak out and make my opinions known, whether by signing a public statement or by participating in the Moratorium protests. To quote one of the greatest of American presidents, Abraham Lincoln: 'To sin by silence when they should protest makes cowards of men.'"

The West Texas town of El Paso, the site of Marty Robbins's hit song, sits nestled at the toe of the Franklin Mountains and adjacent to Fort Bliss, to which it was then tethered culturally, socially, and economically. During the latter half of 1969, El Paso had the distinction of being the site of several antiwar/pro-peace marches that GIs for Peace helped organize and in which many soldiers and their families and local residents participated. These activities were designed, in coordination with the national moratorium movement, to demonstrate that significant resistance to the Vietnam War existed even in conservative and highly patriotic El Paso and its nearby military base.

GIs for Peace and allied organizations hosted an antiwar demonstration in McKelligan Canyon on August 7, 1969. El Paso's first moratorium-related demonstration took place in El Paso on October 15, quickly followed by a second, albeit less robust, rally on November 15. During El Paso's traditional Veterans Day parade, members of GIs for Peace participated in the parade, much to the chagrin of the event's organizers. Some local residents reacted angrily to our protests, claiming we were unpatriotic.

The Army also reacted. On November 13, three members of GIFP—Pfc. James Nies (then chairperson of GIFP), Pfc. Edward Barresi (my Army roommate), and Pfc. Ronald Lund—were summarily dismissed from DLISC and given immediate orders to infantry school in California and Louisiana. All three declined the invitation and speedily headed for the friendly, albeit chillier, climes of Canada, where they bided their time to return home, which they eventually did.

During the lead up to the Moratorium demonstrations, members of GIs for Peace decided to make a statement against the war that all of El Paso would see. Located on the side of the Franklin Mountains facing El Paso and Fort Bliss were some hollow drums, painted white by students from a local school. We decided to adapt those drums for another purpose. Working mostly under the cover of darkness, we relocated them to form the shape of the peace sign, filled them with fuel, and set them ablaze. The fiery scene above the city and environs spoke for itself (and us) and was the talk of the town and base for days to come. Although investigations presumably were launched, nothing came of them.

In January 1970, Gen. William Westmoreland, then the Army's chief of staff and the former U.S. commander in Vietnam, came to El Paso to deliver a speech. When our request to meet with the general to express our opposition to the war was ignored, eighty off-duty soldiers and some of their wives picketed outside the hotel where he spoke to deliver our message for peace.

As I stood in front of the poster replica at the Kroc Institute, shaking hands with Dave, my thoughts slipped back to that time fifty years ago when the two of us and many other soldiers took a principled and courageous stand to oppose an unnecessary and disastrous war. That was the most formative time of my life. It taught me lessons, values, and principles that have guided me through all the years since.

> **Significant resistance existed even in conservative El Paso and its military base.**

Air Force Captain Against the War

Thomas Staten Culver

Special to The New York Times

LONDON, July 8—On the afternoon of May 31, Capt. Thomas S. Culver stood on the fringe of a crowd of 300 other American servicemen at Hyde Park Speaker's Corner. "I feel I've got to speak out against the war," said Captain Culver, a member of the Staff Judge Advocate's

Man In the News

Office at Lakenheath Air Force Base, 82 miles from London. "It's a terrible war." Captain

Culver and the other off-duty servicemen, in civilian clothes, walked silently to the United States Embassy and handed in antiwar petitions signed by 1,000 members of the Air Force, Army and Navy. It was the largest protest against the Vietnam war among United States servicemen stationed here.

"I was the senior man there, probably the only officer," the hefty, intense lawyer said the other day. "I guess that's why they're trying to court-martial me."

Captain Culver is being tried by a court-martial at Lakenheath Air Force Base, the first American officer in Britain charged with taking part in an antiwar protest. He faces up to four years in prison and a dishonorable discharge.

The Air Force specifically charges the officer with violating regulations that forbid demonstrations by overseas personnel and having "solicited other military personnel" to take part.

"We were not demonstrating, we were petitioning," the 32-year-old officer says heatedly. "This is not a play on words. There were no banners, no speeches. We merely handed in the peti-

The New York Times/Nell Libbert

"We were not demonstrating, we were petitioning."

tions. And the regulations say that you can petition."

Captain Culver, a six-year Air Force veteran who spent one year in Vietnam, speaks angrily of the military. "It's quite acceptable in the Air Force to talk about Vietnam as long as you do it privately," he said. "I haven't been popular because it hasn't been private with me."

Thomas Staten Culver was born in Great Neck, L.I. on Nov. 8, 1938, one of four sons of Mr. and Mrs. Frank Culver. His father, who died last year, headed a family retinning busines with factories in Jersey City, Hackensack and Boston. His mother, Dorothy, lives in Westfield, N.J.

Captain Culver grew up in Westfield and graduated from Columbia College in 1960. He spent a year studying law at the University of Pennsylvania, but switched to Stanford and earned a law degree in 1963. Later that year he moved to England where he received a degree in criminology at Cambridge.

Captain Culver joined the Air Force on a direct commission in 1965. At the time, doctors, dentists and lawyers were commissioned directly into the service, obliging them only to remain a minimum of three years.

Captain Culver served in the Staff Judge Advocate's office at Fairchild Air Force Base in Seattle, Wash., from September, 1965, to March, 1967. He was transferred to South Vietnam where he worked mostly at Tonsonnhut Air Base in Saigon.

"I was against the war even before I went," he said, "but I didn't feel that my participation in the Air Force contributed to the war effort. I felt no moral pangs about being a lawyer there."

Despite his antipathy to the war effort, Captain Culver remained in the Air Force to take up the assignment in Britain. "I stayed in the Air Force because I like it here, and living on an Air Force salary is very nice," he said. Captain Culver earns about $800 a month, after taxes.

For the last year, the bachelor has lived in a two-room apartment in Cambridge, 30 miles from the air base.

At the moment, Captain Culver's studies of British law and his one hobby, bicycle riding, have been ignored. He spends mornings and evenings reading Air Force regulations, talking to military lawyers, meeting American supporters from Cambridge and Oxford.

"I'm worried," he said with a tense laugh the other day, "I'm very worried."

The New York Times

Published: July 9, 1971
Copyright © The New York Times

'We were taking these actions as civilians'

Adam Hochschild

A peculiarity of the conflict in Vietnam was that the United States fought one of its largest and longest wars almost entirely without deploying Reserve forces. More than a half-million Americans served in Vietnam at the peak of the war, but except for 35,000 briefly mobilized troops and a small number of volunteers, roughly one million Reservists and National Guard soldiers stayed home.

The reason is simple, and logical. The Pentagon never dared call up the National Guard and Reserves in large numbers because these two similar forces were filled with men who opposed the war. The military's system at the time shows why. Unless you could get a deferment, all able-bodied young American men faced the draft. Draftees were in the Army for two years, with a good chance of being sent to Vietnam. If you enlisted, it was three years, with an even higher chance. But if you joined the Reserves or National Guard, you spent only four and a half months on active duty, getting trained. For the remainder of your six-year obligation, you only had to report to a two-week summer camp each year and an evening's drill every week.[1]

Hence, people like me who didn't want to go to war did everything we could to get into a Reserve or National Guard unit. It was a relatively popular choice among college students and recent graduates, who were far more likely to be antiwar than people from almost any other part of society. The percentage of college graduates among Army Reservists was much higher than among draftees and enlistees. In my own Army Reserve unit in San Francisco, we joked that if they ever did try to send us to Vietnam, so many would refuse that it would be worthwhile to charter a bus to head for the Canadian border.

But hearing the voices of antiwar GIs, seeing the newspapers they published, and reading about those who were prosecuted for refusing orders spurred many Reservists and National Guardsmen to speak out. In 1970, some 2,200 of us signed a petition and newspaper advertisement calling for a full withdrawal of all U.S. troops from Vietnam. We marched in peace parades under banners identifying ourselves as Reservists and Guardsmen. Groups in Boston and Washington, D.C., called press conferences to announce that they were giving their military pay away to peace organizations and peace candidates. Pentagon brass was furious, but powerless to act, because we were taking these actions as civilians.

The Reservists Committee to Stop the War, in the San Francisco Bay Area, and Reservists Against the War, in Boston, helped coordinate our involvement. Did any of our actions stop the war? No, but perhaps they encouraged

Adam Hochschild in 1964.
Source: Courtesy of Adam Hochschild.

Facing page: Air Force captain Thomas Culver was court-martialed and convicted for attempting to deliver an antiwar petition to the U.S. embassy in London signed by one thousand members of the Air Force, Army, and Navy.

Reservists and National Guardsmen Say 'NO' to the War

We, the undersigned, are officers and enlisted men of the United States military Reserve forces.

We wear the same uniform as the American troops being killed and maimed every day in Vietnam. We want those soldiers home — alive.

We demand total withdrawal of ALL our fellow American soldiers from Vietnam now. Not just combat troops, not just ground forces, but ALL troops.

We demand total withdrawal now of all the American soldiers advising the armies of dictatorships throughout Latin America and Asia. We don't want Guatemala, Thailand, or Bolivia to become the Vietnams of the 1970s. One Vietnam is enough; too many people have been killed already to preserve America's overseas empire.

As men who have served in the armed forces, we have seen firsthand the dangerously growing power of American militarism. As soldiers and as citizens, we believe we have a special obligation to speak out against it.

Partial list of signers:
(Full list available on request)

MAJ Harold Jamison, Air Force Reserve
LT Ernest J. Notar, Navy Reserve
CPT William Halal, Air Force Reserve
LT(jg) Francis A. Toth, Navy Reserve
ENS James V. Calio, Jr., Navy Reserve
LT(jg) G. A. Braun, Navy Reserve
AIC David Callow, Air National Guard
LCpl Bruce Hanna, Marine Reserve
PFC Nils Schoultz, Army Reserve
LCpl Richard O. Kraemer, Marine Reserve
E2 Donald L. Harris, Air National Guard
PVT Walter Lobitz, Army Reserve
PFC William D. Hund, Marine Reserve
E3 John P. Van Emmerik, Air National Guard
PFC William T. Weisend, Marine Reserve
E3 David Blakely, Air National Guard
LCpl Kenneth M. Perry, Marine Reserve
SN Richard Holway, Coast Guard Reserve
PFC Edmund Feeney, Marine Reserve
PS2 Stephen Harvey, Coast Guard Reserve
LCpl Stephen Pizzo, Marine Reserve
SGT Dennis S. Thalman, Air Force Reserve
PFC Stephen M. Patras, Marine Reserve
PS2 Thomas Herbert, Coast Guard Reserve
SGT Ronald Gras, Marine Reserve
PFC John Van Orden, Army Reserve
PS2 Ted Perez, Coast Guard Reserve
LCpl Michael John Solomon, Marine Reserve
PS2 Alfonso Roderigues, Coast Guard Reserve
SGT James M. Ballance, Air Force Reserve
SP4 George P. Holmes, Army Reserve
PS2 Frank A. DeOme, Coast Guard Reserve
SGT Michael A. Ryan, Air Force Reserve
PVT Ted Radatich, Marine Reserve
SN David Collins, Coast Guard Reserve
SP4 James Nash, Army Reserve
PVT Craig Sobrero, Marine Reserve
PFC Robert Domergue, Army Reserve
PS3 Terry Minns, Coast Guard Reserve
SGT C. J. O'Hare, Air Force Reserve
PFC Hideo Takahashi, Army Reserve
SN Jerry Isaacs, Coast Guard Reserve
LCpl Timothy C. Beatty, Marine Reserve

MAJ Kent Mayers, Marine Reserve
MAJ Raymond Jenkins, Marine Reserve
LT Meredith Mathews, Naval Reserve
SP4 Arthur Farley, Army Reserve
SGT Bruce Phillips, Air Force Reserve
CPL Robert J. Molini, Marine Reserve
SN T. S. Kelley, Coast Guard Reserve
SP4 Lars Schoultz, Army Reserve
PVT Raymond J. Velati, Marine Reserve
SN Richard Straub, Coast Guard Reserve
LCpl Dave Hope, Marine Reserve
PFC Paul Bell, Army Reserve
PFC George Denise, Marine Reserve
PS3 Henry Darmstaat, Coast Guard Reserve
SP4 John S. Glascock, Army Reserve
PFC Larry Cullen, Marine Reserve
BM2 Glenn E. Torbett, Coast Guard Reserve
SP4 Jonathan Peck, Army Reserve
CPL David Struven, Marine Reserve
PFC Herbert Castillo, Army Reserve
SGT Roger Stowers, Marine Reserve
PFC Philip Grattan, Army Reserve
LCpl Richard Hire, Marine Reserve
PFC Peter Lee, Army Reserve
LCpl Robert Falconer, Marine Reserve
PFC Robert Mattesich, Army National Guard
PS3 Stephen L. Kore, Coast Guard Reserve
SN M. Hurwitz, Coast Guard Reserve
E2 Alfred H. Velarde, Army Reserve
AMN Richard Karlsson, Air Force Reserve
PFC Frank Kallio, Army Reserve
E4 William Wemyss, Army National Guard
SGT Terry W. Hunt, Air Force Reserve
E5 Michael Ennis, Air National Guard
PVT Al Reinhert, Army Reserve
E2 Charles H. Johnson, Army National Guard
SGT Edward Crosby, Air Force Reserve
E4 Gordon L. Jones, Jr., Army Reserve
E1 Richard Heller, Army National Guard
E3 Dennis Pro, Army Reserve
SP4 Robert C. Bernius, Army National Guard
PFC Norman Yee, Army Reserve
HM2 Frank S. Irey, Naval Reserve
SP4 Morris E. Burka, III, Army Reserve

LT Michael W. Freeland, Naval Reserve
LT David L. Kranz, Naval Reserve
LT William W. Cressman, Naval Reserve
E4 William Goodman, Army Reserve
E4 Robert Giorgi, Army National Guard
SP4 Tom Field, Army Reserve
JO3 Albert Spella, Naval Reserve
SGT William T. Morehead, Air National Guard
PFC Eugene L. Zambetti, Army Reserve
PFC Barry Turkus, Army Reserve
SP4 Dean R. Brett, Army Reserve
PFC Joe Strupeck, Army Reserve
SP4 Gerald F. Burns, Army Reserve
PFC Craig Knutson, Army Reserve
PFC Steve L. Rubinger, Army Reserve
E3 James B. Rechtiene, Air National Guard
PFC Rand Levy, Army Reserve
PFC John Adams, Army Reserve
E4 Peter Glennil, Air National Guard
E3 Pete S. Cottrell, Army Reserve
E3 Bill Slimak, Army Reserve
PFC Barry Rubenstein, Army National Guard
E2 Joe Stranger, Army Reserve
PFC Mark Elson, Army Reserve
E4 Harry Siskron, Naval Reserve
PFC David Weener, Army Reserve
SP4 David Schmidt, Army Reserve
SK2 Michael Rainey, Naval Reserve
E5 Charles Parraro, Army Reserve
SP5 Sheldon Barasch, Army Reserve
SGT Thomas Peters, Army Reserve
SP4 Glenn Larson, Army National Guard
E3 David Ruttle, Army Reserve
E4 William P. Campion, Army Reserve
PFC David H. Surles, Army Reserve
E2 Larry Upshaw, Army Reserve
E3 Montgomery Skidmore, Army Reserve
E3 Larry Drill, Army National Guard
E4 Robert Hatcher, Army Reserve
E3 Michael Wolfram, Army Reserve
PFC Robert Gajan, Army Reserve
SP4 David Calchera, Army National Guard
PFC David M. Cazel, Army Reserve

Adam Hochschild in 1971, marching with his Reserve unit. Source: Courtesy of Adam Hochschild.

Overview of the April 24, 1971 march from the *Redline* newsletter. Source: Courtesy of Adam Hochschild

the brave active-duty GIs, who risked military prison for their own protests. And perhaps they contributed to the government's calculus that continuing the war indefinitely meant paying too high a price in dissent at home.

One factor that kept the numbers high in the Reserves and National Guard, we discovered, was that more than 120 U.S. senators and representatives were members. Reserve duty for them often meant service in elite units, where the two-week summer camp involved arduous service inspecting military bases in Europe. They were loath to lose the chance to enjoy such duties and to receive Reserve pay on top of their congressional salaries. Thus they were a part of the powerful lobby that kept the Reserves and National Guard well-funded.

In 1970, our Reservists Committee to Stop the War brought a lawsuit (*Schlesinger v. Reservists Committee to Stop the War*), charging that this situation was unconstitutional. The U.S. Constitution says that no one can simultaneously serve in more than one of the three branches of government. We contended that these men (and they were all men) were in the legislative branch but were unlawfully deciding on matters of pay and privilege that would affect them when, as Reservists and Guardsmen, they served in the executive branch. We won in lower courts and the case finally reached the Supreme Court. However, all of President Nixon's appointees voted against us, and we lost by six to three. Still, our case put the issue on the table and brought attention to the powerful interests that lobbied for an inflated Reserve force. That force included all those congressmen and senators who were no more eager to personally slog through the rice paddies of Vietnam than those of us a generation younger.

Facing page: Adam Hochschild and Robert Scott were editors of *Redline*, the newsletter of the Reservists Committee to Stop the War. In 1970, they collected more than 2,200 signatures of Reservists and National Guardsmen for a petition publicly calling for the immediate American withdrawal from Vietnam. Source: Courtesy of Adam Hochschild

• "Firebase Pace Petition to Senator Ted Kennedy:

We the undersigned of Bravo Company, First Battalion, Twelfth Cav, First Cav Division, feel compelled to write you because of your influence on public opinion and on decisions made in the Senate.

We're in the peculiar position of being the last remaining ground troops that the U.S. has in a combat role and we suffer from problems that are peculiar only to us. We are ground troops who are supposedly in a defensive role (according to the Nixon administration) but who constantly find ourselves faced with the same combat role we were in ten months ago. At this writing we are under siege on Firebase Pace near the city of Tay Ninh. We are surrounded on three sides by Cambodia and on all sides by NVA. We are faced daily with the decision of whether to take a court-martial or participate in an offensive role. We have already had six persons refuse to go on a night ambush (which is suicidal as well as offensive), and may be court-martialed. With morale as low as it is there probably will be more before this siege of Pace is over.

Our concern in writing you is not only to bring your full weight of influence in the Senate, but also to enlighten public opinion on the fact that we ground troops still exist. In the event of mass prosecution of our unit, our only hope would be public opinion and your voice."

On October 9, 1971, six men from Firebase Pace refused to go out on patrol and were threatened with court-martial. Sixty-five out of one hundred men in B Company signed a petition in a show of solidarity. Richard Boyle, the journalist who took these photographs brought their petition back to the United States and delivered it in person to Senator Ted Kennedy. Source: Photos of Firebase Pace on pages 54 and 55 by Richard Boyle.

THE NEW YORK TIMES, SUNDAY, NOVEMBER 9, 1969   E   9

"We are 1,365*active-duty servicemen.
We are opposed to American involvement
in the war in Vietnam.
We resent the needless wasting of lives
to save face for the politicians in Washington.
We speak, believing our views are shared
by many of our fellow servicemen.
Join us!"

"On November 15, join hundreds of thousands of Americans from all walks of life who will march in Washington and San Francisco to demand that ALL the troops be brought home from Vietnam NOW. This will be a legal and peaceful demonstration.

GIs, as American citizens, have the constitutional right to join these demonstrations. In the past, however, military authorities have often restricted servicemen to their bases, thus effectively preventing them from participating in demonstrations against the war.

We ask you to write to the President and your representatives in Congress to demand that GIs not be prevented from participating in the November 15 demonstrations."

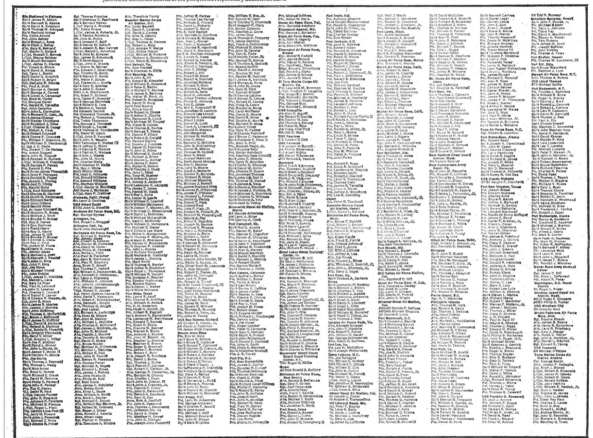

The March on Washington and a similar March on San Francisco the same day are sponsored by the *New Mobilization Committee To End The War In Vietnam*, a broad national coalition of organizations united in antiwar action. The marches have received the endorsement of Dr. Benjamin Spock, Mrs. Coretta King, Rev. William Sloane Coffin, and many other prominent Americans.

Nov. 15 Schedule

6:00 a.m.— Buses leave NYC to Washington
11:00 a.m.— Begin march up Pennsylvania Ave. from Assembly Area in Mall (3rd St., NW).
1-5 p.m.— Massive antiwar rally and folk rock concert at The Ellipse. A special feature of the Washington action will be a memorial March Against Death, Nov. 13-15, involving delegations from every state representing American war dead and Vietnamese villages destroyed. (NYC delegation leaves for Washington on Fri., Nov. 14, 7:00 p.m.)

For all transportation information, New Yorkers should call: Student Mobilization Committee to End the War in Vietnam, 675-8465; or Fifth Avenue Vietnam Peace Parade Committee, 255-0062.

This advertisement is sponsored by the GI Press Service. GI Press Service is a news bulletin and information center for many of the antiwar newspapers published by GIs across the U.S. and overseas. Its editor, Allen Myers, served in the Army from April 1967 to April 1969 and is now a coordinator for the GI task force of the New Mobilization Committee.

Student Mobilization Committee, the nation's largest student and war group, is actively organizing high school and college participation in the Nov. 15 antiwar actions on both coasts. National Executive Secretary of the Committee is Carol Lipman.

Join us in Washington November 15 to Bring all the GIs Home Now.

'We want to shut the whole base camp down'

Dave Blalock

One night we were sitting around the barracks in Vietnam, getting high and smoking dope and passing around this full-page ad in *The New York Times* that a guy who had just come back from R&R in Hawaii had clipped out. Everybody's reading and saying, "Wow, this is great, this is really neat . . . why don't we do something on this date, November 15th." We only had two days to do anything. We came to a decision that we're going to wear black armbands

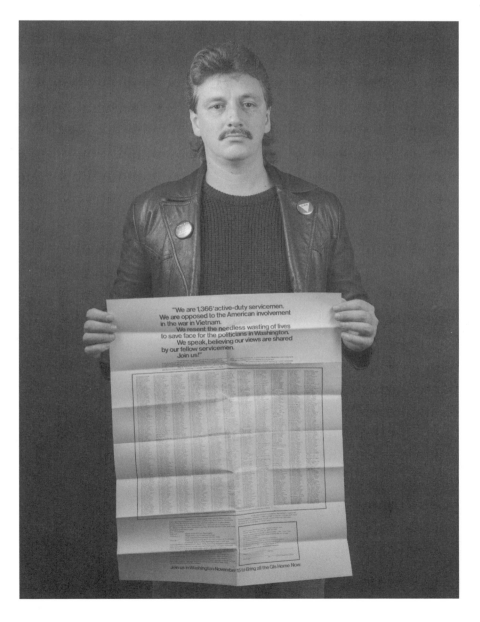

Dave Blalock, 1988.
Source: Photo by William Short.

Facing page: This petition ran as a full-page advertisement in *The New York Times* on November 9, 1969, and called on people to go to Washington, D.C., to protest the war. It was turned into a poster by antiwar groups in Germany and the United States as a tribute to the growing GI movement.

and we're going to refuse to go out on patrol. And then some other guys said, "Why don't we spread this to these other units, to the engineers, to the First Cav guys, and everyone else in our camp."

The next day, we went around to all of our friends and contacts in the other units and put out the word—what do you guys think of this thing; we want to do this; we want to shut the whole base camp down on that day. The word spread and it seemed like everybody was going to do it, but we weren't sure. I remember the night before the fifteenth we were up all night long, wondering what they're going to do or what's going to happen with the First Cav guys, trying to assess what was going to happen, how successful we were going to be. Finally we fell asleep. There was a little MP detachment on our camp; these were dog handlers. The MPs ran the PA system and they played the morning taps—military music—in the morning over the PA system. The morning of the fifteenth we wake up at about five in the morning, and instead of playing the military shit, they put Jimi Hendrix' "Star-Spangled Banner" on. And nobody even told the MPs about this thing! These guys were obviously into it also.

So we went in morning formation with our new commanding officer. The new CO was pretty slick and all the officers were afraid of us at that point. So we went out in morning formation and we're all wearing black armbands. It was like 100 percent of the enlisted men, everybody's wearing a black armband, including some of the war doctors and the helicopter pilots. The CO comes out and he says, "I'll tell you what we're going to do today, you guys. I think we're going to give you guys a day off." He was real slick with it.

So then we jumped in a jeep and cruised around the perimeter to the other units to find out what was happening, whether they were going to be successful. The engineers were in formation. We pulled up on the edge of their company area, and their CO had pulled—he knew who the leaders of the thing were—them out of the ranks and threatened to shoot them on the spot unless they took their black armbands off, and anybody that refused to go out and do their duty for the day would be shot for mutiny. Whether they'd do it or not is another story, but that intimidated a lot of the other people, because only 50 percent of the engineers were wearing black armbands. But they ended up not doing any duty anyway because a guy sabotaged all the bulldozers and everything, and nothing worked. So they couldn't do anything.

Anyway, that was the influence of a full-page ad in *The New York Times*. Somebody saw that and gave us the opportunity to do something bigger than just killing an officer or something like that.

Interviewed 1988 by Willa Seidenberg and William Short

Marching for Peace

5

From Navy Nurse to Protest Leader

Susan M. Schnall

Beginning in 1967, I was a Navy nurse at Oak Knoll Hospital, which was built during World War II in Oakland, California, to care for the Marines wounded in the Pacific. I had joined the service to alleviate suffering by caring for wounded troops from the war in Vietnam. By 1969, I was court-martialed for my actions against the war.

I can still remember the nighttime screams of pain and fear at Oak Knoll. Badly injured young men would dream their nightmares of war, of dead and dying buddies rotting in the dense jungles of Vietnam. They would scream their agony: "My leg, my leg, it's been blown away." "I'm in pain, nurse. Nurse, please give me something for the pain."

On my evening shift I would make rounds through the five buildings for which I was responsible: I would open the narcotics cabinet and dispense pain medication, talking with patients, trying to soothe their fears and quiet their moans.

Nineteen sixty-eight was the height of the war. I watched the battles on TV and lived the war at work. For me, it was very personal. My father, a Marine, was killed on the beachhead of Guam on July 22, 1944. He felt he had to do his share and help give something to this world. I never knew my father except through pictures, letters, and others' memories. World War II was a war I've lived my whole life. It destroyed my mother and her hopes and dreams and future.

As I cared for the wounded of yet another war, I wondered when this destruction would end. I trained the corpsmen who would be sent overseas with the troops and put in harm's way. I helped heal the wounded so they could be returned to the front line. I opposed this terrible destruction and waste and yet I had become a part of it.

I knew I could no longer be silent. As a member of the armed forces, it was imperative to inform the American people that there were active-duty GIs—many thousands of us—who were against the war.

Lt. Susan Schnall speaks at the March for Peace on October 12, 1968, in San Francisco. Source: Harvey Richards Media Archive © Paul Richards.

GI's FOR
GUNG-HO for PEACE
Bring our Husbands Home
Yankee COME HOME
PAUL HOWARD IS HERE IN
Support
G. I.'s
GI FOR PEACE
STOP

Navy Nurse Susan Schnall leads the antiwar march for peace in San Francisco, California, on October 12, 1968. Source: Harvey Richards Media Archive © Paul Richards.

A GI and Veterans March for Peace was being organized in San Francisco for October 12, 1968. We put up posters around our hospital base, publicizing the demonstration, but they were quickly torn down. We knew we had to get the word out.

The TV news showed the U.S. Air Force dropping "informational" flyers on the Vietnamese, telling them to go to "strategic hamlets" away from the fighting and spraying of deadly herbicides. If the United States could drop flyers on the people of Vietnam, then why couldn't we drop flyers about peace in the United States?

A pilot friend and I rented a single-engine plane, filled it with thousands of leaflets, and dropped them over Bay Area military bases: Treasure Island, Yerba Buena Island, Oak Knoll, the Presidio, and the deck of the USS *Ranger* at Alameda Naval Air Station.

One day later, I was given a new Navy order stating that Navy personnel could not wear their uniforms when "participating in a demonstration with knowledge that its purpose was in furtherance of partisan views on political issues."

I wondered about its legality, since General Westmoreland wore his uniform in front of Congress, asking for more money, armaments, and troops. Why couldn't I wear my uniform and speak out against the war? And so I did.

The next day, along with several thousand people, including five hundred active-duty military, I marched down Market Street to Civic Center, wearing my uniform. Soon the Navy determined there was enough evidence against me to convene a general court-martial.

During this time, I continued my nursing duties at Oak Knoll and worked on an underground paper we distributed on the base. We realized that we could speak out against the war and be heard by the American public.

On February 3, 1969, I was convicted of two charges: conduct unbecoming an officer for promoting disloyalty among the troops and disobeying a

Navy Nurse Susan Schnall dropped tens of thousands of this two-sided flyer from a rented single-engine plane over Bay Area military bases in 1968. Source: Image courtesy of Susan Schnall.

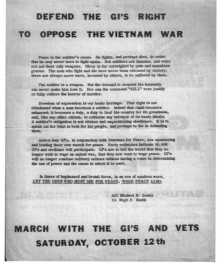

Navy regulation by wearing my uniform in a peace demonstration. I was dismissed from the service and sentenced to six months of hard labor.

More than 58,000 Americans and 3 million Vietnamese were killed in that war.

Our healing and reconciliation continue.

In the fall of 1970, Vietnam Veterans Against the War marched through New Jersey in a mock "search-and-destroy" exercise called Operation RAW (Rapid American Withdrawal) to show Americans the terror inflicted on civilians in Vietnam by U.S. troops. The photographs in the spread were taken by Carolyn Mugar. Source: Courtesy of LAFreePress.com.

Decorated Soldier Becomes a Movement Leader

Dave Cline served as a combat infantryman in Vietnam. He was wounded twice and received Purple Hearts and a Bronze Star. Upon his return, he became active in the GI antiwar movement and helped to publish the *Fatigue Press*, which active-duty GIs smuggled onto Fort Hood, Texas, to build opposition to the war. He later became a national coordinator of Vietnam Veterans Against the War and president of Veterans For Peace.

'A lot of people identified with the demonstrators'

Dave Cline

In training they gave you basically two things: Either you were going over there to help the people of South Vietnam fight against Communist aggression or you were going over to kill Commies. My background made me definitely be against the idea of going over to kill Commies, so I sort of latched onto the idea we were there to help people—I wanted to believe we were doing the right thing. When I got to Vietnam, it really didn't take me but about one day in-country to realize it wasn't true. As soon as you get there, the first thing they tell you is you can't trust any of them, they're gooks, they're not human beings.

On January 20, 1967, we were overrun by NVA and this guy ran off to my hole and started shooting in and I started shooting out and he shot me through the knee and I shot him through the chest and killed him. I laid in the hole all night. When the battle ended in the morning, they pulled me out of the hole, put me on a stretcher, and carried me over to this guy I'd shot. He was sitting there dead, leaning over against this old tree stump, just sitting there, with his rifle across his lap and a couple of bullet holes through his chest. The sergeant said, "Here's this gook you shot; you did a good job." I

Active-duty soldiers lead an antiwar march in Washington, D.C., April 1971.
Source: Photo and copyright by David Fenton.

Dave Cline, 1988.
Source: Photo by William Short.

looked at the guy; he was about the same age as me and I didn't feel any pride in it at all. They gave me a Bronze Star for that. This is the only person I can say with any certainty that I shot, and it blew my mind.

While I was in the hospital in Japan, I found a book which was called *The New Legions,* by Donald Duncan. Duncan had served eighteen months in Nam training ARVNs, and he resigned from the military and basically wrote we're fighting on the wrong side. When I read that book, it made a lot of sense to me because that's what I saw. So I made a decision I was going to come back to the United States and start working against the war.

I was sent down to Fort Hood, and that's when I really got hooked up with the GI movement. They had a coffeehouse in town called the Oleo Strut, and a newspaper called the *Fatigue Press*, which I got involved with. The Democratic Convention was scheduled for that summer, '68, so they began having riot-control training. They called it "the Garden Plot." We decided to organize a movement against it because there was a lot of opposition to the idea of going to Chicago. A lot of guys had just come back from Nam and they said, "We fought the Vietnamese; now they want you to fight Americans." A lot of people identified with the demonstrators on different levels.

We put together a meeting on the base. We met on a big ball field right in the middle of the base, and there must have been about seventy or eighty GIs there—black guys, white guys. We got a sticker mass-produced, a black hand and a peace sign. The plan was we were going to distribute them to all the troops that were opposed to being used. If they put us on the streets

Attitude Check was published by and for Marines at Camp Pendleton. One thousand Marines marched for peace in Oceanside, California near the base.

On April 23, 1971, the Vietnam Veterans Against the War organization sponsored a protest at the U.S. Capitol Building in Washington, D.C. Eight hundred U.S. veterans individually tossed their medals and ribbons onto the steps of the Capitol to denounce the war and proclaim their shame at having been decorated for serving in a war they believed was unjust. Source: Photo by Fred MacDarragh/Getty Images.

Members of Vietnam Veterans Against the War lead a peace march on the Boston Common, spring 1971. Source: Copyright © Diana Mara Henry / www.dianamarahenry.com.

against the demonstrators, we were going to put these stickers on our helmets as a visible sign of solidarity with the demonstrators in opposition to what we were doing. About three days after that, almost everyone that was at the meeting got taken off the Garden Plot roster for being subversive. They told the troops if anyone was caught with a sticker, they would be court-martialed.

Interviewed 1988 by Willa Seidenberg and William Short

Armed Forces Day, May 15, 1971, Fort Hood,
Texas. Source: Photo by Kevin Schaeffer.

Protest

Regarding the latest bombing
that destroyed a friendly village,
here is my medal for good conduct.
For yet another operation
that devastated so many lives,
here are my campaign ribbons.
If that is not enough,
I'll protest until my death
this murderous madness.

Jan Barry

Exposing War Crimes

6

Veterans Take the Lead in War Crimes Inquiries

Michael Uhl

On March 16, 1968, a unit of U.S. soldiers murdered more than five hundred civilians, primarily women and children, who lived in a grouping of Vietnamese hamlets soon known to Americans as My Lai. News of the massacre was suppressed by the U.S. military for more than eighteen months, but when finally revealed in November 1969, thanks to courageous eyewitness whistle-blowers, shock waves of disgust coursed through an American public already increasingly turning against the war in Vietnam.

Many returning veterans were intimately aware from their own combat tours that U.S. forces were routinely committing atrocities, aimed mostly at civilians. They knew what the commanders and policy makers knew, and the public didn't: that in a war viewed by much of the world as genocidal, My Lai was just the tip of the iceberg.

Since the late sixties, many of these veterans had become a familiar presence at mass antiwar mobilizations and were soon to be marching under their own organizational banner, Vietnam Veterans Against the War (VVAW). The anger that led many veterans to become antiwar activists was rooted in what they'd seen and done in Vietnam as unwitting executioners of military policies that inevitably led to war crimes in a conflict so ill-conceived that most of their own compatriots did not support it. These veterans understood that, in applying overwhelming force and firepower for the better part of a decade, the U.S. military had been destroying the very fabric of village life throughout South Vietnam and then grimly measuring its *victories* by counting the bodies of the dead, typically unarmed civilians.

This was my own state of mind in the mid-summer of 1969 when, back from Vietnam, I emerged from the Veterans Hospital on lower First Avenue in Manhattan and enrolled in a doctoral program at New York University. I persevered as a graduate student for three semesters, from the beginning

Soldiers Told the Truth

When the massacre at My Lai was exposed in 1969, dozens of soldiers and veterans gave testimony about similar crimes their commanders ordered them to commit. They organized public events to expose criminal policies such as "free fire zones" and told of numerous incidents of indiscriminate killings against Vietnamese civilians.

Two ex-GIs say troops torture prisoners in Vietnam

By Douglas Crockel
Globe Staff

Two former Army officers charged yesterday that American forces in Vietnam were committing war crimes by the use of electric torture to obtain information.

Speaking to representatives of the National Committee for a Citizen's Commission of Inquiry on U.S. War Crimes, former Army Lts Larry Rottman, 26, of Oliver street, Watertown, and Michael J. Uhl, 26, of New York city, said that American forces had been engaged in action in Cambodia more than two years ago but that the public had not been told of it.

The commission, a private group, was formed following disclosure of the alleged massacre of Vietnamese civilians at My Lai. It has held private hearings in several United States cities.

Jeremy Rifkin, national coordinator, and MIT Prof. Noam Chomsky, recently returned from Southeast Asia, also took part in a press conference here.

They again called for an investigation by an international tribunal into the actions of President Nixon and the military leaders of the United States for their part in what they termed "atrocities."

Uhl, who identified himself as a former military intelligence specialist with the Americal Division, said he had personally witnessed "electrical torture" 15 times.

He said American forces, in attempting to obtain information, attached wires from an electrical devices to sensitive areas of the bodies of men and women and passed electrical charges through them.

Rottmann, who said he was former assistant information officer for the 25th Infantry Division, said he saw nerve gas in storage tanks at Bien Hoa Air Base in South Vietnam, but admitted he had not personally seen it used.

Rottmann, who said he was a humanities teacher in an unidentified "private high school" in Watertown, also said he saw American soldiers decorate themselves with the "scalps, noses and genitals of mutilated Vietnamese peasants."

"This grows out of a Special Forces policy of paying mercenary forces who bring in the left ear of a victim to prove he was killed in action," Rottmann, a former Missouri resident, said.

Rottmann said he was in Cambodia three times during 1967–68 but added he personally had not set foot on Cambodian soil. He was in helicopters, he said.

Prof. Chomsky said the American government was made up of "desperados and lawbreakers" and added; "It's senseless to talk about the law in these times."

He said "American atrocities in Vietnam and Cambodia" were a violation of the Geneva accords.

Rifkin said that 30 former veterans had testified to American crimes in Southeast Asia since his commission's beginning.

He indicated that other former officers would testify at a later date as to the use of nerve gas.

Newsmen were shown photo copies of alleged bombing areas far from actual areas of enemy contact.

TORTURE CHARGED—Two former GIs, Larry Rottman and Michael Uhl, say U.S. used electrical torture in Vietnam. From left, Rottman, Uhl, Jeremy Rifkin and MIT Prof. Noam Chomsky.
(Ed Farrand photo)

The Boston Globe

FRIDAY MORNING, MAY 8, 1970

Prompted by the disclosure of the My Lai massacre, Vietnam veteran Michael Uhl teamed with veterans-rights lawyer Tod Ensign and attorney Mark Lane to create the Citizens Commission of Inquiry in 1969 to investigate and convene public events to expose war crimes committed by U.S. military forces.

Facing page: This leaflet called on veterans to testify to the crimes of the U.S. military in Vietnam as part of an inquiry named the Winter Soldier Investigation. One hundred and nine veterans from all branches of the U.S. military gathered in Detroit, Michigan, for three days in January 1971 to testify about war crimes they had committed or witnessed. A complete transcript was entered into the *Congressional Record* by Senator Mark Hatfield. The investigation's results were discussed in a hearing of the U.S. Senate Committee on Foreign Relations, convened by Senator J. William Fulbright in April and May 1971.

joining in protests with fellow students at local rallies and traveling to Washington, D.C., to attend the major demonstrations in the fall of 1969, but not yet engaged with other disaffected veterans. But after the explosive My Lai revelation, the public increasingly was receptive to hearing about what had turned us against the war. Our ranks quickly grew. Even where pro-war support was still strong, an ethos prevailed whereby folks who would normally tune out antiwar arguments might still listen to "a former soldier who had been there."

The concept that veterans could provide uniquely credible voices to educate Americans on the true nature of the war prompted the creation of an activist project called the Citizens Commission of Inquiry on U.S. War Crimes in Vietnam, or CCI. The initiative was inspired by two international tribunals established by the renowned British philosopher and pacifist Lord Bertrand Russell, and comprised of prominent world intellectuals. Though barely covered by the U.S. media, the tribunals had been convened to indict global opinion against the American war and emphasized the systematic nature of American war crimes.

CCI was the brainchild of Tod Ensign and Jeremy Rifkin, two New York–based civilian antiwar activists. By early 1970, Ensign and Rifkin had grasped how My Lai could accelerate the antiwar veterans' movement by providing a vehicle where veterans could carry an antiwar message, based on their own wartime accounts, to the very communities from which they had gone to war.

I became involved with CCI, combing college campuses in New York City to find veterans willing to come forward and divulge their experiences

WINTER SOLDIER INVESTIGATION

WHAT: An inquiry into U.S. Military Policy in Indochina.

WHEN: January 31, February 1 and 2, 1971.

WHERE: Howard Johnson's New Center Motor Lodge, Detroit, Michigan.

The Winter Soldiers of the American Revolution, unlike the "summer soldiers and sunshine patriots" referred to by Tom Paine, faced up to their responsibility during the long winter at Valley Forge. After our time spent in Vietnam we know that the most difficult and painful part of our service begins now – in telling Americans what is being done in their name.

Join us – former enlisted men and officers from all branches of the military – in sponsoring the investigation. If you have testimony to offer, contact us so that we may arrange for you to come to Detroit on January 31st, 1971.

Please add my name to the list of supporters of the Winter Soldier Investigation. I am a veteran and I have served in Vietnam.

Name _____ (please print) _____ Address _____

Telephone No. _____ Period of Service in Vietnam _____ Outfit _____

Signature _____

I have testimony to offer. Please contact me about arrangements for travel to Detroit.

Mail to: Winter Soldier Investigation, 967 Emerson Street, Detroit, Michigan 48215 or call collect – (313) 822-7700

The Winter Soldier Investigation was organized by the Vietnam Veterans Against the War (VVAW). Source: Photo courtesy of Democracy Now!

publicly. I was selected as one of two American war vets to testify in Stockholm at the International Enquiry on U.S. War Crimes, in my case presenting evidence of the use of torture and beatings of civilians rampant within the interrogation section of our Eleventh Infantry Brigade's First Military Intelligence Team. By that time I had joined CCI as a full-time veteran coordinator. Throughout 1970, CCI would organize events that ranged from community meetings to national press conferences in major cities across the country, creating forums where the disquieting accounts of participating veterans generated prime-time coverage on the nightly news and headlines in the newspapers wherever we went. CCI encouraged all those in a given locale who came forward to join VVAW, if they weren't already members.

A coalition was formed in the summer of 1970 that paired CCI and VVAW with the actress Jane Fonda, who, with a troupe of antiwar actors, had created a show called FTA[1] to entertain GIs outside major U.S. military installations. Fonda also agreed to help plan and finance an event where war crimes testimonies of scores of veterans would be presented.

Ultimately, two events were held. CCI staged its National Veterans Inquiry in early December 1970 over a span of four days in Washington, D.C. Some sixty Vietnam veterans presented their accounts of American atrocities of every category, from unprovoked mass murder, to the poisoning of Vietnam's crops and forests with tons of chemical herbicide, to the widespread use of torture during interrogations. VVAW's Winter Soldier Investigation was held in Detroit a month later and received widespread press coverage.

CCI continued to agitate around the war crimes issue well into 1971, hoping to convince Congress to conduct an official investigation on these allegations that might further shorten the duration of the war. That April, CCI joined forces with a freshman congressman from Oakland, California, Ronald V. Dellums, and a number of his progressive colleagues, to coordinate four days of testimony before an ad hoc panel in the House of Representatives, in conjunction with what would be the war's final and largest mass demonstration. CCI garnered national news with the revelation of another massacre by U.S. forces, which had occurred in April 1969, of at least thirty civilians at Truong Khanh. That atrocity was immediately confirmed by an American journalist stationed in Saigon, who made his way to the village and interviewed survivors.[2]

During that amazing springtime week in 1971 when such intense antiwar commitment erupted in the nation's capital, VVAW occupied the Washington Mall with an encampment of several thousand veterans. Dozens of them participated in another memorable and unprecedented moment, returning their combat medals by throwing them onto the stairs of the Capitol. Antiwar veterans had so thoroughly captured the imagination and support of the American people that when Attorney General John Mitchell ordered our removal from the Mall, the Washington police refused to carry out the order. This was blue-collar solidarity that transcended politics.

A week later, more than ten thousand demonstrators, many of them veterans, were arrested at the May Day mass civil disobedience protest and incarcerated for a day or more in a local sports stadium, an image that conjured the fascist repression of a Pinochet in Chile. Alarm spread that the seams of democracy were coming undone, but in the United States the resistance held.

Two things had become increasingly clear: The antiwar movement, including the GI movement, was of crucial support to the Vietnamese people's superior effort to prevail in the war. And in the face of such explosive popular opposition, and absent the traditional support from soldiers and veterans, the American war-making establishment's objective to deny the Vietnamese people the ultimate victory of their country's reunification was doomed.[3]

'Fifteen unarmed people were murdered that day'

Paul Cox

The Army had been covering up My Lai for an entire year by the time I arrived in-country. I became a squad leader in Bravo Company, First Battalion, Fifth Marine Regiment, and spent much of my time in Quang Nam Province, where I witnessed my own My Lai, on a smaller but no less barbaric scale.

Quang Nam was the land of the sniper and the booby trap, populated by people who were farmers by day and guerrilla fighters by night. We had been on a mission four days when another squad in my platoon took a round of sniper fire and decided to pursue. Not surprisingly, they soon encountered a booby trap that killed one man and wounded three others.

Paul Cox, 1990.
Source: Photo by William Short.

The next day, we left our night position and set off single file toward "Liberty Bridge" to catch trucks back to our base. As we entered a village along the way, the point squad immediately gunned down several women, children, and an old man at the first hut, and civilians at the next hut. Fifteen unarmed people were murdered that day, but there were no repercussions for the perpetrators. No, not as big as My Lai, but it brought into sharp focus the experiences of my entire tour.

It also turned me into antiwar activist. I had decided that the war was wrong and that we were wrong to treat the Vietnamese people like that. I did some reading; I read *The Autobiography of Malcolm X, The Rich and the Super-Rich*, and a book by Noam Chomsky. It really helped draw a lot together for me.

Upon my return to the States, I was assigned to garrison duty in Camp Lejeune, North Carolina. I joined several other Marines there in deciding it was our duty to put out a newspaper and print the truth about the war in Nam.

Until I got out in mid-1972, we wrote, assembled, printed, and clandestinely distributed eight issues of our underground newspaper, *RAGE*. We printed one thousand the first time, two thousand the second issue, and three thousand from then on. Other Marines continued the work until mid-1974—for a total of eighteen issues.

Though *RAGE* definitely was not an example of great journalism, working on it allowed me to redirect my anger and disappointment and try to warn others who were about to be deployed. We weren't alone. During the war, hundreds of underground antiwar newspapers by GIs were published at U.S. bases all over the world—some for many years.

Disaffected draftees and volunteers—enlisted and officers, men and women—formed a diffuse but telling indictment of a war machine and political system gone berserk. Our part of the antiwar movement was perhaps not well known outside the military, but the Pentagon took notice. Many dissidents were imprisoned; others were driven into exile in Canada, France, and Sweden.

These are painful memories. But in dangerous times like these, we should remind ourselves of the evils of war.

'We're all guilty'

Ron Haeberle

I saw a boy walking; he had already been shot. I knelt down to take a photo of him coming toward me. Then a GI knelt beside me and shot him; the boy was flipped end over end.

I stood up and the GI stood up. I asked him why. He looked at me; he stared. Then he just turned and walked away.

That happened about half an hour before I departed My Lai. It was March 16, 1968.

Earlier that morning, I was walking along a trail toward Highway 521 and noticed some soldiers from a distance, guarding what looked like a group of civilians. Minutes later, the soldiers began firing into the group as they were trying to escape. Later I came out to the trail and there were all the bodies I had previously seen being shot. Some were in the rice fields, too; they weren't all in the village.

Through the whole ordeal it was like maybe I wasn't really there. We were trying to find out what was going on. We were trying to find Captain Medina, but we couldn't get to him.

Army combat photographer Ronald Haeberle, in 1967. Source: Photo courtesy of Ron Haeberle.

1st Photos of Viet Mass Slaying

WEATHER
Snow flurries and
colder today.
High in the upper 20s.
Details on Page 5-C.

THE PLAIN DEALER

FINAL
Stocks & Races
Dow-Jones off 5.21

OHIO'S LARGEST NEWSPAPER

128TH YEAR—NO. 324 ★ ★ ★ ★ ★   CLEVELAND, THURSDAY, NOVEMBER 20, 1969   96 PAGES   10 CENTS

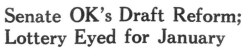

A clump of bodies on a road in South Vietnam.

© 1969, Ronald L. Haeberle

Exclusive

This photograph will shock Americans as it shocked the editors and the staff of The Plain Dealer. It was taken by a young Cleveland area man while serving as a photographer with the U.S. Army in South Vietnam.

It was taken during the attack by American soldiers on the South Vietnamese village My Lai, an attack which has made world headlines in recent days with disclosures of mass killings allegedly at the hands of American soldiers.

This photograph and others on two special pages are the first to be published anywhere of the killings.

This particular picture shows a clump of bodies of South Vietnamese civilians which includes women and children. Why they were killed raises one of the most momentous questions of the war in Vietnam.

Cameraman Saw GIs Slay 100 Villagers

By JOSEPH ESZTERHAS
(c) 1969, The Plain Dealer

U.S. Army troops "indiscriminately and wantonly mowed down" civilian residents of a tiny South Vietnamese hamlet on March 16, 1968, a former Army photographer has told The Plain Dealer.

Along with his eye-witness account, the former photographer has made available to The Plain Dealer a set of photographs taken at the village. They are being reproduced today on two pages of the Plain Dealer. This is the first publication of the photos, which also are in the hands of U.S. authorities investigating the sensational accounts of the village deaths.

RONALD L. HAEBERLE, 28, of Cleveland, then a sergeant and an Army public information staff member, was attached to C Company, 1st Battalion, 20th Infantry Regiment, 11th Light Infantry Brigade when the troops entered the hamlet of My Lai No. 4.

In an exclusive Plain Dealer interview, Haeberle described how U.S. soldiers "recklessly, wantonly and without any provocation" carried out the mass murder of South Vietnamese civilians.

In August of this year, Haeberle provided the Army's Criminal Investigation Department (CID), an arm of the Army Security Agency, with prints of the exclusive pictures he shot in the village during the operation and gave investigators a six-page statement.

Since then, 1st Lt. William L. Calley Jr., 26, of Miami, Fla., and Staff Sgt. David Mitchell, 29, of St. Francisville, La., have been charged in the case — Calley with murder and Mitchell with assault with intent to murder.

Senate OK's Draft Reform; Lottery Eyed for January

WASHINGTON — The Senate passed President Nixon's draft lottery bill yesterday and sent it to the White House. That means the next men inducted may be chosen under the new system.

Based on a national drawing of birthdays, and designed ultimately to concentrate the draft on 19-year-olds, it will supplant induction rules under which the oldest eligible men are the first summoned to military service.

The bill passed by voice vote after a scant hour of sparsely attended debate.

Sen. Mike Mansfield of Montana, the Senate Democratic leader, cast the only opposing vote, saying the measure does not adequately deal with the inequities of selective service.

Sen. John Stennis, D-Miss., chairman of the Armed Services Committee, promised he would open comprehensive hearings by Feb. 15 in an effort to fashion a general draft reform bill.

SECRETARY OF DEFENSE Melvin R. Laird said the next draft call would come in January and the administration would try to have the system in operation by then.

When the new system is fully effective, it will mean a single year of draft liability for most young Americans instead of the seven uncertain years they now face.

While the program is being phased in, however, all draft-eligible men up to 26 years of age will face equal liability to selection by lottery.

Under present law, the President is empowered to designate the prime age group, but once he does so the oldest men in that group must be summoned first.

Continued on Page 5, Col. 1

Reporter Eszterhas, left, and eyewitness Haeberle.
Plain Dealer photo (Richard T. Conway)

Army combat photographer Ronald Haeberle took these photographs. Explaining why he submitted them to his hometown paper, he said, "I wanted to tell my story [about My Lai] because there is a greater truth which must be told." Source: Reproduction copyright *Cleveland Plain Dealer*.

The top brass had to know. Officers were flying around above the site, observing. And the bodies were everywhere.

The cover-up was right from the top on down. I mean, 109 VC killed? Only about nine weapons? It was false reporting. The whole investigation was done to try to cover up this massacre. That's the way it was back then. If you wanted to get promoted, the whole objective was body count.

After I got home, I was giving talks about my time in Vietnam. During one talk I showed the pictures of My Lai. People couldn't react; they just stared. One woman said it was a staged production. No one wanted to accept it.

In mid-August, the CID questioned me. The lead investigator came and talked to me. They knew everyone in Vietnam carried a personal camera.

He asked me if I had seen any mutilations or rapes at My Lai. I said, "No, I didn't see anything like that; did that happen?"

He said yes, and he started telling me what happened: babies, women, teens raped and mutilated. It bothered me, and I thought to myself, You know, maybe the public ought to know what is going on in Vietnam.

I had taken twenty-one photographs with my personal camera, in color, and an additional forty black-and-white photographs with an Army-issue camera.

I destroyed two images. They were of a couple of GIs, where you could identify them doing the killing. I figured, why should I implicate them—we're all guilty—there were one hundred–plus of us there.

I went to the Cleveland *Plain Dealer* and talked to a reporter I knew. At first, he thought I was a kook while I was telling him the facts of what happened on March 16, 1968. But he called Fort Benning and talked to Lieutenant Calley's prosecutor.

The Army tried to stop the *Plain Dealer* from publishing. The publisher said, "Print." That edition of the *Plain Dealer* sold out; it was all over the news.

I didn't believe in the antiwar protests and the violence, but as soon as I knew it was women and girls—and what age they were—I couldn't accept it. Everybody said, Oh it was Charlie Company, Charlie Company. But what about B Company, where ninety-plus civilians were massacred in My Khe?

I had to testify at two trials. There were only two trials because certain soldiers had been called before the House Armed Services Committee and they couldn't be tried because information was kept from their military defense lawyers by the House committee. The numbers of potential defendants kept coming down until it was just Calley—he was the only one charged out of 100 or 125 people. I had reservations. We're all guilty.

• Documenting the My Lai Massacre

Twenty-five years after the My Lai massacre, Vietnam veteran Ron Ridenhour wrote, "My own investigation into My Lai—which took place between April and November 1968, while I was a soldier in Vietnam—convinced me that even the distressingly enthusiastic Calley, like everyone else in Charlie Company, was following orders.

"What happened at My Lai was not the consequence of some lowly second lieutenant who went berserk. It was, instead, the logical outgrowth of overall U.S. policy in Vietnam, one of two massacres that day, one of what I believe were many such massacres during the course of the war and, without question, the specific act and responsibility of officers much further up the military food chain than Calley."

Vietnam Veteran Ron Ridenhour turned over the information he gathered about the My Lai massacre to journalist Seymour Hersh after his letters to thirty members of the U.S. Congress and the Pentagon were ignored. Hersh won a Pulitzer Prize for his reporting on My Lai. Source: AP photo.

'The chaplain tells me you're being a troublemaker'

Dennis Stout

On my first operation we took this village and we were told to clear the bunkers, but they were really bomb shelters. They put me with an old-timer and said, "Do what he does." We came up to a bunker and he went to the back; I went to the front. He held up a grenade and pulled the pin, so I pulled the pin out of mine. He yelled in English, "Get out of there, you dirty gooks"; then he threw his grenade in and I threw mine in. They exploded and we heard kids screaming, so he pulled another grenade and threw it down and the noise stopped inside.

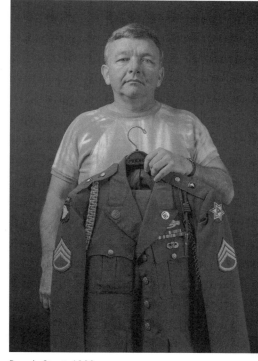

Dennis Stout, 1989.
Source: Photo by William Short.

We took a break, let the smoke clear, and went down to count the bodies. It was all mothers, small children, and old people. I decided to learn Vietnamese enough to talk people into surrendering because I didn't want that to ever happen again. I learned to speak maybe two hundred words of Vietnamese and, because I learned a little Vietnamese, they wanted me to interrogate prisoners. I could ask a question, but I couldn't really understand the answer.

Occasionally they would send a real interpreter, a guy we called "Baron Von Phuc." We were questioning this guy that we captured with his wife and two kids. I had talked them into surrendering. Our lieutenant said, "Ask him if he's ever worked for the NVA or helped the NVA." Phuc asked him and the guy said, "They made me carry a bag of rice into the jungle. They had guns, so I carried rice for two days and left it in a clearing. They gave us a political lecture and paid us." Phuc translated and said, "Yes, he did." So the captain said, "Shoot him." Just as I turned around to argue with the captain, Phuc pulled out his pistol and shot the guy.

Another time, we rounded up about forty civilians in a field. The people tried to save themselves by bunching up in the middle of the rice fields so nobody would execute them all at once. Our lieutenant ordered them shot. This colonel, who was hovering overhead in a helicopter, landed and locked that lieutenant's heels. I thought he was going to chew him out for shooting civilians, but he said, "Don't leave those bodies out here in the open where they can be seen. Take them in the brush." I refused to do it, and as far as I know, I'm the only one that refused.

I was ten months in-country and short. After I was wounded for the second time, I was made battalion public information officer and reporter for the battalion newspaper. I went back to my combat unit, the Tiger Force Platoon, to do some stories. They set up a little road barrier and started robbing the civilians. This one woman came along, so they took her and held her in a pit, along with a couple of other supposed suspects. Anybody between fifteen and fifty was suspect. They were torturing one old man, slapping him around, just for amusement.

aboveground

VOLUME 1, NUMBER 6   FROM THE HOME FRONT   FEBRUARY 1970

THIS PUBLICATION IS YOUR PROPERTY—IT CANNOT LEGALLY BE TAKEN FROM YOU

The newspaper *aboveground* was published by and for soldiers at Fort Carson, Colorado. GI underground papers regularly carried stories and photos by returning veterans about U.S. war crimes. Source: GI Press Collection, Wisconsin Historical Society.

At night they got the woman and started raping her on the other side of the perimeter and then carrying her from position to position. I could hear them slapping her. I didn't know what I was going to do when they came to me. I really cared about these guys; I was close to them, closer than brothers, closer than family, and I didn't know what to do. The position just before me was our new medic. They carried her to his position, and he said, "No, this is wrong and it's not moral." They beat him, broke two of his ribs, put a pistol against his head, and told him they would shoot him if he ever said another word about anything like that.

Then they came to my position and I said, "I'm going home pretty soon and I don't want to get any diseases or anything." They said okay, and they passed on and took her around to everybody else. The next morning, they tried to get her to run so they could shoot her. She wouldn't, so they threw a grenade at her feet. The grenade blew one leg almost completely off and the other one partially. And then one of the guys shot her in the head a couple of times. I decided I couldn't take any more.

I went to the sergeant major, my direct superior, to report it. He told me to keep quiet or I'd get a lot of good people in trouble. Then I went to the captain and he said pretty much the same thing. So I went to the chaplain. I thought he could get word out to the CID so they could investigate and put a stop to it. I told you, I was real naïve. Within half an hour I was told to report to the sergeant major and he says, "The chaplain tells me you're being a troublemaker. If I hear another word about this, you're going to go out on the next operation and you're not going to come back alive." I knew he really meant it.

I had about a year and a half left to serve. I wound up going to Fort Huachuca, Arizona, close to my home. I kept my mouth shut about my time in-country because I was afraid if I made any more noise while I was in the military, they would make me disappear. I had my wife and daughter with me, and my wife was pregnant with my second daughter. But then the My Lai massacre happened just as I was about to get out of the Army.

Six days after I got out, I officially reported eight war crimes that I could closely document. I had the time, date, names, and locations. I turned them in with the idea of not so much getting the individuals prosecuted, but I wanted the way people were trained and prepared for the war to change.

I called a reporter first because I didn't know how to report it through the military. [The reporter] did these stories on me, and the CID immediately came to see me. They said, "Okay, we're going to pursue this, and you should turn your evidence over." I gave them all the evidence, which they immediately made disappear.

I came under terrible harassment: My neighbors were asked to spy on me and my GI Bill payments were withheld for ten months. I made a speech on June 8 at the Federal Building in Phoenix before five thousand people. The night before, two agents with CID identification came to the house. The agent said, "if you make that speech, you know that you could go to work some morning and disappear, and no one would ever know what happened to you?" And he took his finger and poked me really hard in the chest and said, "You know we can do it, too, don't you?" I made the speech, stayed at a friend's house that night, hitchhiked to California, and caught a plane to Hawaii.

Interviewed 1989 by Willa Seidenberg and William Short

Postscript

William Short

Dennis Stout's eight documented accusations of war crimes by members of the Tiger Force Platoon, First Battalion, 327th Infantry of the 101st Airborne Brigade were investigated by the U.S. Army. In 1970, he received a letter saying the investigation was halted because investigators could not interview necessary witnesses in Vietnam. Actually, investigators interviewed dozens of witnesses over a two-year period. They identified several soldiers from the Tiger Force who were suspected of killing and raping Vietnamese civilians, including the ones that Dennis Stout spoke of in this interview. The investigation ended with no charges brought against the service members. In 1973, Army officials claimed that records of these events were destroyed "in anticipation of a cease-fire," but the investigation lasted until 1975. News articles say that many of the documents are most likely still in the National Archives, and a 2003 article in the Toledo *Blade* corroborated Stout's claims of deadly assaults on civilians in the Song Ve Valley.

• Senate Testimony by John Kerry

On April 22, 1971, John Kerry testified before the U.S. Senate Committee on Foreign Relations, representing Vietnam Veterans Against the War. Kerry described how more than 150 U.S. veterans had spoken before the Winter Soldier Investigation in Detroit months earlier, trying to bring to light the horrific crimes that had been "committed on a day-to-day basis with the full awareness of officers at all levels of command."

Excerpts from Kerry's Testimony

"It is impossible to describe to you exactly what did happen in Detroit—the emotions in the room and the feelings of the men who were reliving their experiences in Vietnam. They relived the absolute horror of what this country, in a sense, made them do.

"We rationalized destroying villages in order to save them. We saw America lose her sense of morality as she accepted very coolly a My Lai and refused to give up the image of American soldiers who hand out chocolate bars and chewing gum.

"We fought using weapons against those people which I do not believe this country would dream of using were we fighting in the European theater. We watched while men charged up hills because a general said that hill has to be taken, and after losing one platoon or two platoons they marched away to leave the hill for reoccupation by the North Vietnamese. We watched pride allow the most unimportant battles to be blown into extravaganzas, because we couldn't lose, and we couldn't retreat, and because it didn't matter how many American bodies were lost to prove that point, and so there were Hamburger Hills and Khe Sanhs and Hill 81s and Fire Base 6s, and so many others."

John Kerry represented Vietnam Veterans Against the War, testifying before the U.S. Senate Committee on Foreign Relations on April 22, 1971. Source: AP photo.

"Each day to facilitate the process by which the United States washes her hands of Vietnam someone has to give up his life so that the United States doesn't have to admit something that the entire world already knows, so that we can't say that we have made a mistake. Someone has to die so that President Nixon won't be, and these are his words, 'the first President to lose a war.'

"We are asking Americans to think about that because how do you ask a man to be the last man to die in Vietnam? How do you ask a man to be the last man to die for a mistake?

"We are here in Washington to say that the problem of this war is not just a question of war and diplomacy. It is part and parcel of everything that we are trying as human beings to communicate to people in this country — the question of racism, which is rampant in the military, and so many other questions, such as the use of weapons; the hypocrisy in our taking umbrage at the Geneva Conventions and using that as justification for a continuation of this war when we are more guilty than any other body of violations of those Geneva Conventions; in the use of free fire zones, harassment interdiction fire, search and destroy missions, the bombings, the torture of prisoners, all accepted policy by many units in South Vietnam. That is what we are trying to say. It is part and parcel of everything."

Making the Children Behave

Do they think of me now
in those strange Asian villages
where nothing ever seemed
quite human
but myself
and my few grim friends
moving through them
hunched
in lines?
When they tell stories to their children
of the evil
that awaits misbehavior,
is it me they conjure?

W. D. Ehrhart

Seeking Asylum Beyond Our Borders

For Deserters, a Solitary Decision to Register Dissent

Ron Carver

In April 1965, I drove to Washington, D.C., from Olive Branch, Mississippi, where I had been working with the Student Nonviolent Coordinating Committee in the fight against segregation and for voting rights. I was on my way to attend the first national protest against the Vietnam War, at a time when the direct involvement of American troops there was just beginning.

I had seen the FBI refuse to protect my brothers and sisters fighting for voting rights, so I was skeptical about President Lyndon B. Johnson's views on Vietnam. I rejected his claim that we had to send ground troops because Vietnamese patrol boats had, allegedly, attacked American warships in the Gulf of Tonkin. I couldn't accept that napalming and shelling Vietnamese peasants should be part of a fight for "freedom."

As soon as I returned to Mississippi from the antiwar march, I submitted my conscientious objector application, hoping to avoid wartime service. But I was from a small conservative town outside of Boston and my local draft board turned me down, berating me for even applying.

By early 1968, hundreds of thousands of troops had been deployed to Vietnam, with ever-greater numbers of men being poured into the meat grinder of war, notwithstanding the Pentagon's repeated promises that victory was just around the corner.

By then, hundreds of soldiers had refused to participate in the war, fleeing to Sweden, France, and Canada for refuge, even though Canada's border was officially closed to them.

I was determined to help them. I couldn't know it then, but eventually it was clear that the scale of desertions, along with refusals to fight, significantly limited the Pentagon's ability to conduct the war.

And so, at eleven o'clock one cold December night in 1968, I found myself turning off Highway 5 in Derby Line, Vermont, heading onto Caswell

Terry Klug enlisted in the Army from 1966 to 1971. He refused to go to Vietnam, went AWOL to Europe, and in May 1967 established RITA/ACT, a Paris-based GI antiwar group, with Dick Perrin and Max Watts. Terry returned to the United States in January 1969 and was charged with desertion. In June 1969, he helped to organize the Fort Dix stockade rebellion. He was sentenced to three years in the Leavenworth federal prison and served fourteen months before he was released. Source: Photo, 1991, by William Short.

Avenue, and then hooking a left onto the Pelow Hill road. Moments later, we were safely into Quebec, having crossed the border unnoticed between official points of entry. I was worried but not scared for myself. The "goods" I was smuggling across the border were two active-duty soldiers who had been stationed at Fort Dix, New Jersey.

The worst I risked was some small penalty. But if we were stopped and questioned, I knew the dissenting soldiers could be detained and turned over to American authorities, charged and tried for desertion or treason, and jailed in a Federal penitentiary.

At the time, I myself was protected from the draft by a student deferment. Ferrying soldiers across our northern border was the least I could do to show my solidarity with those on the front lines.

By early 1969, under pressure from its own antiwar movement, the Canadian government finally opened its border to deserters. During spring break, fellow antiwar activist Bo Burlingham and I borrowed my girlfriend's VW bus for our antiwar version of Paul Revere's ride. We playfully adopted code names and dubbed our trek "the CS3," after the Army's own Combat Services Support System. But our serious mission was to alert antiwar GIs and their civilian supporters that deserters no longer had to come up with plane fare to Europe, or sneak into Canada in the middle of the night.

Now they could enter Canada lawfully, and English-speaking communities in Vancouver, Toronto, and Montreal would welcome them with open arms. We brought the news to troops at military bases in New Jersey, the Carolinas, Georgia, Kentucky, Louisiana, and Texas.

Eight months later, I was ordered to report for a preinduction physical, after I graduated from college and lost my student deferment. By then I was working full-time at an antiwar coffeehouse that occupied a former fast-food restaurant less than a mile from the Fort Dix main gate.

The morning I showed up for my physical in Philadelphia, I was greeted by two dozen members of the Fort Dix Soldiers Liberation Front. They picketed the center with placards demanding that the Army induct me, along with my coffeehouse compatriot Saul Shapiro, so we could join the GI antiwar movement from the inside.

I had decided that, if accepted, I would join; I would use the skills I had honed opposing the Klan to take on the Army brass and the war itself. But I also knew that, before I would allow them to ship me off to Nam, I would travel the now-familiar route to Montreal to join the ranks of deserters. The Army must have sensed that I would be trouble for them and declined to accept me.

In 1970, four of us—myself, Josh Gould, Jay Lockard and Wendy Forbush—drove a donated Ford Falcon from army town to army town, down the East Coast, across the South, and up the West Coast. We were funded by the Center for Constitutional Rights (CCR), with an assignment to collect sworn statements from GIs back from Nam, detailing the war crimes they had witnessed or participated in. CCR attorneys Peter Weiss and Morty Stavis would later use those affidavits to support deserters' assertions that they chose to go absent without official leave (AWOL) because the alternative was to violate international prohibitions against crimes against humanity.

Historians Richard Moser and David Cortright cite Department of Defense testimony before the U.S. House of Representatives Appropriations Committee to conclude that by 1971, desertion and AWOL rates had reached the highest levels in modern U.S. history. According to Moser, "From 1966 to 1971 army desertions rose from 15 to 70 per thousand."

Cortright notes that, "Unlike those of World War II, most Vietnam-era desertions did not take place under fire, indicating that soldiers did not take off because of danger but because of disgust." [2] Similarly, sailors stationed on aircraft carriers were in little danger, and only a small percentage of U.S. pilots were shot down, yet AWOL and desertion rates climbed in those services, as well.

For many young working-class soldiers, the prospect of relocating to Montreal, Quebec, Paris, or Stockholm—with their unfamiliar cultures and languages—was a much more frightening prospect than heading into a jungle in Quang Tri Province. But they, and many other dissenting sailors and airmen, often felt morally compelled to take such a life-changing step.

By the war's end, more than thirty thousand draft resisters and deserters had left for Canada. Yet each soldier, alone, faced the decision to refuse to fight. As Mike Wong, a deserter from San Francisco, related in his interview with Willa Seidenberg, "It was questions of manhood, giving up your country, your family, your friends, giving up everything you knew." [3]

As the ground troops in Vietnam became increasingly unreliable, the Pentagon turned to B-52 bombers and fighter jets aboard aircraft carriers—and desertion rates exploded in the Navy and Air Force. Again, using Department of Defense figures, Cortright shows that the Air Force AWOL rate increased by 59 percent in 1971 and by 83 percent in 1972, the peak year of the air war, and continued at record levels during the bombing of North Vietnam and Cambodia. [4]

For decades after the war, a sort of conspiracy of silence or forgetfulness seemed to erase the significance of these events in helping to end the war. That "forgetting" was reversed when the exhibition that inspired this book opened.

"Waging Peace: U.S. Soldiers and Veterans Who Opposed America's War in Vietnam" was displayed at the War Remnants Museum in Ho Chi Minh City during March and April 2018. At the opening, thirty American military veterans joined dissenters like me and more than a dozen Vietnamese veterans for a conversation about the war.

Among the Americans were four former deserters, including Mike Wong; Lee Zaslofsky, who lives most of the year in Toronto but spends months each winter in Saigon; and two deserters still living in Sweden: Steve Kinneman, who deserted from the Army while stationed in Thailand, and Mike Lindner Sutherland, who deserted from the aircraft carrier USS *Intrepid* stationed in Japan.

Military Capability Deteriorates

By 1971, the rate of unauthorized absence in the military, including desertion, reached 17 percent, the highest rate in modern American military history.

"It is estimated that absenteeism deprived the military of about one million man-years of service . . . [which] forcibly curtailed military capabilities and contributed to the aura of chaos that hung over the armed forces by the early 1970s." [1]

I never set foot in Vietnam until 2016. But my experiences during the war helped define my life and they still reverberate—in some ways, painfully. The chance to connect with others through that conversation in the War Remnants Museum closed a circle and felt like a homecoming.

'It was questions of manhood, giving up everything you knew'

Mike Wong

I was born and raised in San Francisco, in the Polk District, which at that time was mostly a Chinese district. The Chinese have a real different slant on war. They see it as one of the miseries of life that comes around periodically, like famines, and it was never glamorized. In Chinese society, the hierarchy was nobles at the top, scholars directly under them, farmers, then merchants, and last of all soldiers.

I got my draft notice in 1968. I didn't know what to do. I was no longer convinced the war was right, but I wasn't totally convinced it was wrong, either. I finally decided I would volunteer in order to get into the medics. One time we were in the line for the mess hall, a real long line. We could see people whispering to each other and passing it down. And when the whisper

By the spring of 1969, Canada opened its borders to American deserters. Thousands streamed across the U.S. northern border. Here, three GIs and a child stand in front of the Toronto office of the American Deserters Committee.

Mike Wong, 1990.
Source: Photo by William Short.

got to me, the guy in front of me said, "They're killing women and children in Vietnam." I said, "Who's killing women and children? The Vietcong?" And he said, "No, we are." When we got to the front, we saw this newspaper rack with pictures of My Lai on the front pages. I can't describe what that did to us. There could no longer be any doubt as to who's right and who's wrong.

I received orders for Vietnam and decided to go AWOL and then turn myself into the Presidio Stockade, plead guilty to AWOL, and then they'd have to throw me in the stockade. That would become my permanent duty station and I could apply for CO. They had me in the stockade for, like, twenty minutes and a guard comes and pulls me back in the office. This lieutenant wants me to sign this thing saying they're releasing me from the stockade and putting me back on Vietnam orders, and I was to proceed immediately to Oakland Army Terminal for shipment to Vietnam. My lawyer says, "Just sign it." So they released me, and my lawyer took me back to his office and said,

Dr. Benjamin Spock was a prominent pediatrician and the revered author of *Baby and Child Care*, which has sold fifty million copies and been translated into more than thirty-nine languages. Here, Dr. Spock meets with members of the American Deserters Committee in Montreal. Some sixty thousand deserters and draft dodgers were in Canada at the time. Left to right, Stephen Texas Moon Argo, Dave Beauchene, Barry Sunderstrom, Dr. Spock, and Laurence M. Svirchev.

"They were going to stick a gun in your face and put handcuffs on you and then put you on the plane. I managed to talk them into releasing you into my custody. My legal responsibility is to take you to Oakland Army Terminal. If you resist, of course, you're a trained soldier, I can't very well stop you." I was so young and naïve, I had no idea what to do. I finally got the hint and I split.

I knew Canada was my only remaining option. But to go to Canada was to desert, to run away, to say I'm a coward. I was just going around and around in circles. So I went to this Chinese movie theater to stop thinking about it. What was showing was a movie about Chinese guerrillas fighting the Japanese during World War II. I came out and realized I only had two choices: Either I could go to Vietnam and do to the Vietnamese what the Japanese had done to the Chinese in World War II or I could go to Canada. The question had been framed in black and white: Do you want to be a murderer or do you want to be a coward? And I finally decided that the worst thing that can happen with a coward is he hurts himself, but a murderer not only hurts himself; he hurts other people, too. And so I went to Canada.

People think we make these decisions lightly and that all the people that went to Canada just ran away. I was prepared to go to prison and fight my case for as long as the war lasted. Going to Canada was the hardest decision of my life. It was questions of manhood, giving up your family, your country, your friends, giving up everything you knew. I went to Canada with the assumption I would be there for the rest of my life, that I would be an exile, a criminal, wanted by the FBI . . . and that I could never come home again.

Interview 1990 by Willa Seidenberg and William Short

NOTICE: THIS PAPER IS YOUR PERSONAL PROPERTY. IT CANNOT BE LEGALLY TAKEN FROM YOU FOR ANY REASON.

Blind Nationalism

Pvt. Richard Perrin, RA11748246

Since the first printing of ACT, an American Embassy official told the press that our effect on troop morale was "potentially calamitous". Some of us are and some have been in the Army. We know the type of information you are receiving either from the STARS AND STRIPES or the brass. It is the job of the STARS AND STRIPES and officers to keep up your morale; of course to do this they indoctrinate you with pro-war ideas. They must make you believe that U.S. policies in Vietnam are just.

We all know high morale is necessary for a successful war effort. Stop and think for a minute about how Germany kept up their troops' morale during W.W. II. The Nazi cause was unjust, yet the German troops were tough and difficult to defeat. How did the Nazis accomplish their high troop morale? They did it by appealing to German boys' blind nationalism. A good German accepted the draft, fought, killed, and died for Germany. They did it because Hitler was their <u>elected leader</u>. Germany was at war and a "good citizen" is not afraid to die for his country.

If someone asks you to kill and die, we say you should know why. The ACT shows you the other side of the story, all we ask is that you question U.S. government policies and your involvement with them.

RITAS LAUNCH ACT AT INTERNATIONAL PRESS CONFERENCE
From left to right: Terry Klug, Cornell Hiselman, G.Wuerth Dick Perrin and Philip Wagner.

Flicker of Light

Pvt. Ralph David Denzman, RA16930188

As a deserter of the United States Army a question arises in the minds of my countrymen. Was he just another one of the misfits who was unable to adjust? Or, perhaps he has tangible and sincere beliefs.

The everlovin' undecided homosapiens have freewill as a gift from the creator. It is only natural for a man to make use of this gift, rather than conceal it behind a cloak of conformity as a vast majority of people choose to do.

I have denied myself the expression of my innermost convictions for the majority of my life. But now that some unknown flicker of light is visible for the first time I staunchly refuse to surrender my integrity to the force of social pressure.

You as a soldier and human being have reached the time in your life where an important decision must be made. That is, a decision between conformity to the common belief that our government's position is righteous, or that a stand must be taken against our shoddy administration.

If you have a sincere desire for a decent and peaceful life, do something about it. Don't allow yourself to settle into the inevitable stagnation.

The RITA's Newsletter
Vol. 1, No. 2
Western Europe

United we stand

G.W.Wuerth Jr., RD 3, B202678

The country which preaches "life, liberty, and the pursuit of happiness," the country whose principles I would defend to the death, has become immorally and illegally involved in a war of aggression. This realisation is difficult to accept.

"It's your country, right or wrong". Right or wrong the United States leaders are allowed to decide who lives and who dies, and with which type of government a country will be endowed—all this in the name of freedom and democracy.

Is the "pursuit of happiness" coming home to find one's father and mother dead and one's village completely destroyed? Is that happiness! Dropping bombs on innocent people, or anyone for that matter, destroying schools, hospitals and land, spreading poisonous gases and inhuman chemicals throughout south Vietnam; is this our interpretation of "of the people, for the people and by the people.

What corruption, what madness renders our country the sole protectorate and ultimately, the destructor of humanity? What derangement, what stupidity continues our brutal aggression? Our leaders have rejected negotiations, the courageous Vietnamese can never be defeated, and each escalation further enflames and involves the "red" powers of China and the U.S.S.R. Are we destined towards a world wide showdown? Must all humanity be deprived of life itself because of the deranged audacity of our leaders and the blind obedience of their subservients.

My fellow Americans, I appeal to you, to your conscience, to your sense of justice and righteousness, and to your love of life.

The war must be stopped! Now! It is the individual responsibility of each American to clarify and to realize the true meaning of "life, liberty, and the pursuit of happiness".

> THIS NEWSLETTER IS WRITTEN BY DESERTERS AND RITAS FOR THE PURPOSE OF PROVIDING INFORMATION TO AMERICAN SERVICEMEN.

Dear Sirs,
I am a GI serving in Germany. I read your paper called GIs ACT and agree with a lot of what you say. Many of my friends have got orders for Vietnam. I think I will get orders to go too. I would like to resist this rotten war but am afraid to do anything by myself. Can you send me some information that could help me decide what to do? I am so confused about my position in the Army and no one here will give me any help. I hope that you can help me.

From a soldier stationed near Frankfurt.

American servicemen unite! You have nothing to lose but your stripes!

An edition of the *ACT* underground paper for deserters in France featured the announcement
of a new organization, RITA (Resisters Inside the Army), at a 1968 Paris press conference.

'You're going to have to decide who you are'

Gerry Condon

Basic training was really brutal and rude. It kind of shocked me, and the in-humanity of it reinforced my doubts about war. Just to survive the day-to-day routine, I suppressed my antiwar feelings for a period of several months. The training reality is so intense around you that it doesn't leave room for much else. I got an ulcer when I was going through Special Forces medical training. I sat down with myself and said, I think you know what this ulcer's about. I had, in a sense, become a little schizophrenic. I told myself, You're going to have to decide who you are and who you're going to be. So I finagled a leave

Gerry Condon, 1990.
Source: Photo by William Short.

back to the San Francisco Bay Area. I sat down in the backyard of my home and wrote this long, dramatic letter to the papers and had my picture in both papers. The *Chronicle* said, "Anti-war Green Beret Drops Out." I went back to Fort Bragg to face the music. I went through about six months of pretrial legal maneuverings, and realized they were going to make an example of me. Eventually, they convicted me of two counts of refusing orders to go to Vietnam, and sentenced me to ten years in prison. But I wasn't present at my court-martial. I had already deserted—I decided my freedom was more important than I thought.

I got a passport sent to me in Canada, which was really a godsend. After a couple of months, I decided to go to Europe. I lived in Germany for six months and I was totally broke, so I called home. My mom told me the FBI had been there the day before and for the first time they got her goat, which is great, because my father was a cop and she's used to cooperating with the system. The first couple of times they had Navy Intelligence visit her and she said, "Oh, they were such nice young men." But this time they called her a liar because they couldn't get the information from her they wanted, because she didn't have it. So I just happened to call the next day and she says, "They know where you are; they're getting closer." I'd been postponing doing the obvious thing of going to Sweden. I arrived in Sweden in November of 1969, the day of the first snowfall there.

If you arrived at the wrong port and got into the wrong hands in Sweden, you could have some troubles, because despite being a very progressive country, it's still got right-wing, fascist elements. There's cops in Sweden that wear American flags on their shoulders, even at that time, and they supported Nixon and the war. But Stockholm was pretty well set up. There were U.S. social workers that were on the government payroll to help out. And there was the American Deserters Committee, which had gained a lot of political allies and was on top of things. So when we arrived, we were basically accepted with open arms, and given a stipend, to buy a good winter coat, for rent and language training.

The majority of the guys there were deserters rather than draft resisters. Most of them, frankly, were not strongly motivated by antiwar idealism, although certainly antiwar attitudes were part of the total context that we were in.

On the other hand, a significant minority of us were extremely active—that's where I became politically active and aware. We did a lot of good work in conjunction with the Swedish antiwar movement. Of course, you have to keep in mind that during the entire war, no more than eight hundred men came to Sweden, and there were never more than five hundred at one time at the height, and they were spread around Sweden, as opposed to Canada, in which there were at least sixty thousand men who came up there fleeing the war.

Interviewed 1990 by Willa Seidenberg and William Short

A poster by a German antiwar group called on U.S. soldiers stationed in Germany to desert and seek sanctuary in France.

'Staying in the military would be a crime against humanity'

Mike Sutherland

Mike Sutherland in Ho Chi Minh City, March 2018. Source: Photo by Ron Carver.

My name is Mike Sutherland. People from my past know of me as Mike Lindner. That is the name I had when I was a sailor in the U.S. Navy during the American War in Vietnam.

I never wanted to put myself in a situation where I would be forced to kill another human being or be killed. So, instead of waiting to be drafted into the Army, I joined the Navy. I thought it was the patriotic thing to do.

Was this a just or legal war? I didn't know. I figured our government had already thought about that. But it didn't take long after I came aboard the aircraft carrier USS *Intrepid* that I realized that being in the Navy wasn't as honorable as I had been hoping.

At that time our ship was located in the Gulf of Tonkin. I saw with my own eyes the enormous quantity of bombs that our planes hurled on the Vietnamese. The scene was staggering. I saw how the A-1 and A-4 jet fighter planes were continually taking off, laden with bombs. At times, they did not return.

All this caused me to think about the nature of the war. I understood that thousands of people were dying. These airplanes were wiping villages from the face of the earth, destroying cities, burning children with napalm.

This was really murder and impossible to justify.

I knew I was doing something terribly wrong on a daily basis and I could no longer shrug it off with the cliché "I'm in the military and just doing what I'm told."

Talking about desertion wasn't something you did with just anyone. But in September of 1967 on our ship's flight deck, I met new friends who had the same thoughts with regard to the war and our participation in it.

We finally came to the conclusion that staying in the military, knowing how we felt, would be a crime against humanity.

So, on October 23, 1967, while our ship was in Yokosuka, Japan, the four of us changed into civilian clothes and took a train to Tokyo, where we met with a Japanese peace group. With their help, we filmed a statement to be released to the press.

"We four—Craig Anderson, John Barella, Richard Bailey, and Michael Lindner—are against all aggressive wars in general and are against the American aggression in Vietnam in particular.

"We consider it a crime for a technologically developed country to be engaged in the murder of civilians and to be destroying a small, developing, agricultural country. We believe that the Vietnamese people themselves should determine their own fate. We are in favor of the total withdrawal of all forces of the U.S.A from Southeast Asia."

A meeting at the office of the American Deserters Committee on Kungstaten in Stockholm in 1971. Left to right, Barry Fockler, Mike Powers, Laura (surname unknown), Gerry Condon and Susie Kaufman. Source: Photo by Jeanne Fockler.

Joint Statement by the Four Patriotic Deserters of the USS Intrepid

You are now looking at four deserters, four patriotic deserters from the United States Armed Forces. Throughout history, the name deserter has applied to cowards, traitors and misfits. We are not concerned with categories or labels. We have reached the point where we must stand up for what we believe to be the truth.

This overshadows the consequences imposed by the categories.

Why Have We Done This ?

We oppose the escalation of the Vietnam war because in our opinion the murder and needless slaughter of civilians through the systematic bombing of an agricultural, poverty stricken country by a technological society is criminal.

We believe that the U. S. must discontinue all bombing and pull out of Vietnam, letting the Vietnamese people govern themselves.

We believe that a majority of the people in Japan and the U.S. oppose the war in Vietnam, but are individually indifferent in taking actions to move towards peace. We appeal to the people the world over to realize that each one of us is responsible for the slaughter in Vietnam.

We believe that further escalation in Vietnam will eventually lead to a direct confrontation with China, resulting in a world war.

We oppose the war as true Americans, not affiliated with any political party.

We face military disciplinary action as a result of our beliefs, therefore we seek political asylum in Japan, or any other country not engaged in the war.

We believe that the people in Japan, seeking peace in Vietnam, should unite with the Americans, and all others peaceful people of the world, in a united stand against the war.

We oppose the militaristic impression the U.S. is forcing on the world. Through military occupation and economic domination, the U.S. controls many small countries.

We oppose American military forces in Vietnam, but not Americans. With only seven per cent of the world's population and control of one third the world's wealth, Americans should make a humanitarian stand rather than a military stand.

We believe that all military expenses should be cut. The money now spent for the war effort, should be rechanneled into health, education and welfare, throughout the world.

It is our fervent hope that our actions will move you, wherever you are, whoever you are, to do whatever you can to bring peace to Vietnam.

To conclude, we think that we have made it clear that our decision to publicize our action in deserting from the military has been made in the hope that other Americans, particularly those in military, the people of Japan and of all countries can be spurred into action to work towards stopping this war.

We appeal to all of you wherever you may be to take action in whatever way you can to bring peace to the troubled country of Vietnam. Let all of us unite together and work for peace.

Nov. 1, 1967, Tokyo

John Michael Barilla
Richard D. Bailey
Michael A. Lindner
Craig W. Anderson

The Japanese peace group Beheiren hosted the Intrepid Four's press conference and helped them board a ship to seek asylum. Left to right, Beheiren Chairman Makato Oda, Michael Lindner, Craig Anderson, Richard Bailey, and John Barella.
Source: Flyer courtesy of Beheiren.

American Deserters Committee members marched in Stockholm in 1971.
Source: Photo courtesy of Bruce Beyer.

When the filming was done, we were able to board a ship heading to the USSR. In Japan, in Russia, and in Sweden, good people helped to make it possible. It was like they were saying "You're doing good; keep going!" And we did.

But it wasn't easy. We, of course, would feel the great distance from our families and friends at home and the loss of the social support that being at home would have meant. Yet we felt we had no choice. And so we wound up in Sweden.

The Intrepid Sea, Air & Space Museum, on Pier 86 at 46th Street, on the West Side of Manhattan. Source: Photo courtesy of Intrepid Museum.

Special permanent exhibit on the Intrepid Four within the Intrepid Museum. USS *Intrepid*, permanently docked in Manhattan, has been converted to a museum. Source: Photo courtesy of Intrepid Museum.

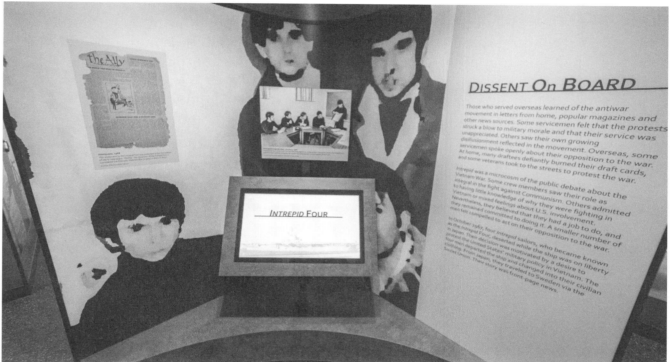

Craig moved back to the States quite early and John went to Canada and started a new life there. Rick Bailey and I acclimatized to Sweden. It has been our home, along with a lot of other guys who refused to cooperate with the American War. Sweden is where our wives and our kids and grandkids are. And, of course, we now have lots of friends there, too. It has been good.

Letter to My Brother from the Onondaga County Jail

In the snow, in the blinding snow—
I thought of you
the sullen, gray winter day
they brought me there.
Handcuffed, shackled
I wondered what you would think
if you could have seen me:
stumbling into the long cellblock—
in my winter dress green uniform
trying to seem aloof, hard-edged,
I had just turned twenty.
Now I wonder where you were
that winter—
did you know where they'd taken me?
Did you know I never even said
Goodbye—
I say it now—*Goodbye*,
there's grace in that,
the way time has of fooling us
of fouling up the mechanics
of our lives—so we learn too late
how precious the hours are,
how I wish you might
have seen me then,
how alone & lost I felt without you.

Gerald McCarthy

Uprisings and Rebellions

8

Black GI Resistance

David Cortright

The most consistently rebellious troops in Vietnam and throughout the military were African Americans. The civil rights struggles and urban uprisings that shook American society during the 1960s emerged within the military, as well. Many African American troops came into the military with a bolder, more assertive consciousness of black power and a sense of deep skepticism about the war. Influenced by the civil rights movement and growing black militancy at home, African American troops tended to group together (the "bloods," they often called themselves).[1] They were among the most defiant troops in fighting against racism and the war and posed a significant challenge to the military's mostly white power structure.

Many major racial uprisings occurred in the military during the Vietnam War. One of the largest and most explosive was the prison rebellion at Long Binh Jail at Bien Hoa, northeast of Saigon, in August 1968.[2] The overcrowded prison was packed with African American troops who experienced squalid conditions and constant harassment from untrained guards. GIs called the jail "LBJ," a contemptuous reference to their commander in chief in the White House. Nearly 90 percent of the inmates were black, and currents of black power identity surged through the jail.[3] The exact spark that touched off the uprising is unknown, but on the night of August 29, a melee broke out in which hundreds of prisoners fought with military police. Dozens of prisoners and MPs were injured, and one soldier died. Much of the prison was burned to the ground.[4]

All of the services experienced major racial rebellions. One of the largest in the Marine Corps occurred at Camp Lejeune, North Carolina, in the summer of 1969. The fighting broke out on the night of July 20, after a dispute over an incident of racial discrimination at an enlisted men's club among Marines of the First Battalion, Sixth Marines. Many African American and Puerto Rican GIs were involved, most of them Vietnam veterans. The episode

Resisting Racial Discrimination

African American, Latino, and Native American soldiers often opposed the war and resisted the pervasive racial discrimination they experienced in the military. Many were imprisoned in overcrowded jails and stockades. Dozens of major uprisings occurred during the war.

quickly turned into a sprawling melee that left fourteen Marines injured and one dead.[5] The troops blamed the violence on a persistent pattern of racial harassment and discrimination from local commanders. That pattern of unequal treatment was documented in an internal Marine Corps report a few months before the uprising. The unheeded report, later obtained by *The New York Times*, warned local commanders that "an explosive situation of major proportions" existed on the base and that "many white officers and NCOs retain prejudices and deliberately practice them." [6] Afterward, criminal charges for the violence were pressed against twenty-six Marines, all of them black and Puerto Rican. The minority troops responded by creating their own organization, the Council of Concerned Marines, a network of representatives from each company that sought to free their imprisoned colleagues and defend against continued harassment and abuse.

Travis Air Force Base in northern California was the major debarkation point for troops deploying to Vietnam. It was also the scene of the largest mass rebellion in the history of the Air Force, a racial uprising that traumatized the base and the surrounding community. As with most of the other black rebellions in the military, the roots of the May 1971 rebellion lay in patterns of racial discrimination, growing militancy among African American troops, and a general crisis of morale at the base. According to a 1981 study in *Air University Review*, conditions on the base "resembled the ghetto environment described in the Kerner Commission Report." They were the result of the "impersonality, insensitivity, and indifference" of military commanders.[7] The uprising was sparked by complaints about loud music and an incident at an enlisted men's club. Fighting began on a Saturday afternoon and continued sporadically through the weekend, resulting in the arrest of several black airmen. On Monday evening, more than two hundred enlisted members, including some whites, marched in several groups to free the arrested troops. They were met by a force of more than three hundred military police and more than seventy civilian police called in from surrounding communities. More than six hundred airmen were drawn into the resulting brawl. An officers' club was burned to the ground and dozens of troops were injured. One hundred and thirty-five service members were arrested, most of them black; ten people were injured, and a civilian firefighter died.[8] For several days, this vital center of military transport for the Vietnam War was in a virtual state of siege as commanders sought to end the violence and restore order.

The most serious racial uprising in the Navy occurred in October 1972 aboard the USS *Kitty Hawk*, when the aircraft was on bombing duty in the Gulf of Tonkin. The racial explosion occurred when the giant warship was unexpectedly ordered back to Vietnam from shore leave in the Philippines rather than returning to the United States as planned. Groups of angry black sailors armed with pipes and chains clashed with members of the ship's Marine detachment. Fighting continued into the early-morning hours before subsiding. Forty-seven sailors were taken to the ship's medical center with injuries.[9] At one point during the chaos, the ship's executive officer believed that the captain had been killed and issued emergency orders over the ship's public-address system. The unhurt captain quickly countermanded the XO's announcement and pleaded with the crew to keep calm. "I know everyone is hot under the collar. I know you are disappointed at not going home as planned. So am I, but we've got to live with it, so cool it." [10] It was a remarkable admission by the captain that part of his crew was in open rebellion and that the violence racking his ship was partly due to the sudden return to bombing operations.

A nonviolent rebellion among sailors occurred aboard the USS *Constellation* a few weeks later. The episode was described as the "first mass mutiny in the history of the U.S. Navy." [11] As the aircraft carrier prepared for air operations after refitting in San Diego, word of the *Kitty Hawk* action arrived. Strongly motivated to support the brothers on the *Kitty Hawk*, black sailors on the *Constellation* intensified their demands for improved conditions and an end to racist policies. On the evening of November 3, a group of sailors gathered on the ship's mess deck to discuss their grievances and refused to leave until the ship's captain agreed to meet with them.[12] The captain refused and decided instead to return to port to off-load the dissident group as a beach party. A few days later, on the morning of November 9, the defiant sailors gathered at the dock as the ship prepared to sail. Supported by antiwar lawyers, and with a large press contingent on hand to witness the drama, the sailors refused direct orders to return to the ship and responded instead with clenched-fist salutes.[13] A total of 120 sailors were charged with disciplinary violations for the action.[14]

The resistance of African American members of the military against racism and war was a major factor in the collapse of discipline, morale, and combat effectiveness during the Vietnam War.

'There was a lot of rage; it just began to build and build'

Greg Payton

I was in a supply unit in Vietnam located in Long Binh. We went out on the field depot and I worked a location deck. What they told us was, if we come in and do the right thing in the beginning, that we're doing the menial jobs now and as other groups come in they will get the jobs and we will get a better situation. So I accepted that for words. So in the beginning we had a lot of dirty jobs: burning feces, cleaning out urine pits, and all kind of different

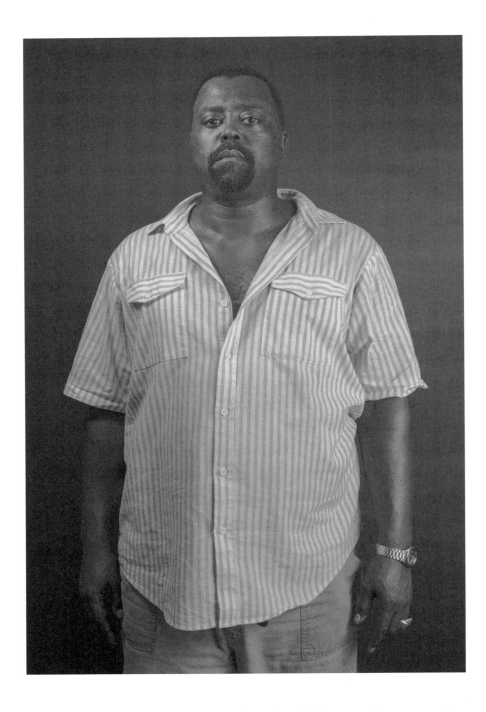

Greg Payton, 1988.
Source: Photo by William Short.

things. But what I began to notice is that a lot of white recruits were coming in and they weren't getting the same assignments I was getting. It seemed like we were always pulling up the short end of the stick.

One time the first sergeant was talking about these gooks or something, and I replied, "Yeah, the gook is the same thing as a nigger." It was like a light went off; it was a real revelation. I was naïve about a lot of things. I had to develop a racist attitude. I never was raised with that. The first sergeant told me I was a smart nigger; that's just what he said.

One incident that really opened my eyes was with a white GI named Muncey, from Kentucky. He was really a typical superartificial macho guy.

LBJ

The U.S. Army's Long Binh stockade, or jail, in Vietnam was commonly referred to as "LBJ," the initials of the U.S. president who escalated the number of troops in Vietnam. Source: Courtesy of the National Archives.

A group of Vietnamese kids came up to our truck as we were coming back from guard duty. We had food and stuff and we'd feed the people out in the field. We had leftover food, bushels of apples and oranges and stuff. These kids came up to the truck begging and you could see it in their faces; these kids had that "I'm hungry, feed me" kind of look. So Muncey says, "Look at these gook kids," and he took a bite out of an apple and threw it in the dirt and about four or five kids dove on it. It was just like when you drop a piece of bread in the fish tank. It just really set me off. I damn near threw him out of the truck, and it was still moving. I was brought up on charges for that.

I had three courts-martial and I went to the stockade and it was all these black people . . . all these brothers. That blew my mind. After I'd been in the stockade about two months, I made it to minimum security and I had a work detail. I used to bring in kerosene to burn the feces with. Some guys got together and said they were going to have a riot in the stockade. They asked me to bring in an extra can of kerosene every other day so they couldn't see buildup. So I did. It started in minimum security, but they went to maximum security and broke the locks and let everybody out. They picked noon because that's when the guards change, and most of them were eating in the mess hall. They broke the gate, broke the lock, let everybody out of maximum security,

These locks were broken off cell doors at the maximum-security section of the Long Binh stockade. The photo was part of the U.S. Army's official investigation of the rebellion there. Source: Courtesy of the National Archives.

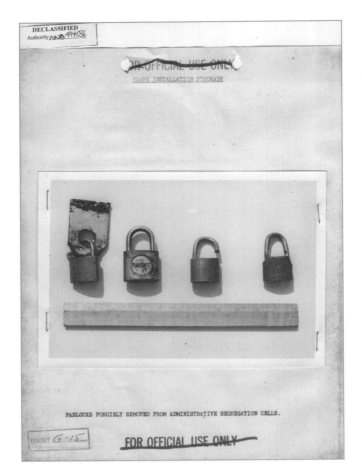

DECLASSIFIED
Authority AND 994086

FOR OFFICIAL USE ONLY
USARV INSTALLATION STOCKADE

RABBIT

PADLOCKS FORCIBLY REMOVED FROM ADMINISTRATIVE SEGREGATION CELLS.

EXHIBIT G-15

FOR OFFICIAL USE ONLY

This photo shows the Long Binh stockade after the prisoners revolted and destroyed many of the buildings in 1968. Source: Courtesy of the National Archives.

and started burning the hooches and whatnot. There was a lot of chaos. A lot of people got hurt and I imagine some people got killed. I remember seeing white guys, in particular, and guards getting beat up with bunk adapters. If you were white, you were in trouble, whether you were a good guy or a bad guy.

I've never been as violent as I was in Vietnam. There was a lot of rage; it just began to build and build. I did so many things that were unnecessary and hurt some people and it really wasn't their fault. But I had to take it out somewhere; I had to vent this anger in some way. Today I work on not becoming violent; I'm scared of violence.

Interviewed 1988 by Willa Seidenberg and William Short

'That year in Vietnam was like twenty years'

Clarence Fitch

My father was in the military in World War II, and even though he was in a segregated army, it was very much a part of his life experience. Being a veteran wasn't something that was looked down on; it was one of the few things black men had that they could hold up as being honorable, as being accepted, as being proof that you had just as much right to anything that was going to be given out, even though you didn't get it all the time. That's why a lot of the hostility and resentment came, because they didn't get their just due. But they did get some things out of it. My father went to mechanics school on the GI Bill. The house my mother lives in right now was bought on the GI Bill. We probably would not have been able to do it without the GI Bill. My father talked about his personal experiences in the war all the time. I could tell you where he was stationed because he told us a thousand times. He made us sit down and listen to the stories, but he didn't really elaborate on the negatives and the racism.

For me and other black GIs in Vietnam in 1967, things were changing. Things going on in the States affected our behavior there. Some of the same black consciousness, the whole black power movement, was taking place there, too. We were growing Afros, expressing ourselves through ritualistic handshakes, black power handshakes, African beads, hanging around in cliques, trying to eat up as much of the black music as we could get our hands on. We kind of segregated ourselves; we didn't want to integrate into what we considered the white man's war. For the first time I was looking at the enemy not so much as the enemy, but as another minority, brown people. The North Vietnamese reminded us of it, too.

Clarence Fitch, 1988.
Source: Photo by William Short.

People started really trying to educate themselves about how the war started, where the war was going. We read a lot of the books, *The Confessions of Nat Turner*, *Soul on Ice*, all of the black publications, *Ebony*, *Jet*, as much as we could see, because we wanted to be a part of it. There were some nights we had twenty, thirty, fifty brothers hanging out. When we went into a mess hall, we ate together in certain parts of the mess hall. They were trying to make us get haircuts, cut those Afros off, and people were going to jail to keep their hair. We tried to spend almost all of our time together, the "Bloods" in Vietnam, we tried to have all-black hooches. The brass would try to prevent this; they would try to assign us to integrated hooches and stuff like that.

When I was put in the brig, it was like another awareness. Because the brig was like— there were white Marines in the brig, but the overwhelming majority were black, much like the jails were back in the World. It just made you more bitter, more conscious, more hard, more militant, gave you more of a reason for being what you were and to resist and to fight, and make sure you educated yourself and educated others.

You laid down at night and there was just so much tension going through you, with all the racial stuff, the war itself, and we were so young. But it felt like we were so much older. It felt like you had lived a long time. That year in Vietnam was like twenty years, you saw so much and witnessed so much.

Interviewed 1988 by Willa Seidenberg and William Short

'I couldn't quite believe my eyes'

David Fenton

OBEDIENCE TO THE LAW IS FREEDOM.

I couldn't quite believe my eyes seeing this sign hanging at the entrance to the Fort Dix, New Jersey, stockade. It was 1969, and this was where the Army imprisoned American soldiers who refused to go to Vietnam to fight the immoral war. The stockade was the site of numerous demonstrations in support of the soldiers. It became a big rallying cry for the antiwar movement.

David Fenton at Liberation New Service office in New York City, 1970.
Source: Photo and copyright by David Fenton.

THE TIME HAS COME FOR A LONG-NEEDED

SHAKEDOWN

Vol. I, No. 8   P.O. Box 68, Wrightstown, N.J.   September 12, 1969

This paper is written and published by a group of Ft. Dix GI's who in doing so have freed their minds from the involuntary servitude of the military machine. This is our "Ultimate Weapon."

FREE TO SERVICEMEN   **25¢ FOR CIVILIANS**

Demonstrate at Fort Dix
SUNDAY, SEPT. 28   HIGH NOON

FREE THE FORT DIX 38

FREE ALL POLITICAL PRISONERS

The movement has come to the stronghold of American Imperialism – the U.S. Army. Coffee houses and GI underground newspapers are educating and organizing GI's against the war in Vietnam and against white racism and fascism here on the home front. We are now fighting the Amerikan oppressive system from within. The Army is in Vietnam profiting on the lives of GI's. The Army has been to Chicago, Newark, Berkeley, Watts, and other cities, keeping people down who are fighting for their human rights. We must get together – the people oppressed on the outside and the people oppressed within the Army. RALLY WITH US – BEGINNING AT HIGH NOON – AT THE COFFEE-HOUSE, AND THEN MARCH ON POST WITH US, WITH GI'S, AGAINST THE WAR MACHINE.

On June 5, 1969, over 200 prisoners at the Fort Dix stockade rebelled against conditions in the pound. Prisoners on June 5th were forced to stand formation in the hot sun for 6 hours. One prisoner that day left his seat in the mess hall to get his water bowl. He was immediately thrown into Maximum Security Segregation, the dungeon of the Army Stockade. The rebellion to protest these conditions was suppressed by the Military Police, and some of the activists in the Pound are now facing over 40 year court-martial sentences for their attempt to survive. Their courts-martial will be coming up in October. The Fort Dix 38 are political prisoners of war, just like Huey Newton, the N.Y. Panther 21, the Presidio 27, and countless others. Together, we can help free these GI's and political prisoners all over this country.

THE POUND

Since the invention of the Vietnam War, the population in Army stockades has greatly increased. The Fort Dix stockade, which was condemned over 20 years ago, was originally built to house 350 men and now holds over 800. (There were 300 men in the pound before the Vietnam buildup began.) 90% of the men in the pound were not convicted of any "crime" -- they went AWOL, a personal form of rebellion against the Army (either because of opposition to the war in Nam or Newark, or because of hardship at home). Conditions in the Fort Dix stockade are standard for Army prisons: brutality, sadism, starch fillers and water for meals, lack of medical or psychiatric care, almost no hygienic facilities, purposelessness, idiotic details, etc. Men in seg (solitary confinement)

sit for months with very little human contact, are fed "D.S. chow" ("rabbit chow"), i.e., dry cereal, water, lettuce, and stale bread – often because of voicing "political" issues. Medieval tortures, for example, STRAPPING a prisoner's hands and ankles behind his back, and then DROPPING him on his stomach are applied to those who deviate from military discipline (like epileptics, political activists, and black or Puerto Rican GI's who don't appreciate their sergeant's racism). A number of prisoners are driven to suicide (by banging their heads against the steel or concrete walls) while in the pound.

Now why does today's Action Army have to keep such a horrid stockade system? It's because the Army has something even more murderous on its hands – the Vietnam war. And so GI's are given a motivating choice (we're a "democracy," remember) -- Vietnam or the pound. That's why most draftees become robots at the command of the Nazi brass. And that's why all of us must demonstrate on post and demand, forcefully, the abolition of the stockade system within the military.

continued on p. 4

SHAKEDOWN is your personal property and cannot legally be taken from you for any reason. If any individual attempts to confiscate this paper or any other literature from you, you should read him Army Regulation 381-135 (d): "Unit commander shall further ensure that there is no interference with the U.S. Mails, and that every individual under his command has the right to read and retain commercial publications for his own personal use."
This is the legal situation, but we all know that most of what the Army does is illegal. Don't be afraid to make a stand. If you're really hassled, call the New York Draft and Military Law Panel at 212-683-8180, or drop us a line.

On June 5, 1969, more than two hundred prisoners rebelled at the Fort Dix stockade. Most had been jailed for being AWOL. Thirty-eight antiwar soldiers were charged with leading the rebellion and faced forty-year federal prison terms. Four months later, more than five thousand antiwar protesters marched onto the base in support of the Fort Dix 38. The next morning, *The New York Times* covered the story for the first time and the Army released three hundred prisoners. Soon after, the Army dropped charges against the thirty-eight men.

And the frequent demonstrations there put more and more attention on the plight of the soldiers.

My photograph of the obedience sign at the stockade entrance went viral, at least its 1969 equivalent. It was published in antiwar newspapers across the United States and, indeed, across the world. It got so much attention that an embarrassed U.S. Army felt compelled to finally take the Mussolini-like slogan down. A small victory but satisfying nonetheless.

I was a photographer for the Liberation News Service (LNS), which was the AP/UPI of the underground, antiwar, countercultural press of the late 1960s. LNS was also a chapter of Students for a Democratic Society (SDS).

Facing page: OBEDIENCE TO THE LAW IS FREEDOM. The stockade (prison) at Fort Dix, in Wrightstown, New Jersey, was built originally to house up to 350 prisoners. By 1969, it was filled to overflowing, with more than eight hundred incarcerated soldiers. Source: Photo and copyright by David Fenton.

SHAKEDOWN   Oct. 17, 1969   9

Letter From One of Many

I feel it is time to say something. I am one of the Ft. Dix 38, the youngest member in fact. I am only 17. My name is Thomas Catlow, I am facing 40 years for the June 5th revolt at the stockade. I have read alot of articles on the revolt and about the treatment of the prisoners in the stockade. The army denies cruel treatment but I have proof that this is false. I have been beaten three times since June 5th in Maximum Security.

The army would like to know why there actually was a revolt in the Ft. Dix stockade on the evening of June 5th. It's simple! You can only deprive men of their essential manhood and treat them like animals for so long until finally they stand up and fight back.

I say down with military dicipline, for if the American people really believe men should be jailed for going home or refusing to kill in a war that we do not have any interest in, please send me to another country. I would rather go to jail than be forced to murder Vietnamese people in a needless war.

What has become of our sense of reasoning? Nothing beneficial ever comes out of any war! Is going to jail the only way to stop ourselves from being forced to murder?

I have been confined in the Ft. Dix stockade for a period of 7 months now. I would like to be cut. I would like to be free, but I will not be a slave! Yet if the military establishment believes that by locking me, a 17 year old boy, away for up to 40 years will stop men fracm fighting back when they cannot take it any longer, then I say do it! I also say that if the military does this, I will make a request for execution and if it is denied, I will end my own life. If I cannot live in this world without having to be forced to kill needlessly, I would rather be dead.

I only hope that someday this world will realize we can only live together in peace.

Yours truly,
Thomas W. Catlow
One of many

I Read The News Today....OH BOY!

-The number of retired high ranking military officers working for the defense industry tripled in the last decade to the figure of 2,072, including these figures for the top five defense contractors in the nation: General Dynamics- 113, Lockheed - 210, Douglass - 141, Boeing - 169, American Rockwell - 104.

-New York Post: (Headline) Fort Dix Salutes Peaceful Protesters.

-New York Post: Colonel Nealon said,"They sure organized a hell of a march".

-National Guardian: The demonstrators marched down Main Street chantting, "Free the Fort Dix 38, Power to the People" in a joyous discipline.

-Dailey News: Girl Officers appeal to military policemen behind barbed wire during the march on Fort Dix.

-New York Times: Several marchers approached the growing line of soldiers. "We are with you", They shouted, "The brass lives high and G.I.'s die, where are your Generals while they send you to fight girls and boys".

'I turned and half the formation was coming toward me'

Keith Mather

My mother gave me an address and phone number of the War Resisters League. I met up with these people and they introduced me to other AWOL GIs. A connection, finally! All these people with short hair, all AWOL, all doing the same thing—resisting the war. People at WRL suggested the idea of taking sanctuary in a church. Out of that idea came chains connecting our arms with those of priests and ministers. This represented the bonds between men, and between the clergy and these AWOL servicemen. We became known as the "Nine for Peace." At the close of the service, we were arrested by the Military Police.

Keith Mather, 1990.
Source: Photo by William Short.

Facing page: A letter to the Shakedown newspaper from Thomas W. Catlow appeared October 17, 1969. Source: GI Press Collection, Wisconsin Historical Society.

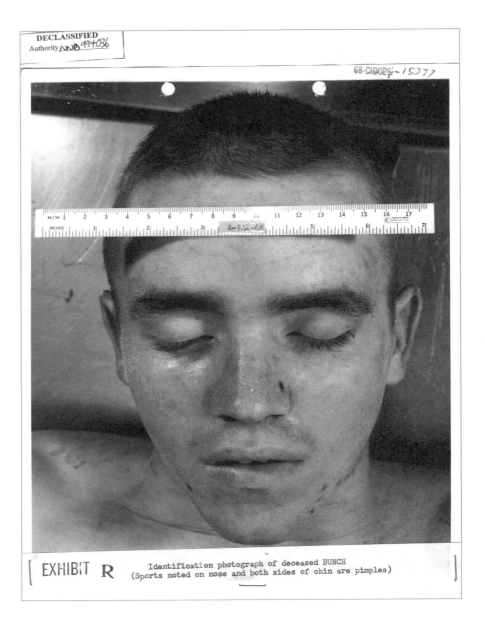

Richard Bunch, shown in a postmortem photograph. A soldier with psychological problems, Bunch was sent to the Presidio stockade in San Francisco, where he was frequently denied his medication. On October 11, 1968, a guard shot him in the back and killed him as he walked away from a work detail. Source: Photo courtesy of the National Archives.

All the Army guys were sent to [the] Presidio. They paraded NCOs by to look at us—"Oh, these are those peace freaks" and "We're going to send you off to Vietnam anyway; we're going to take you out and put you on an airplane tonight." That scared us. I heard somebody talking about this guy sitting there in his cell in his underwear, refusing to wear his uniform. I'm going, all right; there's people here resisting. We started to network.

Richard Bunch was a disturbed kid who had been to Vietnam and was in prison on an AWOL charge. The guards would withhold his psychiatric medication. I didn't know him well, but I spoke to him briefly several times and then the next thing I knew he was murdered by a prison guard. It scared the shit out of us all. We were all nervous, itching to get out and itching to figure out what happened. There was a miniature riot, people were going, "It ain't worth it anymore; they're killing us."

Then they had a memorial service. We all went because he meant something to us. He was one of us, not one of them. The chaplain stated it was justifiable homicide. We started throwing chairs in every direction and yelling. We knew then that the chain of command was trying to cover up the murder. We realized we had to do something. We decided to do something at roll call after chow. A name was called, a couple people shuffled, so I took a step and I brushed a guy aside. I heard steps behind me, so I kept walking. We got over to the lawn; I turned and half the formation was coming toward me. We all locked arms and sat down. From that time on, we were known as the "Presidio 27." Walter Pawlowski stood up and read the list of grievances. The captain ordered us to get up and then opened the book and started reading us the mutiny act. About that time, about sixty MPs arrived. They got us inside. Walter and I were thrown into solitary confinement and named as the ringleaders right off the bat. We felt we could do a lot of damage if we took away their two-star defendants, so after solitary we started planning our escape. Christmas Eve day, 1968, we bailed out of a window while we were putting our work tools away and jogged off the post.

An illustration showing where the guard, Bryce Gordon Wolverton, was standing when he shot Bunch. Source: Photo courtesy of the National Archives.

DECLASSIFIED
Authority AND 994036

For Official Use Only

STATEMENT BY ACCUSED OR SUSPECT PERSON
(AR 195-10)

PLACE	DATE	TIME	FILE NUMBER
Presidio of San Francisco, California	11 Oct 68	1130	68-CID026-75337

LAST NAME, FIRST NAME, MIDDLE NAME	SOCIAL SECURITY ACCOUNT NO.	GRADE
WOLVERTON, Bryce Gordon	FOIA(b) 6	SP4

ORGANIZATION OR ADDRESS
Headquarters Company, U.S. Army Garrison, Presidio of San Francisco, California

PART I - WAIVER CERTIFICATE

I HAVE BEEN INFORMED BY Robert M VALERA

OF Detachment B, 6th MP Group (CI), Presidio of San Francisco, California 94129

THAT HE WANTS TO QUESTION ME ABOUT A FATAL SHOOTING

OF WHICH I AM ACCUSED OR SUSPECTED. HE HAS ALSO INFORMED ME OF MY RIGHTS.

I UNDERSTAND THAT I HAVE THE RIGHT TO REMAIN SILENT AND THAT ANY STATEMENT I MAKE MAY BE USED AS EVIDENCE AGAINST ME IN A CRIMINAL TRIAL.

I UNDERSTAND THAT I HAVE THE RIGHT TO CONSULT WITH COUNSEL AND TO HAVE COUNSEL PRESENT WITH ME DURING QUESTIONING. I MAY RETAIN COUNSEL AT MY OWN EXPENSE OR COUNSEL WILL BE APPOINTED FOR ME AT NO EXPENSE TO ME. IF I AM SUBJECT TO THE UNIFORM CODE OF MILITARY JUSTICE, APPOINTED COUNSEL MAY BE MILITARY COUNSEL OF MY OWN CHOICE IF HE IS REASONABLY AVAILABLE.

I UNDERSTAND THAT EVEN IF I DECIDE TO ANSWER QUESTIONS NOW WITHOUT HAVING COUNSEL PRESENT, I MAY STOP ANSWERING QUESTION AT ANY TIME. ALSO, I MAY REQUEST COUNSEL AT ANY TIME DURING QUESTIONING.

I (DO) (DO NOT) WANT COUNSEL.
I (DO) (DO NOT) WANT TO MAKE A STATEMENT AND ANSWER QUESTIONS.

X *Bryce G Wolverton*
(Signature of Person To Be Questioned)

INTERROGATOR: *Robert M Valera* (Signature)
Robert M VALERA
Det B, 6th MP Gp (CI), PSFC
(Typed Name and Organization)

WITNESS: *Mark T Wurgess* (Signature)
Mark T WURGESS
Det B, 6th MP Gp (CI), PSFC
(Typed Name and Organization)

PART II - SWORN STATEMENT

I, Bryce Gordon WOLVERTON WANT TO MAKE THE FOLLOWING STATEMENT UNDER OATH: X BGW

Q: WOLVERTON, please relate all knowledge you have concerning a shooting which occurred during the morning hours, 11 October 1968, in which you are suspected of shooting a stockade prisoner, Private Richard BUNCH, who was in your charge, when BUNCH allegedly attempted to escape from a work detail.

A: I am a member of a prisoner guard detail and my duties consist of picking up prisoners from the post stockade and then escorting them to various work details on the Presidio Post. I am required to be armed, usually with a shotgun, issued by the Detail NCO at the stockade. I have guarded prisoners in this capacity on about six previous occasions. This morning I reported to the stockade about 0715 to take a detail out. I received a list of prisoners which included Privates COLIP, BUNCH, REUM, and BLACK. I drew a shotgun, serial number 1007164, from the Detail NCO and also five rounds of number 4 bird shot. I loaded the shotgun and then cleared the chamber of the weapon. My instructions were to take the four prisoners to the medical company at Letterman General Hospital and there to report to the First Sergeant for the location of the work site. I left the stockade about 0920 and marched the prisoner in a column of twos to the medical company orderly room. We arrived about 0950 hours, without incident. The First Sergeant sent us with an NCO to a building later identified as Building 238 where we were, that is the prisoners were, to assemble wall lockers. Before starting to work, I decided to give the prisoners a smoke break as we had walked a long way. I asked the NCO if there were any objections to the prisoners smoking and he said no.

EXHIBIT	INITIALS OF PERSON MAKING STATEMENT	
D	X BGW	PAGE 1 OF 5 PAGES

ADDITIONAL PAGES MUST CONTAIN THE HEADING "STATEMENT OF___TAKEN AT___DATED___CONTINUED." THE BOTTOM OF EACH ADDITIONAL PAGE MUST BEAR THE INITIALS OF THE PERSON MAKING THE STATEMENT AND BE INITIALED AS "PAGE___OF___PAGES." WHEN ADDITIONAL PAGES ARE UTILIZED, THE BACK OF PAGE 1 WILL BE LINED OUT. AND THE STATEMENT WILL BE CONCLUDED ON THE REVERSE SIDE OF ANOTHER COPY OF THIS FORM.

The statement given by Wolverton as part of the official investigation into Bunch's murder. Source: Photo courtesy of the National Archives.

For Official Use Only   68 CID026-15337

STATEMENT (Continued)

Accordingly, I told the prisoners to take a smoke. They were sitting around on some crates and BUNCH happened to remark something to the effect of wether I would shoot anyone. I attempted to ignore him and he may have repeated the question. Anyway, I told him that if I did not shoot then someone would shoot me. What I meant was that if I were to permit one of the prisoners to escape, then I would be punished. I am sure BUNCH knew what I was talking about. As we started to work, BUNCH asked for some water. I asked the NCO where the nearest water fountain was and he directed me to Building 244, across from the building we were in. I then marched the four prisoner to Building 244. We entered and the went to the water fountain at the other eand of the room. After the prisoners drank water, and as were were walking back to the exit, BUNCH said something to the effect "Will you promise to shoot me. I won't run unless you promise to shoot me". I didn't really know what to reply to him. I was upset over the question, of course. At any rate, we exited the building and I was walking behind the prisoners. As we were crossing the street, I noticed that BUNCH started to lag behind. By this time, COLIP, REUM, and BLACK had crossed the street and were next to the building. BUNCH then turned and said something to the effect "I don't really think you'll shoot". At that time he started moving away from me and I said "don't start running". He suddenly turned and started running in the direction of the commissary. I chambered a round and I though he had heard me do so. He kept running and I then yelled "halt". He failed to stop and I brought the weapon to my shoulder and yelled "halt" again. When he continued to run, I removed the safty and fired once at him. I aimed toward the lower part of his buttocks when I fired. I saw that he was hit when he fell to the ground. I ordered the other prisoners to get on the ground. Shortly thereafter, the military police arrived and took the other prisoners in custody.

Q: Why did you shoot BUNCH?
A: I shot at him to prevent him from escaping. I wanted to disable him.
Q: How far from you had BUNCH moved when you fired at him?
A: About fiftenn yards.
Q: At the time you fired, was BUNCH running with his back to you?
A: Yes.
Q: I show you a 12 guage shotgun, serial number 1007164. Is this the weapon you fired at BUNCH?
A: Yes. x BGW

AFFIDAVIT

I, **Bryce Gordon WOLVERTON** HAVE READ OR HAVE HAD READ TO ME THIS STATEMENT WHICH BEGINS ON PAGE 1 AND ENDS ON PAGE **3**. I FULLY UNDERSTAND THE CONTENTS OF THE ENTIRE STATEMENT MADE BY ME. THE STATEMENT IS TRUE. I HAVE INITIALED ALL CORRECTIONS AND HAVE INITIALED THE BOTTOM OF EACH PAGE CONTAINING THE STATEMENT. I HAVE MADE THIS STATEMENT FREELY WITHOUT HOPE OF BENEFIT OR REWARD, WITHOUT THREAT OF PUNISHMENT, AND WITHOUT COERCION, UNLAWFUL INFLUENCE, OR UNLAWFUL INDUCEMENT.

(Signature of Person Making Statement)

WITNESSES:

Mark T WURGESS
Det B, 6th MP Gp (CI), PSFC
ORGANIZATION OR ADDRESS

Subscribed and sworn to before me, a person authorized by law to administer oaths, this **11** day of **October**, 19**68** at **Presidio of San Francisco, Calif**

(Signature of Person Administering Oath)
ROBERT M VALERA
Criminal Investiga tor
(Typed Name of Person Administering Oath)
ART 136 (b), (4), UCMJ 1951
(Authority To Administer Oaths)

ORGANIZATION OR ADDRESS

INITIALS OF PERSON MAKING STATEMENT
X BGW

PAGE **2** OF **3** PAGES

For Official Use Only

EXHIBIT D

The Presidio 27: Three days after Bunch was killed, twenty-eight prisoners sat in protest of stockade conditions and against the war. They sang "We Shall Overcome," a song made famous by the U.S. civil rights movement. One prisoner returned to work when they were ordered to disperse. Captain Robert S. Lamont read the Army's mutiny article. Some of the Presidio 27 were sentenced to up to sixteen years at hard labor. Source: Photo courtesy of the National Archives.

On New Year's Eve, we went to Canada. I lived there until 1980, when I came back to live with my two children. In 1984, I was going along like there was nothing wrong. I got a call that someone had found my driver's license. When I went to the police station to get it, they arrested me on my old warrant. They took me to the Presidio, then to the stockade at Fort Ord, and then to Fort Riley, Kansas. I was thirty-eight, in prison with twenty-year-olds. While I was imprisoned, [the] former Presidio 27 and others campaigned to get me released. After serving four months, I was released from the military in April 1985. My dishonorable discharge states I had been in the military for seventeen years and two months.

Interviewed 1990 by Willa Seidenberg and William Short

Fragging

9

An Army at War with Itself

David Cortright

The most horrific indication of the breakdown of the armed forces was the prevalence of fragging, an attack with a fragmentation grenade. As Republican Senator Charles Mathias told the Congress in 1971, "In all the lexicon of war there is not a more tragic word than 'fragging' with all that it implies of total failure of discipline and depression of morale, the complete sense of frustration and confusion and the loss of goals and hope itself."[1]

The army began keeping records on assaults with explosive devices in 1969. By July 1972, with the last troops on their way out of Vietnam, the total number of fragging incidents reached 551, according to army figures, with eighty-six fatalities and over seven hundred injuries.[2] This does not count an estimated 100–150 fragging attacks that occurred in the Marine Corps.[3] Exact figures for the total number of fragging incidents in Vietnam are not known, but a recent study estimates that the number of grenade attacks within the military ranged from "600 to 850 or possibly more."[4] The targets of these fragging attacks were mostly officers and noncommissioned officers (NCOs).[5] The frequency of fragging in the Vietnam War provided grim evidence of the anger and social decay that were tearing the military apart. It was an indication of an army at war with itself.

In an attempt to reduce the threat of fragging, the Army and Marine Corps began to limit access to weapons in Vietnam, especially in base-camp areas, where most of the attacks occurred. In the Americal Division, Army commanders issued a letter warning of "an increasing number of incidents involving the unauthorized detonation of explosive devices . . . in the vicinity of NCO and officer quarters." The circular called for removing grenades from rear-area bunker lines and consolidating weapons in centrally located arms rooms.[6] The 173rd Airborne Brigade issued a circular limiting access to ordnance, ordering that grenades were not to be used for base-camp defense without the express approval of the gate commander.[7] Despite these

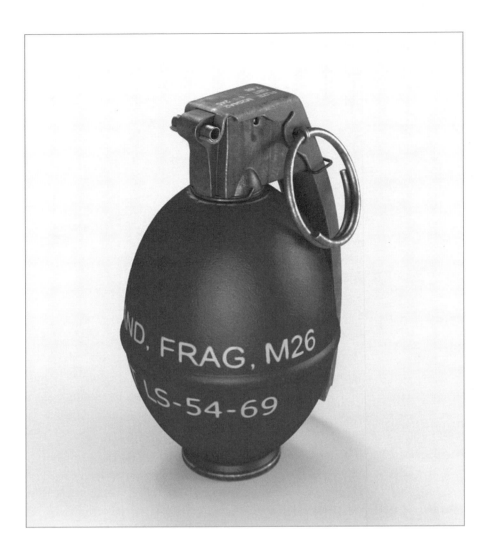

The M26 fragmentation hand grenade was the weapon of choice for enlisted men seeking to intimidate, injure, or kill their superior officers. At four inches tall, it was easy to hide, readily available, and left no fingerprints. A soldier could toss it into his officer's billet with the same practiced ease as he would toss it in battle.[9]
Source: Illustration by Andrea Genovese.

An NCO was killed at this bunker in D Battery, Eleventh Marines, at Liberty Bridge (Phu Lac 6), February 1969.
Source: Courtesy of the National Archives.

FOR OFFICIAL USE ONLY

200   USARV Cir No 190-3

HEADQUARTERS UNITED STATES ARMY VIETNAM
APO San Francisco 96375

CIRCULAR   15 May 1971
NUMBER 190-3

(Expires 15 May 1972)
Military Police
CONTROL OVER FIREARMS AND DANGEROUS WEAPONS

1. <u>PURPOSE</u>: To provide a procedure to improve control over firearms and dangerous weapons within this command to eliminate shooting and grenade incidents.

2. <u>GENERAL</u>: a. The number of shooting and grenade incidents occurring within RVN is unacceptable. The loss of life and injury resulting from intentional use of these weapons in attempts to intimidate, assault, and murder, as well as accidents, is a growing matter of concern. This circular is designed primarily to restrict the availability of firearms and dangerous weapons to those personnel who require them to accomplish their duties. In particular, a concerted command-wide effort must be made to eliminate the detonation of explosive devices by an individual with the intent of killing or doing bodily harm to the victim(s) or intimidating the victim(s).

   b. An analysis of past incidents reveals that many of the young men involved did not feel that their leaders had established an atmosphere conducive to discussion of problems. The situation had created barriers to communication and had generated mistrust and disillusionment on the part of the younger men toward their officers and noncommissioned officers.

   c. Positive leadership on the troop level will solve most, but not all, of the problems. Officers and noncommissioned officers must actively demonstrate their interest and sincere willingness to provide the necessary guidance and assistance. The control measures in para 3, below, are a partial solution. The resolution of this situation rests in positive unit leadership and supervision. This applies equally to combat service support, combat support, and combat units. Discipline, law and order remain a function of this command.

3. <u>POLICY</u>: The following will be effective 15 May 71:

   a. Reports of incidents. All incidents involving the use of explosive devices, as defined at Appendix I, for suspected attempted intimidation, assault, or murder are reportable as Serious Incident Reports (SIR) in accordance with para 5, USARV Reg 190-47.

   b. Command-wide inventory.

   (1) A one time command-wide inventory of all weapons listed at Appendix I will be conducted on 15 Jun 71. A moratorium on issue of these items will be in effect from 15 Jun 71 to 22 Jun 71.

   (2) On 15 Jun 71 all issues by ammunition logistical installations, except for validated Combat Essential (CE), Emergency Resupply (ER), and Tactical Emergency (TE) requirements, of DODIC's listed at Appendix I, will cease. This

FOR OFFICIAL USE ONLY

> **"Especially heinous and despicable is the form of assault and attempted murder known colloquially as 'fragging.'"**
>
> From a Marine Corps antifragging order, December 13, 1970. Source: Courtesy of the National Archives.

The first page of the Army's antifragging directive, May 15, 1971. Source: Courtesy of the National Archives.

extraordinary measures, fragging continued. In May 1971, the Army issued Circular 190-3, placing a moratorium on the issuance of grenades in nearly all units in Vietnam, as shakedown inspections were conducted to find stolen or hidden ordnance. It was a radical step, "unprecedented in the annals of warfare," wrote historian George Lepre.[8] Soldiers could not be trusted with weapons, for fear they would use them against their own commanders.

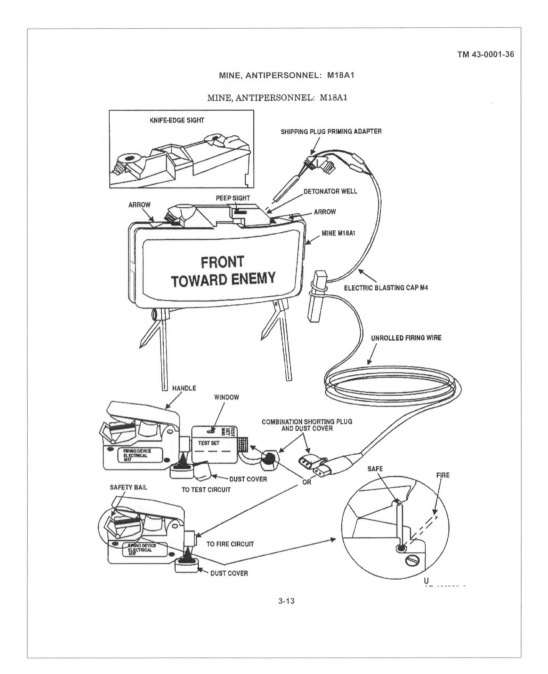

A weapon used in fragging incidents was the M18A1 Claymore antipersonnel mine. According to George Lepre's *Fragging*, "The Claymore was a small rectangular affair that could be detonated by a handheld firing device or trip wire. When it exploded, its effect was devastating: the mine sprayed hundreds of steel fragments into a sixty-degree, approximately fifty-meter-wide kill zone. Few survived run-ins with Claymores."[10]
Source: Courtesy of the Department of the Army.

The most significant impact of fragging was to undermine the functioning of military authority. The threat of fragging became a pervasive presence that loomed over many units in Vietnam and fundamentally altered the relationship between commanders and their troops. For every one of the hundreds of violent attacks, there were many more instances of intimidation and threatened attack. A protocol of fragging developed in which increasing levels of threat were used to force concessions from superiors or fellow soldiers. First was the unexpected appearance of an unexploded grenade on the target's bunk or desk. Often that was sufficient to send the message to back off on aggressive combat missions, drug busts, or racial abuse—whatever was the complaint in that unit. If the initial action did not work, the next step was to set off a smoke grenade. That would cause a small explosion and send a powerful message of threat. It also made clear what the next step could be. Once an officer or non-commissioned officer became the target of fragging threat or attack, their authority was compromised. In conditions such as these, which were widespread by 1969–1970, the effectiveness of the armed forces in Vietnam disintegrated.

One Soldier Remembers

In 1969, Stanley Fanaras was a spec 4 with the Fourth Infantry Division stationed at Camp Enari, a base camp east of Pleiku, in Vietnam's Central Highlands. Fanaras describes walking into a VA hospital in Baltimore, Maryland, twenty-six years later, dazed and disoriented. He said the doctor asked if this was the first time he had come to a VA hospital. When he asked how the doctor knew, he was told, "I can take one look at you and see you have PTSD."

'Smoke billowing out of the NCO hooch'

Stanley Fanaras

It was always at night when they did this.

I was asleep in my hooch—that's what we called our barracks in Nam. We heard a loud explosion and jumped out of our bunks. I grabbed the M16 and bandolier of bullets I always slept with. But right away we knew it wasn't enemy incoming rounds, because no siren went off.

We ran outside into the company area. That's when we saw, at the end of the pathway, smoke billowing out of the NCO hooch.

I asked, "What's going on?"

This fellow answered, "They have fragged the 'lifer hooch' as a warning because they were getting too gung ho. They are increasing the number of ambush patrols."

Ambush patrols. That's what we called them. They drop you off and you wait until night. Sometimes we would ambush the VC who came out at night. But sometimes the hunter would become the hunted.

Interview by Ron Carver, February 14, 2019, College Park, Maryland

Fragging

Five men pull straws
under a tree on a hillside.
Damp smoke & mist halo them
as they single out each other,
pretending they're not there.
"We won't be wasting a real man.
That lieutenant's too gung ho.
Think, man, 'bout how Turk
got blown away; next time
it's you or me. Hell,
the truth is the truth."
Something small as a clinch pin
can hold men together,
humming their one-word
song. Yes, just a flick
of a wrist & the whole night
comes apart. "Didn't we warn him?
That bastard." "Remember, Joe,
remember how he pushed Perez?"
The five men breathe like a wave
of cicadas, their bowed heads
filled with splintered starlight.
They uncoil fast as a fist.
Looking at the ground, four
walk north, then disappear. One
comes this way, moving through
a bad dream. Slipping a finger
into the metal ring, he's married
to his devil—the spoon-shaped
handle flies off. Everything
breaks for green cover,
like a hundred red birds
released from a wooden box.

Yusef Komunyakaa

Redefining Patriotism

10

Standing on Principle, Facing the Consequences

Tom Wilber

On June 16, 1968, flying off the aircraft carrier USS *America* on his twenty-first mission over North Vietnam, my father, Gene Wilber, parachuted from the spent hulk of his burning F-4J, hit by a missile. He landed on the bank of a rice paddy in Nghe An Province. A week later, he was in Hanoi, beginning his fifty-six months of internment, the first twenty months living in solitary confinement at Hoa Lo Prison. He was thirty-eight years old.

My father was born in rural Bradford County in north-central Pennsylvania. A son of sharecroppers, in 1948 as a recent high school graduate, he knew that he was a prime candidate for Truman's soon-to-be instituted peacetime draft. Dad joined the Navy, hoping to have a say in what he would do. He wanted to fly, and he got his wish. In his early twenties, he made two deployments to Korea, flying off of carriers. He continued to deploy over the years. In combat situations, Dad was confident in the Navy's system of accountability for mission assignments and target choices; the chain of command that rose to the civilian leadership level, with the president as commander in chief. "I was fighting for peace," he would later remember.

However, in the mid 1960s his trust in this system began to fade.

In captivity, Dad had time to listen to his conscience. He thought through the things that he knew and examined them word by word: words from the Constitution, the Declaration of Independence, Bible verses he had committed to memory, lessons from his high school civics teacher, the words of the commissioning oath to support and defend the Constitution of the United States. He pondered how he was fulfilling the obligations and principles inherent in those words and teachings. The religious, conservative, right-leaning, career military officer that he was, Dad worked through his own thoughts and concluded that the war was wrong. It was not declared through international or national protocols and it was being directed and

Walter Eugene Wilber (left) and Ray Slingerland walking on the tarmac leading to the flight line at Naval Air Station (NAS) Kingsville, in Texas. Source: U.S. Navy Photo.

sustained by a succession of executive administrations, not by a legal declaration of Congress.

To support and defend the Constitution of the United States as best he could from Hanoi, he decided to speak out. Through letters, taped broadcasts, and interviews, he called on Congress to stop the war, urged U.S. citizens to voice their opinions, and exhorted all who might hear him to work for peace. On my fifteenth birthday, in 1970, his tape-recorded voice, broadcast over Radio Hanoi, told me that I was "old enough now to work for peace."

Among the many communications he initiated from prison camp, Dad sent a simple, consistent message that the war was wrong and we must end it: *We have to admit the facts as they lie, and stop the war. And, of course, we must withdraw our troops to stop the war.*[1]

The Paris Peace Accords were signed in late January 1973. On February 12, my father left Hanoi with 115 other newly freed captives. The simmering controversy of his principled position would soon reach full boil.

Dad's story had challenged the "official story" of the POW experience. While other prisoners who had spoken out against the war accepted an "amnesty" when they recanted their antiwar statements before they returned, Dad did not recant. Rather, he announced publicly that the statements he made while in captivity were voluntary. Throughout his time in prison, he received shelter, clothing, hygiene, and medical care.[2] He never went a day without food. On the television program *60 Minutes*, he acknowledged that the circumstances among POWs varied and that each POW would have his own story to tell. He further stated, "I was not tortured."[3]

That is when the controversy began to boil over. A fellow returnee initiated formal charges of collaboration with the enemy against my father and one other officer returnee. The charges were later dropped, although Dad was prepared for the trial. He remained steadfast that we never should have gone to Vietnam and that speaking out against the war had been the right thing to do, and his right to do. He remained unswerving in his personal values, as well: religious, conservative, and believing in the higher principles that our country stood for.

Bob Chenoweth grew up wanting to fly. He joined the Army after high school in 1966 and became a crew chief on a UH-1 helicopter. He completed a one-year tour in Vietnam and returned for a second tour. On February 8, 1968, his helicopter was hit and went down in Quang Tri Province, and he and his crewmates were captured.

After several weeks in the jungle, then walking for nearly two weeks to the Ho Chi Minh Trail, Bob went by truck for two weeks more to a camp in the countryside in North Vietnam. As Bob witnessed the massive human effort on the Ho Chi Minh Trail, he realized who would win the war. Only twenty years old when he was captured, Bob used his time in Vietnam to learn about his captors, their history and culture. In November 1970, Bob finally moved to Hanoi, to a prison that the captives referred to as "Plantation." He ended up in Hoa Lo prison (nicknamed by prisoners the "Hanoi Hilton"), arriving there on the second night of the December 1972 "Christmas bombing" campaign and staying until his release in March 1973.

He has described his overall experience as life changing … for the better.

> *"These are people from whom I learned a new way of looking at the world, who protected me and sent me home a better person than when I left."* —Bob Chenoweth, in a speech at Hoa Lo Prison Museum, November 29, 2017.

But like my father, Bob would face accusations for his beliefs. He had spoken out against the war. He was one of eight enlisted returnees, all labeled as members of a so-called "Peace Committee" by other POWs. Bob and the other seven were charged with violations of the Uniform Code of Military Justice by an Air Force colonel who had been held captive with them in the Plantation camp.

During the anxious period that followed, one of Bob's fellow charged enlistees, Marine sergeant Abel Larry Kavanaugh, died from a self-inflicted gunshot wound.

> *"The North Vietnamese kept him alive for five years and then his own country killed him."* —Sandra Kavanaugh[4]

Bob and five of the others who had been charged served as pallbearers at Kavanaugh's funeral. The charges against the enlisted POW returnees were dismissed days after Larry Kavanaugh's death, as would be the charges against Dad a few months later.

Bob Chenoweth was discharged from the Army, and my dad retired from the Navy. But for both, the ostracizing continued. More than a decade and a half after returning, with a degree in anthropology and nine years of work experience at the Smithsonian, Bob was forced out of his job as a historian for the Navy because of his prior antiwar activities. In October 1988, more than fifteen years after he returned from four years and nine months of captivity, the Department of the Navy denied my dad the award of the POW Medal. In a 2007 book, "official POW historians" further stigmatized the POW dissenters with unsubstantiated assertions, including that they lived the rest of their lives in shame.[5]

Neither Bob nor my father, however, would consider themselves as victims, nor would they be silenced; rather, they stood on the same principles that had driven their actions while in captivity.

Others who stood on principle, and against a system that would attempt to silence them, include Hugh Thompson and Ron Ridenhour.

Thompson was the Army helicopter pilot who took action to intervene during the ongoing massacre at My Lai and was unfaltering in reporting the atrocious crimes and cover-ups. Thompson persisted as an unrepentant whistle-blower for decades. It took more than thirty years for the Army to finally award Thompson the Soldiers Medal in 1998. In the meantime, he experienced withering criticism in the media, the halls of Congress, and the Army for doing what he believed was right and for telling the truth.[6]

In the month after that horrible massacre of civilians at My Lai, Ron Ridenhour was assigned with some of the troops who had participated in the slaughter. As they told him the horrifying stories of March 16, 1968, Ron began to put together a dossier of what happened and how it was covered up. Upon his return to the States and his discharge—anticipating that any single authority could suppress a report—Ron simultaneously mailed copies of his two-thousand-word letter documenting his findings to more than thirty government officials in Washington, D.C.[7] Ron's actions were instrumental in exposing My Lai to the light of scrutiny.

We see in the words and actions of Chenoweth, Ridenhour, Thompson, and Wilber a principled and conscientious call for accountability. In late November 1969, after reading news of the Moratorium demonstrations in the U.S., Dad taped a statement of support and encouragement to the antiwar movement:

> *The recent unification of the many anti-Vietnam war groups, along with millions of peace-loving citizens, for an early end to the Vietnam war, brought floods of joy into my heart . . . may God bless each of you as you struggle to bring peace on earth.*[8]

My Journey, from POW to the Antiwar Movement

Bob Chenoweth

Every year I commemorate the date my UH-1 helicopter was shot down in Quang Tri Province, Vietnam. I mark February 8, when I was captured by people we called the Viet Cong, because it was the beginning of a process that led to my own opposition to the war.

I had already served one tour in Vietnam at the time of my capture. While I had many questions about what we were doing in Vietnam, I did not have a political consciousness that allowed me to answer those questions. But it broadened my perspective to travel through liberated zones, up the Ho Chi Minh Trail, and to live in the countryside of Nghe An, and later Ha Tay Province.

I learned about Vietnam's history, culture, and people. Along with other POWs, I learned about the growing antiwar movement at home, and what

Bob Chenoweth in Vietnam, 1968. He was captured and spent five years as a prisoner of war. Source: Photo courtesy of Bob Chenoweth.

antiwar leaders were saying about the war. My own experience confirmed what they were saying and convinced me to raise my own voice against the war.

When we saw films about the antiwar demonstrations—and especially about the Winter Soldier Investigation undertaken by Vietnam Veterans Against the War (VVAW)—we felt great moral support. Americans visiting North Vietnam during the war brought us copies of underground newspapers published by active-duty members of all the services. We received about two hundred different papers. We read each paper and book with great interest and followed stories of stateside activities, GI trials, and the VVAW.

GI activists and veterans educated the antiwar movement in so many ways. They provided an undeniable voice about what was being done in our name. That voice needs to be part of the history of the antiwar movement and of the war itself. It became difficult for the United States to continue the war when so many warriors turned against the effort.

We must remember that people's understanding was based mostly on their experiences. It does not surprise me that many vets still think the war was a noble cause, but people all over the world understood what Americans could not. Our government installed and supported a government in South Vietnam that had no popular support, against the desires of world opinion. Our leaders lied to us about why we went and what we were doing.

The Right and war apologists would have us believe that peace activists could only spit on veterans and GIs. In fact, GIs were an integral part of the peace movement, and should be honored and remembered.

Bringing POWs Home

Cora Weiss

The Nixon administration played on the public's sympathies and used the prisoner of war issue as a pretext for continuing the war. In the late sixties, it was just another excuse in a long line of justifications. We heard the argument, If the North doesn't stop torturing our prisoners, we are going to bomb the hell out of them.

People had no idea how many prisoners existed, whether the missing pilots were dead or alive, or what condition they were in. A few letters from POWs had trickled in over the years, but there was no regular channel of communication and not even a list of how many Americans were in detention.

I was in the leadership of Women Strike for Peace (WSP) and the New Mobilization Committee to End the War in Vietnam. A few of us got together in 1969 to address the POW issue at the urging of Stewart Meacham of the American Friends Service Committee. Meacham suggested that we send an

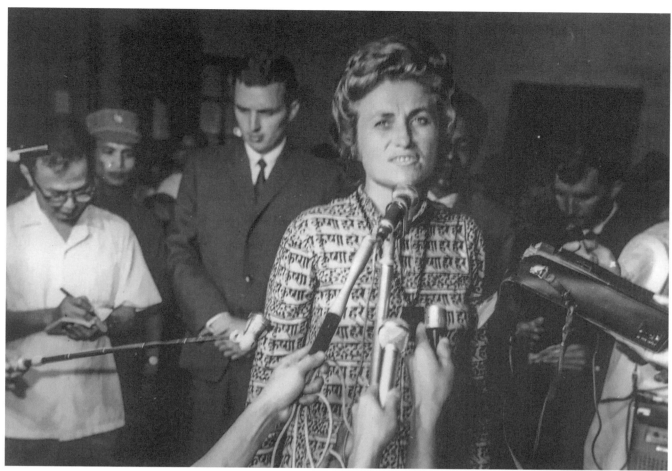

Cora Weiss speaks at a press conference in Hanoi on September 17, 1972, after the DRV People's Army released three U.S. prisoners of war. The three are shown behind Weiss; left to right: Navy pilots Mark Gartley and Norris Charles (somewhat obscured) and Air Force pilot Ed Elias.

Source: Photograph in the Committee of Liaison With Families of Servicemen Detained in North Vietnam Records (DG 227), Swarthmore College Peace Collection.

aide-mémoire, a diplomatic communication, to the other side. We would offer to hand-carry mail to Vietnam from family members who thought their husbands, sons, fathers, or brothers might be prisoners.

To address this issue and undercut the administration's argument, I joined with Meacham, David Dellinger, Richard Falk, the Reverend Richard Fernandez, and others to form a new organization called the Committee of Liaison with Families of Servicemen Detained in the Democratic Republic of Vietnam.

On July 4 of that year, I accepted an invitation from Voice of Women in Canada to meet members of the Vietnam Women's Union, who were visiting. I remember that day as if it were yesterday. We were sitting on the lawn at a farm just north of the U.S. border, licking ice-cream cones together with the Vietnamese women. Nguyen Ngoc Dung, a journalist, activist, and member of the Vietnamese delegation to the UN, who became a close friend, told me, "We want you to come to Vietnam and bring two other women with you."

So, in December, I traveled to Vietnam with WSP president Ethel Taylor, from Philadelphia, and Madeleine Duckles of Women's International League for Peace and Freedom, from San Francisco. We brought with us the aide-mémoire that Meacham had suggested, written with the help of Falk, an international lawyer. Our message to the Vietnamese said that we would bring mail from family members in the U.S. if they would allow prisoners to write back to their families. We would serve as a liaison for the exchange of mail. We proposed to send three people each month, who would carry the letters back and forth.

We were careful to make all of these arrangements with the Vietnam Women's Union. We were mindful that, as U.S. citizens, we were prohibited by the Logan Act from negotiating with an enemy government during wartime. We brought back more than three hundred letters during that first trip in December 1969.

At one point, I testified at a hearing in Congress, chaired by Congressman Benjamin Rosenthal from Queens, New York. I had a box of correspondence from the prisoners with me and I spread the mail on the hearing room table. A hush went over the room as people in the audience gasped. The congressman called me "a great patriot."

Our trips to Vietnam allowed us to comfort many families who hadn't even known if their servicemen were alive. More concretely, we were able to establish a list of detainees by checking the names of the prisoners on their envelopes. More names were added as those captured in the South were transferred to the North and as additional planes were shot down. Military sources had placed the total number of POWs at more than five hundred by the end of the war, in January 1973.

The Nixon administration was embarrassed that an ordinary group of citizens, including a "housewife from the Bronx," as I was called by the press, were able to get information that the government could not provide. Most important, through the Committee of Liaison we were able to contest the use of the POW issue by Nixon and Kissinger as a justification to continue the war.

In September 1972, I was part of a delegation that brought back three of the pilots, Lt. (jg) Norris Charles, Maj. Edward Elias, and Lt. (jg) Mark Gartley. The delegation included Richard Falk, the Reverend William Sloane Coffin, Jr., David Dellinger, and me. With us were Minnie Lee Gartley, Mark's mother, and Norris's wife, Olga Charles. (Relatives of Edward Elias declined our invitation to come along.) Also with us was Peter Arnett, at the time a cub reporter for AP, who was married to a Vietnamese woman and spoke a bit of Vietnamese.

The procedure for freeing the pilots was carefully orchestrated. They were released to the Vietnam Women's Union and then handed over to our custody to escort them back to the United States. A large press delegation attended the release ceremony. After the event, we took the three men back to our hotel in Hanoi, where a huge feast awaited us, including beer—the first time the pilots had alcohol in a long time. We had a wonderful evening and began to build friendships with Arnett, the family members, and the pilots.

Arnett was able to file an AP story on the POW release through serendipity. Right after our plane landed in Hanoi, air raid sirens sounded, and we were hustled into an underground bomb shelter. There by chance was Richard Dudman, the well-known reporter for the *St. Louis Post-Dispatch*, who was leaving on the next plane out of Hanoi. Arnett wrote the story and gave the article and a roll of film to Dudman, who delivered them to AP upon his arrival in the States. AP syndicated a big story across the country, which appeared on the front page of the New York *Daily News*, with a photo showing the mother and wife of two pilots shaking hands with Vietnamese officials.

Before we left Vietnam, our hosts took us on a long drive in the middle of the night from Hanoi to the southern provinces of North Vietnam to see the damage done by American bombing. The freed pilots were with us. As we reached the banks of a river, our drivers suddenly stopped the vehicles and dived into a ditch and we were rushed into an old French-built bunker. Overhead we could see a distant bomber crossing the face of the moon. "Nixon's flying," said our Vietnamese guide. In the distance we could hear bombs and antiaircraft fire.[9] The pilots ironically had to join us in hiding from bombing attacks by their own Air Force.

The U.S. military had sent planes to Vientiane, in Laos, and were waiting to take the men into custody, but our agreement with the pilots was that they would stay with us until we landed in the United States. So we found another route out of Hanoi with the help of Jean-Christophe Oberg, a friend who was the much-admired Swedish ambassador to Vietnam. Oberg arranged for a plane to take us to China, then to Moscow, and then on SAS airlines via Copenhagen to the United States. He had to do this furtively, because at the time the Chinese government was negotiating with Kissinger over a trip to China by Nixon and did not want to be seen as cooperating with the antiwar movement. In Beijing, we were kept in a hotel in Tiananmen Square under virtual house arrest before boarding the plane to Russia.

When we arrived in Moscow, the chargé d'affaires of the U.S. embassy tried to convince the pilots to go with him. But the pilots stuck with their agreement and stayed with our delegation at a hotel in central Moscow. The next day, we headed to Copenhagen. When we landed, an SAS van took us to a nearby restaurant for a lovely meal while we waited for the flight to New York. As we boarded the plane for the last leg of our journey, there was Seymour Hersh, who was then a reporter for *The New York Times*. He had declined to accompany our delegation earlier, but now he was able to take over from Arnett in reporting on our mission.

As the plane approached the United States, a military officer who had boarded the plane took the pilots to the upstairs lounge of our 747 jumbo jet. When the pilots reappeared, they were in military uniforms, with medals and proper rank, ready for the cameras when we landed. The military tried to downplay our role in the mission, but we had accomplished our goals.

A GI's Report from Vietnam

"They have set up separate companies for men who have refused to go out to the field. It is no longer a big thing here anymore to refuse to go. . . . Vehicles don't work for lack of maintenance; helicopters are just falling to the ground, airfields are falling apart. . . . Many guys don't even put on their uniform anymore. It used to be they would get a couple of months of work out of new people but that is no longer the case. Lately they have been segregating new guys, whom they call 'new meat.' "

—October 26, 1970[11]

'I sat down on my duffel bag and said, "I'm not leaving here" '

Carl Dix

I got the first draft notice in April 1968, a couple of days after Martin Luther King was killed and the rebellion swept the cities. I was in no mood to show up at the Army. I sent them a notice back and said I'm too busy right now. So then they hand-delivered me a notice saying I should show up in June—the people who delivered it said they were Military Police. After going through testing they sufficiently scared me about the prospect of going to Vietnam that I switched to a three-year enlistment, which I thought would get me out of going to Vietnam. It turned out that wasn't true.

I was sent to Fort Bragg, North Carolina. We go by this big sign, WEL-COME TO KKK COUNTRY, outside the base and it was like, What did they get us into here? What really introduced me to reading more about Vietnam was a developing black consciousness. Malcolm X wrote quite a bit on Vietnam—what the U.S. was doing there and how ridiculous it was for people to talk about they were for justice, but then go off and help America oppress other people, especially when your people are oppressed at home in America.

I was sent to Germany, and about a week after Nixon's speech about the withdrawal from Vietnam, they levied half of my unit to Vietnam. Very interesting timing. I came back to the States with orders to Vietnam. I talked with a lot of GIs to try to get the deal on what the war was really about. They would say things like, the My Lai massacre, that was SOP—standard operating procedure.

I got orders to report for Vietnam on December 31, and on the fifth I heard that Fred Hampton and Mark Clark were murdered. The Chicago police staked out the house, and at three in the morning they shoot their way in and blow these guys away. Then I hear the Black Panthers' side of the story, and I said, "Wow, the police carried out a search-and-destroy mission in the middle of Chicago!" Then they attacked the L.A. Black Panthers' headquarters, and there were tanks and mortars set up in the streets of L.A. It's like, This war isn't just something over there, it's here, too, and I have to decide what side I'm on. I decided I couldn't be a part of the war in Vietnam; I couldn't go fight for America.

Usually you leave your unit in the morning and you have until midnight to report to your next duty station. So that morning a company commander calls out to the first sergeant, "I want you to go to the weapons room, draw out a .45, keep this man in your sight, and if he makes a false move, you have my authorization to shoot him." I get my stuff and there's a truck waiting and the commander says, "I'm giving you a direct order to get in the truck." I say, "I don't have to because I got until midnight." And he says, "I'm going to have you over there by ten in the morning and then you're going to be out of

LEWIS-McCHORD FREE PRESS

"Three hostile newspapers are more to be feared
than a thousand bayonets" --Napoleon

The Lewis-McChord Free Press is published by active-duty GIs and
airmen stationed at Fort Lewis, Washington, and McChord Air Force Base,
Washington, sharing the views expressed in the Declaration of
Independence and the Constitution of the United States. It is dedicated
to peace, justice, and freedom to all, including those being held without their consent on active duty in the United States Armed Forces.

| Volume 1, No. 4 | Free to Servicemen | Donations 25¢ | November 1970 |

Green Machine Sentences F L Six

Carl Dix, Jim Allen, Paul Forrest, Manuel Perez, Larry Galgano, Jeff Griffith. These are the Fort Lewis 6. They are conscientious objectors who refused to go to Viet Nam. In seperate trials on October 26,27,and 28, they were found guilty of the courts-martial charges pending against them. All are now in prison. What do they have to say to us?

DIX: (two years and a bcd) " I just have to exist, be my own man, and accept the consequences. If I had continued to participate in the Army, I wouldn't be able to relate to my-self or humanity."

ALLEN: (three years and a DD) "Off the system, that's all there is to say."

FORREST: (two years and a DD) "They asked me to violate my own being. There is nothing I can do in the Army but go to jail."

PEREZ: (one year and a BCD) "A man who hurts somebody or kills somebody is less than a man."

GALGANO: (one year and a BCD) "Any person who wears the uniform supports the effort to kill."

GRIFFITH: (two months and no discharge) "The newsreels I used to see of for-eign armies training always repulsed me. Very naively, I thought my own country's army could never be like that."

Dix is Black, a ghetto child with a high IQ. Allen's father is an E-7

with 28 years of Army service. Forrest is a British subject, born in Liverpool. Perez is a Cuban who refused to fight in Castro's Army. Galgano is an artist from Brooklyn. Griffith is a schoolteacher from Maine. Three of the men are married. Two are Catholics, one is a Methodist, one a Buddhist, and two are non-sectarian Christians. All are opposed to war in any form.

Each man first applied for recognition as a conscientious objector in January of 1970 at the Overseas Replacement Station at Fort Lewis. They were then transferred to Company B, USATCI to await processing of their applications. In March, their first applications were returned from DA disapproved.

The men then tried to submit second applications. At first they were not allowed to do so. Later the Commanding General granted them permission when they filed complaints stating that they had been denied their rights in the first application processing routine.

The second applications were returned without action late in June. They were judged to be substantially the same as the first.

Immediately upon the return of the second applications, the men were handed written orders to report to ORS for shipment to Viet Nam. Each man went through the motions of process-ing out of Company B. However, when issued a direct order to board a vehicle bound for ORS, five of the six refused. In the confusion the sixth man, Jeff Griffith, was never

(Continued on Page 4)

DIGNITY COSTS BLACK 3 YEARS

—DALE BORGESON, PFC (RET.)

October 15 was one of those rare autumn days when the sun manages to cut through the smog and touch us with a cold light. I spent most of the day inside a General Court Martial room at Ft. Lewis.

Theoda Lester, a 21 year old Black GI, was being tried for dis-obeying a direct order to shave and be fingerprinted. The maximum sen-tence for these charges is ten years confinement at hard labor, a dishon-orable discharge, and complete for-feiture of pay and allowances.

Meanwhile, Fersch checked with the Army Chaplain's Office at the Penta-gon. They told him that the Army did not recognize Black Nationalism as a religion. There have been a few in-stances of the beard and haircut reg-ulation being waved in the past. One of the GI's now serving at Lewis is a Sikh from India who took a vow as a youth never to cut his hair or shave. The Army honored that vow.

On Tuesday, August 18, Fersch call-ed Lester in again. He advised him of his rights, explained that in the Army soldiers are expected to follow the orders of their superior commissioned officers, pointed out that the Army would not recognize Lester's religious position, and ordered him to shave. Lester refused.

The day of the trial, I met Les-ter with his attorney and several friends at a Ft. Lewis snack bar for noon lunch. Lester has a splendid Afro, and a full beard with moustache. He was wearing his dress green uni-form and drawing incredulous stares from other GI's.

A Sergeant with a Courtesy Patrol arm-band approached our table and tried to give Lester a DR for his haircut and beard. Jim Vonasch, Lester's attorney, explained that his client was already under general court-martial charges. The CP seemed to feel cheated. He made us leave the snack bar.

The courtroom holds about eighty people. By 1:30, the officers still hadn't shown, and the room was nearly packed. I counted over twenty blacks

(Continued on Page 6)

Dale Borgeson was one of the editors of the Lewis-McChord Free Press until he was discharged from the Army as a conscientious objector. He is now a counselor with the Pacific Counseling Service in Tacoma.

my hair." I sat down on my duffel bag and said, "I'm not leaving here." I had heard stories of people being forcibly put on the plane and I figured no sense in going any closer than right here. If they're going to forcibly put me on it, they're going to have to drag me across the base in broad daylight with a lot of people around. I ended up in the stockade that morning.

The trial happened four months later. The military judge made it very clear he was not listening. He says, "You guys can make your arguments for the record; I am not going to consider them. I don't care what you have to say; it seems fairly cut-and-dry to me." He would lay his head down on the desk, look out the window. He got up at one point and said, "I'm going to the bathroom; it would expedite things if you continued to make your arguments while I was gone." They sent a group of us to Leavenworth, including five people out of the "Fort Lewis Six," the name we got for refusing.

Interviewed 1991 by Willa Seidenberg and William Short

'Later that night I heard the grenades go off'

Bill Short

I served with the Blue Spaders First Battalion, 26 Infantry Regiment, First Infantry Division, otherwise known as the "Bloody Red One," from February 1969 to July 1969. I was an infantry platoon sergeant with Mike Platoon in Alpha Company. My tour of duty was cut short by my own volition.

My unit patrolled the Michelin rubber plantation, operating in company strength by day and splitting up into platoon-size ambushes for the night. We usually spent three to five days doing this before we rested in a fire-support base for a couple of days. Whenever we made contact or blew an ambush, the body count came next. I would never view the bodies; I was afraid to. I didn't want to know what I was doing. So when the guys would say, "Hey Sarge, we got to check out the dead gooks," I always made up some excuse. I knew it was my responsibility as platoon sergeant to be on top of all situations, but somehow the body count was something I had no desire to be part of. After a firefight, I felt drained and empty; it seemed pointless. Our battles were never decisive and tomorrow always came with the welcome of surviving one day, only to have to face another. The last thing I wanted to do was count bloody body parts, so we could compete with the Second of the Twenty-eighth, the Black Lions, our sister battalion, for first place in the division.

I carried my weapon and fired many rounds through it, but I always felt protected against taking another life because twenty or eighty other guys fired,

William Short, 1991.
Source: Photo by William Short.

too. For years after the war, when people would ask the inevitable question, "Did you kill anyone?" I always answered, "I don't know," but in reality I did.

On one company-size operation, we broke for a rest at midday. My RTO, because he had a feeling, put his Claymore mine out, something we only did for ambush. Halfway through our lunch, all hell broke loose. Barney blew his Claymore, and after a three-hour firefight, things were calm again. The attack came from three Vietcong, two of whom we got. When the body count came, I went for the first time to see the remains. Both VC had been killed by the blast from one of our grenades, and as I approached, the first thing I noticed was a piece of bone protruding from the hand of one of the bodies. It seemed to glow white-hot; I thought it was the brightest thing I had ever seen. The next thing I noticed was how heavy the body seemed to my eyes. It looked as if it were glued to the ground.

One of the new NCOs, a staff sergeant and second-timer, decided we should booby-trap the bodies, and he asked for my help. We rolled them over and pulled the secondary pins on two grenades, leaving the primary detonation lever in place. Each grenade was placed lever side up and under the rib cage beneath the dead men. Later that night, while positioned in a company-size ambush, I heard the grenades go off. I knew the comrades of the men we had killed had come to claim the bodies and quite possibly had gotten something extra to go with their grief. I *knew* I was responsible for taking human life. Two months later, I refused to go out on any more combat missions.

Interviewed 1991 by Willa Seidenberg

Bill Short, with two Cambodian scouts, Chau and Ung. "They worked with me as trail scouts in my infantry platoon. Both from Chou Doc, a Cambodian village inside Vietnam, northwest of the Mekong Delta, right along the Cambodian-Vietnamese border. We are hanging out in the rear at Lai Khe Fire Base."
Source: Photo courtesy of William Short.

Airing His Views? Cable splicer Anthony Ciccone comes out of his manhole just in time to catch a couple of mini-skirted cuties pass at Ann St. and Broadway yesterday. Ciccone was coming up for a breather as the 94-degree heat at 2:20 p.m. made life miserable for most of us. Mini-happy returns, Tony. —*Other pictures in centerfold*

The New York *Daily News* bannered this startling headline about the first reported incident of mass mutiny of U. S. troops in Vietnam. A Company of the Third Battalion,196th Infantry had been pushing through the Sonchang Valley south of Da Nang for five grueling days and had suffered many casualties. On August 24, Captain Eugene Shurtz ordered the sixty men remaining in the company to move out again and proceed down the dangerous slope of Nuilon Mountain. The exhausted, disgruntled men simply refused to go, all sixty of them.[10] Source: Getty Images.

'They were not supposed to bring me back alive'

John Tuma

At my first duty station in Vietnam, a Military Intelligence detachment, I refused to work with South Vietnamese interpreters who were using physical coercion in order to extract "the truth" from North Vietnamese and Viet Cong soldiers. There were four or five ARVN interpreters who were working with the Military Intelligence unit. And although I was language-trained in Vietnamese, it was standard operational procedure to have a Vietnamese interpreter with Americans, in order to make sure no nuances of the language escaped anyone, and maybe to check up on us.

The first person I was to interrogate was an NVA soldier who had been brought in during Operation Iron Mountain. I started doing basic debriefing of the individual and realized that the Vietnamese interpreter was pulling and twisting on the man's earlobe and had it stretched down somewhere below his chin line. I told him to stop, and he did, only to start again after a few moments. I stopped the questioning and requested another Vietnamese interpreter, and the same thing happened. I decided to end the debriefing session.

My next interrogation was of a suspected Viet Cong who had been shot. He was from a small village on the Laotian border. We had nothing that showed he had ever been a Viet Cong and I classified him as being civilian, possibly civilian defendant. The South Vietnamese I was working with to debrief the fellow kept pinching off his IV tubes while we were talking. I told him several times to stop, but it was totally out of my control. I tried using three other Vietnamese interpreters after that, and they also abused the prisoner—either cutting off his IV or pulling and twisting on his earlobe or twisting a handful of flesh from his side in order to create pain. I refused to work with them. As a result, I was transferred out of the MI detachment.

I was later asked to interpret at the evacuation of a refugee camp and was sent in unarmed to an area with several South Vietnamese from the Province Recon Unit. I felt something was wrong . . . very, very wrong. I was told we were looking for a woman and some children who were supposed to be on the farthest edge of the village. We got to the village edge and they told me it was just a little farther. We went through the tree line, and still farther. I realized they were acting very nervous and suspicious. They ran forward to a small ravine and I started running back. When I got to the edge of the village, I heard gunfire behind me. The fire was directed at me; they were not supposed to bring me back alive. Earlier I had reported the use of a "birdcage" [a cage constructed of barbed wire wrapped around a captive and then hung in a tree] in a Vietnamese compound, and they were forced to take it down. Shortly after this incident, my hooch was fragged with a percussion grenade.

I was threatened with courtmartial several times, but I always thought about what would my parents have done. What would be the right thing to do, not from the Army's point of view, but from my family's and my community's. I consciously thought about that and came to the conclusion there were things I had been raised not to do and couldn't and wouldn't do.

Interviewed 1987 by Willa Seidenberg and William Short

John Tuma, 1987.
Source: Photo by William Short.

'We were seeing bodies everywhere'

Hugh Thompson

In Vietnam, I flew an OH-23 Scout helicopter. Our job was to draw fire from the enemy, then peel back as the big gunships came in to take them out. On board with me were Larry Colburn, my gunner, and Glenn Andreotta, my crew chief.

On the morning of March 16, 1968, around 7:30 a.m., we were flying in support of a ground operation at My Lai, which we called "Pinkville." There was supposed to be a whole battalion of Vietcong fighters there—but that

From the air, helicopter pilot Hugh Thompson observed American soldiers slaughtering Vietnamese civilians in My Lai. He landed his craft multiple times in an effort to end the massacre. Photo courtesy of Trent Angers, Hugh Thompson's biographer.

Thompson speaks to the press on December 4, 1969, immediately after a closed-door Army hearing about the massacre. Thompson was strongly condemned by many, including Congressman Mendel Rivers, chairman of the House Armed Services Committee, who publicly stated, according to *The New York Times*, that Thompson was the only soldier at My Lai who should be punished (for trying to stop the massacre). Source: AP photo.

report was wrong. There were no combatants—only women and children and old men in the village that day. And our own people were shooting them.

We were seeing bodies everywhere. At first, we didn't know what was going on. And we surely couldn't believe our own people would do this. Then it finally sunk in—U.S. soldiers were killing unarmed civilians.

We were really, really upset.

We continued circling the village and trying to figure out why this was happening. Then Glenn spotted a little group of GIs chasing some Vietnamese civilians—three, I believe. They were running for their lives and headed toward a bunker.

In that instant, I knew what I had to do. I knew what would happen if we didn't do something. So, I told Glenn and Larry, "We're going in."

Then I radioed my buddies in the low gunship to ask for backup. I told them, "I'm setting down. Would appreciate some help. I'm not going to let these GIs kill any more of these people."

I set my aircraft down between the civilians and the GIs, and I told my crew, "Y'all cover me. If these bastards open up on me or these people, you open up on them." They said, "Yes, sir, we're with you."

I got out of the aircraft and walked up to the lieutenant in charge [Stephen Brooks]. I told him, "Hey, listen, hold your fire. I'm going to try to get these people out of the bunker. Just hold your men here."

And the lieutenant said, "We can help you get them out—with a hand grenade!" Then I told him, "I think I can do better than that. Just hold your men here."

I walked to the bunker and saw three people looking out: an old man, an old woman, and a little kid. Turned out, there were six more people in that bunker besides them. Nobody was armed; they were completely helpless.

Vietnam war heroes Hugh Thompson and Larry Colburn pose with two of the women they protected from fellow American soldiers during the My Lai massacre. The photo was taken in March 1998, when the Americans returned to My Lai for the ceremony commemorating the thirtieth anniversary of the massacre. Left to right: Colburn, Pham Thi Nhung, Pham Thi Nhanh, Ms. Nhanh's daughter, and Thompson.
Source: Photo by Trent Angers.

I told them, "Y'all come with me now. I'm gonna get you out of here. Don't worry, no one's gonna hurt you."

I put my hand out, offered to help the old lady up and out of the bunker. She hesitated, then took it. Then a bunch more people came out—women, children and two old men. And I was thinking, What the hell am I going to do with all these people?

I talked to them as if they understood English—which they didn't. But I think my tone of voice told them I was there to help them.

I went back to the helicopter, and all of them followed me. They stuck close. I'd move, and they'd move right with me. They sort of hid behind me.

I stood by the aircraft and radioed to my gunships. I said, "Danny [Millians], Brian [Livingston], I need some help. Can y'all come in and get these civilians out of here before someone kills them? Please, y'all. I need help!"

One of the gunships came down and the other stayed in the air to provide cover. We helped the civilians onto the gunship—in two batches—and they were flown off to safety.

I thank God to this day that none of the GIs on the ground tried anything. Larry knew what he had to do, and he would have done it if he was forced to. We were serious about saving these civilians.

We flew back to our base and I went to see our platoon leader. I threw my helmet down and started shouting that our people were acting like a bunch of Nazi executioners.

I said, "There's a ditch full of dead women and children over there. We saw one armed VC all day. We never captured one damned weapon. They're killing the women and children!"

Then I said, "I'll stay on the ground before I'll ever take part in anything like that. I don't want to have anything to do with an operation like that—ever. That's *not* what this country stands for!"

Then my CO [Maj. Fred Watke] came over and tried to calm me down. I told him what we were seeing. Then he talked to the top brass [Lt. Col. Frank Barker], who, I understand, called for a cease-fire.

And the killing stopped.

Navy and Air Force Resisters

The Stop Our Ship Resistance in the U.S. Navy

John Kent

During midshipman training at the U.S. Naval Academy in Annapolis, Maryland, I went to Vietnam in 1967, on board a guided-missile frigate in the Gulf of Tonkin. I graduated from the Academy in 1968, and the next year I was in the jet-training pipeline at a Naval Air Station in Beeville, Texas. One day I was in a classroom full of eager pilots who had just been introduced to their guest lecturer for the day, a Marine major with a chest full of ribbons, fresh from combat in Vietnam. He was telling war stories to psych us up. He used his hands to describe skimming his A4 over the jungle canopy at more than five hundred miles per hour:

> *I dodged enemy flak as I approached the target, jigging left and right, until I spotted the bridge, a key munitions route for the NVA.[1] I pulled the joystick back and slammed the throttle forward climbing to the top of my run. Then I dove toward the bridge, aimed and dropped my load. Kaboom! Then, I'm outta there.*
>
> *But wait, I'm not done. Now I can go looking for some real fun. I still had a Sidewinder. I circled back away from the enemy concentrations—no reason to risk anything now. I found an old man riding a bike on an open path, a perfect target. With the heat-seeking missile I barely had to aim. I fired and blew him to smithereens. Made my day. I reported it as a confirmed kill of a munitions transport vehicle.*

The major grinned while the trainees laughed and applauded in approval and admiration. They couldn't wait for their turn.

But I wasn't laughing. Holy shit, I thought. Is this what I've been training for? Are these the same guys I was having a beer with last night? Is this what the war is about? I read and questioned and thought and concluded that the

John Kent after his first solo flight, September 14, 1968.
Source: Photo courtesy of John Kent.

Antiwar activists in San Diego hired an airplane to fly over the area, encouraging sailors aboard the USS *Constellation* to stay home. Source: Photo by Bob Fitch Photography Archive, Stanford University Libraries.

major's story was exactly what the war was about: a bully's war, a war of domination and conquest, an imperial war.

In November 1969, I marched against the war with half a million others in Washington, D.C. A few months later, at Miramar Naval Air Station, north of San Diego, in the last phases of training in F-8 jets prior to my return to Vietnam, I turned in my wings.

With the help of civilian antiwar friends, I began organizing within the Navy, at first among officers, forming the San Diego Chapter of the Concerned Officers Movement. As many joined us from the enlisted ranks, we renamed ourselves the Concerned Military. San Diego, the principal home port of the U.S. Navy's Pacific Fleet, was the perfect place for the start of the Stop Our Ship (SOS) movement.

We joined with San Diego Nonviolent Action and began a campaign to stop an aircraft carrier from returning to Vietnam; we selected the 75,000-ton USS *Constellation*. It was an outrageous but contagious idea that soon attracted antiwar activists from all over California, including Joan Baez and David Harris. Harris suggested organizing a citywide referendum on whether the *Constellation* should set sail, and soon hundreds of activists, including sailors and veterans, were canvassing the city, organizing the *Constellation* Vote. In late September 1971, 54,721 votes were cast in a straw poll. More than 82 percent voted to keep the ship home, including 73 percent of the military personnel who voted.

Large numbers of antiwar officers and enlisted men had become involved in SOS, which allowed us to use creative methods to get our message out. For example, a CONSTELLATION STAY HOME FOR PEACE banner was frequently seen being towed over the city by recently retired navy flight instructor Lt. John Huyler, and *Constellation* Vote stickers were found everywhere on board the ship, including in the captain's personal bathroom. When the captain lined up the crew and demanded to know who was behind the stickers, a mysterious Lieutenant Harvey was blamed. It wasn't until the captain ordered Lieutenant Harvey to a disciplinary captain's mast that an investigation by Naval Intelligence discovered he didn't really exist, despite being in the ship's personnel records.

On the day the *Constellation* set sail for Vietnam, nine of its crew publicly refused to go and took sanctuary in a local church. The commander in chief of the Pacific Fleet was quoted as saying, "Never was there such a concerted effort to entice American servicemen from their posts." [2]

As news of the *Constellation* campaign spread, crewmen aboard the USS *Coral Sea*, stationed at the Alameda Naval Air Station, near San Francisco, circulated a "Stop Our Ship" petition in September 1971 that officially gave the SOS movement its name. Before the ship sailed, more than one thousand members of the four-thousand-member crew had signed, and when the *Coral Sea* passed under the Golden Gate Bridge on a training run, a large SOS banner hung over the side of the bridge, thanks to mobilization by the Bay Area's civilian antiwar movement. Seventy crewmen responded by forming

With the USS *Constellation* in the background, the singer Joan Baez declares her support for the "Connie Vote" at a San Diego press conference. Source: Photo by Bob Fitch Photography Archive, Stanford University Libraries.

UP AGAINST THE
BULKHEAD

THIS PAPER CANNOT LEGALLY BE TAKEN FROM YOU. ACCORDING TO DOD DIRECTIVE 1325.6 "POSSESSION OF UNAUTHORIZED MATERIAL MAY NOT BE PROHIBITED."

98 Chenery Street, San Francisco, California 94131   Issue 13   January 1973   Free to GIs

MILITARY REVOLTING!

Constellation brothers photographed in the middle of a vote on whether or not to reboard the ship.

At the same time many Americans feel powerless to change the course of Nixon's ship of state, a hundred and thirty black sailors forced a United States aircraft carrier to turn around dead in its tracks and return from sea trials to its port in San Diego.

The 130 had staged a sit-down strike in the mess deck of the attack carrier USS Constellation. They settled in for a long stay, and remained calm, disciplined and unified in the face of everything from sweet-talking Human Relations counselors to a riot squad toting loaded M-16s with fixed bayonets. Unable to feed the rest of the ship's 4000 men, and unable to split up the group, Captain Ward was forced to turn "his" ship around in order to get "the problem" off the boat.

But even when the 130 were on the pier and off the boat, they remained a problem to Capt. Ward. They stuck together and refused to get back on until their demands for fair and equal treatment by the ship's command were dealt with. Again, they sat down together, refused to work, and disobeyed a direct order to get back on the boat. See the full story on page four.

VIETNAM

What Lies Behind the Peace Talk?
How Will It Affect You?
See Page 8.

PHILIPPINES

When Martial Law Was Declared,
American Friends of the
GI Movement
Were Jailed & Deported.
Interview on Page 9.

BILLY DEAN SMITH

Acquitted of Fragging Charges
At Fort Ord, California
See Page 15.

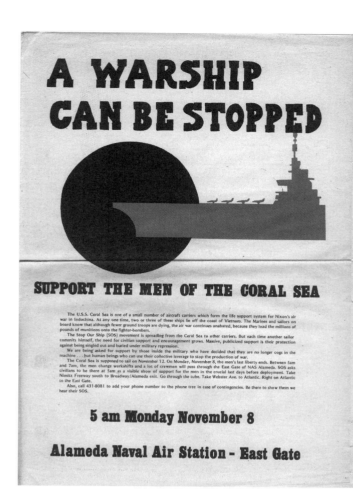

Flyer calling for a protest at the Alameda Naval Air Station in Northern California to stop the USS *Coral Sea* from departing for Vietnam.

the letters SOS on the flight deck as the ship passed under the bridge. On November 6, over three hundred crewmen marched with more than ten thousand others in an antiwar demonstration in San Francisco. When the ship set sail for Southeast Asia, around twelve hundred protestors demonstrated outside of the base to encourage sailors not to sail, and at least thirty-five crewmen failed to report for duty. After a brief port stop in Hawaii, another fifty-three sailors were missing.

Back in San Diego, another aircraft carrier, the USS *Kitty Hawk*, was preparing for deployment to Southeast Asia. Sailors on board, with help from Concerned Military and civilian supporters, began publishing their own newspaper, *Kitty Litter*, and organizing a campaign called "Stop the Hawk." They circulated a petition, attended antiwar rallies, and when the ship set sail for Indochina, seven members of the crew publicly refused to sail and took refuge in local churches.

Similar activity occurred on other aircraft carriers on both the East Coast and the West Coast of the United States, including the USS *Midway*, the USS *Ticonderoga*, the USS *Enterprise*, the USS *America*, and the USS *Oriskany*. When the *America* began to leave port on June 5, 1972, thirty-one activists in thirteen canoes and kayaks positioned themselves in front of the massive

Facing page: Sailors vote on whether or not to sail on the USS *Constellation* to Vietnam. Source: GI Press Collection, Wisconsin Historical Society.

Sailors Bobby Muse and Larry Harris from the Stop Our Ship campaign lead a peace march down Market Street, San Francisco, on November 6, 1971, carrying a model of the Navy aircraft carrier USS *Coral Sea* on their shoulders, like a coffin. Source: Photo by Steve Rees.

ship. As the Coast Guard moved in to clear the demonstrators, hundreds of sailors on the deck of the *America* jeered and pelted the cutters with garbage. When the *Oriskany* left port on June 6, an estimated twenty-five crew members refused to sail, including a group of ten who turned themselves in to naval authorities and issued a bitter public statement, including, "the only way to end the genocide being perpetrated now in South East Asia is for us, the actual pawns in the political game, to quit playing." [3]

Aircraft carriers weren't the only ships affected. Crew members aboard the USS *Nitro*, a munitions ship loaded with armament at the Naval Weapons Station in Earle, New Jersey, staged a dramatic protest. On April 24, 1972, as the ship was pulling out of port, it was greeted by an antiwar blockade of seventeen canoes and small boats. As the Coast Guard attempted to disperse the demonstrators, they were first confronted by dissent from within their ranks; then one of the *Nitro*'s crew stood on the deck rail, raised a clenched fist, and jumped overboard. Six more crew members followed, including one nonswimmer in a life jacket.

Nonwhite grunts often faced racial prejudice, were sent to the front lines in combat, and found themselves assigned to the toughest, dirtiest jobs. In the Navy, these issues found acute expression among Filipino waiters, non-white boiler crews working in 120-degree heat, and the southern goodold-boy leadership. The seething anger that resulted was combined with growing antiwar sentiment and made for explosive situations. In September 1972, the Navy shipped more than two hundred enlisted "troublemakers" back to San Diego from the Philippines. Once in San Diego, a racially mixed group of thirty-one of them held a press conference to expose the conditions and racial prejudice they had been experiencing. They demanded an end to the mistreatment and harassment they had endured while working between fourteen and sixteen hours a day, at times going up to thirty-six hours without sleep. They condemned the brass for taking "out their frustrations on the enlisted people and especially on people of color."[4]

On board the *Kitty Hawk*, where black crew members felt they had been "treated like dogs," an actual riot was brewing.[5] While at sea in October 1972, a white officer began an investigation into black/white fights that had occurred in the Philippines. When he summoned only black sailors to be questioned, one of them brought nine friends to find out why, and a heated confrontation ensued. The nine stormed out to join other black sailors on the mess deck, with the crowd soon growing to more than one hundred. The captain deployed the ship's Marines and soon a fight broke out between the blacks and Marines.

Navy wives Vicky Kelly (left) and Rose Hills unfurl their banner at the Alameda, California, Naval Air Station as the USS *Coral Sea* prepares to depart for Vietnam on December 5, 1974. Source: Photo by Steve Rees.

Navy wife Rose Hills squares off with a base security official, refusing to surrender the banner in her hands. It reads good luck on your captain's suicide mission. Source: Photo by Steve Rees.

Confusion and fighting raged on for much of the night, with forty white and six black sailors injured, including three who had to be evacuated to onshore medical facilities. Twenty-five sailors were arrested—all of them black.

As word spread in the fleet about the incidents on board the *Kitty Hawk*, many of the black sailors on the *Constellation* were holding meetings and "swearing an affinity with their beleaguered brothers on the *Kitty Hawk*."[6] The ship's command, in a typical Navy response, started giving administrative and less-than-honorable discharges to those they considered troublemakers. Feeling they were being singled out for retaliation for their activism, more than one hundred sailors, including several whites, staged a sit-in and refused to work on the morning of November 3, 1972. The captain cut sea operations short and put 144 crew members off the ship, including 8 whites. When the ship returned a few days later to pick up the mutinous sailors, most of them staged a defiant dockside strike, which was called "perhaps the largest act of mass defiance in naval history."[7]

In tandem with the SOS movement, naval sabotage increased in 1972 as the air war dramatically expanded. In July, fires were started on the *Forrestal* and the *Ranger*. On the *Midway*, three thousand gallons of oil were deliberately dumped overboard, and the captain of the *Constellation* told a press conference that "saboteurs were at work" during the rebellion on his ship. The Navy reported seventy-four instances of sabotage during 1972, most on aircraft carriers.

Despite the very difficult organizing conditions within the military, many thousands of sailors found ways to resist and express their discontent with the military and the war. The overall result of the SOS movement was to make it even harder for the United States to continue the war effort. There is no doubt that, while it was the Vietnamese who won the war, the antiwar sentiments and resistance within the Navy played an important role.

• The Ripple Effects of Sabotage

David Cortright

Two major incidents occurred in July 1972 that had significant impact on the Navy's ability to carry out its mission and helped to make a volatile climate aboard ships even more unstable. First, an intentionally set fire aboard the carrier USS *Forrestal*, based in Norfolk, burned the admiral's quarters and extensively damaged the ship's radar communication system, resulting in more than seven million dollars in damage. It was the largest single act of sabotage in naval history.[8]

Later that month, sabotage struck the carrier USS *Ranger*, based in San Diego. The ship had already experienced some twenty acts of sabotage in the months before its scheduled departure for Vietnam.[9] In July, shortly before it was to leave port, major destruction occurred when a paint scraper and two twelve-inch bolts were dropped into the one of the ship's reduction gears. This seriously damaged the engines and caused a three-and-a-half-month delay in the ship's sailing.[10] When the ship finally made it to the Gulf of Tonkin, it was disabled again, this time by an intentionally set fire.[11]

These sabotage incidents played a role in precipitating one of the worst racial uprisings in naval history, the violent upheaval that rocked the USS *Kitty Hawk* in October 1972, when, already on its way home from a long deployment, the ship was unexpectedly ordered back into battle.[12] The crew's bitter disappointment at being sent back to battle exacerbated racial tensions and sparked rebellion among black sailors.

The House Armed Services Subcommittee investigating disciplinary problems in the Navy at that time concluded: "The rescheduling [of the *Kitty Hawk*] apparently was due to the incidents of sabotage aboard her sister ships U.S.S. *Ranger* and U.S.S. *Forrestal*.[13]

Dissenting Airmen

Carolyn Eisenberg

By 1972, if not earlier, it was widely recognized that the exigencies of the ground war were yielding dangerous levels of dissent. However, as the Nixon administration shifted its emphasis to the air war, resistance among the airmen became an unexpected problem. During the eleven days of Operation Linebacker II (referred to as the "Christmas bombing"), President Nixon had authorized more than one hundred B-52s, plus fighter jets to conduct multiple air strikes on Hanoi and Haiphong. The danger to civilians was clear, as was the risk to the airmen. Since the spring offensive, the North Vietnamese had significantly improved their antiaircraft capability, with hundreds of surface-to-air missiles able to retaliate.

With the war winding down, the purpose of this air campaign was murky at best, and the continued killing was hard to justify. At the American air base in Guam, morale was low, with reports of heavy drinking and rowdy behavior. Some men were calling in sick, some interfering with plane maintenance, others offering excuses for not flying.[14] Among those declining the mission was Capt. Michael Heck, whose widely publicized refusal was explicitly political. "The goals do not justify the mass direction and killing," he explained. "I'm just a tiny cog in a big wheel. I have no illusions that what I'm doing will shorten the war, but a man has to answer to himself first." [15] The captain had already flown 175 B-52 missions but had concluded that "any war creates an evil that is far greater than anything it is trying to prevent."

The negativity at Guam persisted into the months that followed the Paris Peace Accords. In the immediate aftermath, the Nixon administration shifted the armada of planes that had been used to attack North Vietnam to hit targets in Cambodia. The next six months saw the most intense bombardment of that country. Under the rubric of Operation Freedom Deal in northeast Cambodia, some of these air strikes were aimed at North Vietnamese troops near the border, while the majority went deeper into the country, in support of the Lon Nol government against local insurgents.

However, back on Guam many American airmen were disgusted with this project and did what they could do to avoid it. More important perhaps was the effort to stop it by appealing to members of Congress. Since the spring of 1971, when members of VVAW went up to Capitol Hill to lobby against the war, there had been ongoing efforts by dissenting Vietnam veterans to influence legislators. In a less formal way, personal relationships between returning soldiers and elected officials could also make a powerful impact. Over the past four years, as members of Congress turned against the war, the reports they received from relatives, neighbors, or even friends had played a role.

Now in the early months of 1973, the United States was continuing an air war, which was both a violation of the 1970 Cooper-Church Amendment and at odds with Article 20 of the Paris peace agreement, which had called on all foreign countries to "put an end to all military activities in Cambodia and Laos, totally withdraw from and refrain from reintroducing into these two countries troops, military advisers and military personnel . . . "

To bring this to a halt, some of the pilots and crew members wrote to members of Congress, who were now actively debating whether to force an end to the air war in Cambodia by cutting off government funds. Senator William Fulbright chose to include some of these letters in the *Congressional Record*, while leaving out the names:[16]

> *I write to you today with much despair in my heart. I had mulled over these words in my mind many a time but now I must sit down and bear my conscience...*
>
> *I am an AC-130 gunship navigator fighting the war in Cambodia on a day to day basis. I come as close as one can get to observe the conflict at hand. What I see is an absurd effort by my Commander in Chief to preserve an unpopular, corrupt, dictatorial government at any expense. We have become once again involved in a civil conflict and as a result of our involvement have escalated the death and destruction on a massive scale . . .*
>
> *I love my country and have served it faithfully for five years, but I fear my conscience can no longer endure this senseless, indiscriminate bombing by B-52s and F-111s that kill and injure thousands of civilians and create hundreds of thousands of refugees. As a crew member in an AC-130 gunship I feel a terrible sense of guilt. We do not use bombs-only artillery shells over a battlefield, but we contribute to the prolongation of this meaningless, unconstitutional war. [May 4, 1973].*
>
> *I fly my bombing missions as often now as I did before the so-called peace agreement ... I do not understand how the President can criticize the North Vietnamese for sending arms and supplies into Cambodia and then expect people to accept his continued bombing of that country as being within the provisions of Article 20 of the Vietnam cease fire. It seems that we are equally at fault. ... It is obvious to me that the United States is choosing sides in a civil war and that despite what the President says we are indeed trying to force a particular outcome.*
>
> *I hope you and your colleagues in the Senate will continue to battle to cut off funds for Nixon's private war. I don't feel that he should be allowed to maintain an army for hire at the expense of the American public any longer. [May 8, 1973].*

Other senators were also hearing from military personnel. Among them was Senator Ted Kennedy, who throughout the previous four years had been a constant voice for peace. Along with Fulbright, Kennedy shared some of his correspondence with *The New York Times*, which decided to print them just days before the Senate was slated to vote on cutting off funds for war in anywhere in Indochina.

Please do not misjudge this letter as the ravings of a wild-eyed radical. I am, as my father before me, an officer of the United States Air Force . . .

Ostensibly there are no American ground troops in Cambodia and yet the bombing continues "at the request of the Cambodian Government." What about the American Government? Where are the American people? Where is the Congress? Congress may offer token protests but we are the ones who must subjugate our conscience and carry out the day by day business of preparing and flying the aircraft. Sixty sorties each day, over 600 tons of high explosives. Congress debates, we destroy. The American people wonder, we kill... [April 15, 1973] [17]

At present I am a staff sergeant in the Air Force serving a second six-month temporary tour of duty assignment in Guam, with the distasteful prospect of returning for a third, to assist in the murder of more innocent people. . . . The obviously insane slaughter of innocent people is not at all conducive to restful nights.

The flight crews are simply "fed up" with the "useless killing." Aborted takeoffs are becoming increasingly common. The uninviting prospect of becoming an un-retrievable prisoner in Cambodia coupled with the graver prospect of losing their lives for something they do not believe in is the prime reason. [May 9, 1973].

Throughout the Vietnam War, another important vehicle for military dissent was use of the courts. In the spring of 1973, Air Force captain Donald Dawson, who had been flying B-52s over Vietnam, had become increasingly conscience-stricken about his own actions.[18] When ordered to bomb Cambodia, he refused the order. As court-martial proceedings began, he joined an American Civil Liberties Union suit filed by three other B-52 officers and Congresswoman Elizabeth Holtzman, declaring the American bombing of Cambodia as illegal. The initial decision by a Republican judge was in support of the plaintiffs, who then issued an injunction against further bombing, scheduled to go into effect in forty-eight hours. The government, in turn, sought a stay of the injunction, with a Supreme Court decision never reaching completion.

Before this case could be settled, Congress had finally acted decisively on the matter of continuing the war. By late June, both the House and the Senate had passed amendments cutting off all funds for any U.S. combat operations in Southeast Asia, without congressional consent.[19] Thus the ongoing skirmishing over American bombing operations in Cambodia had the salutary effect of shutting the door on further military action anywhere in Indochina. This reflected an array of pressures, which had been building over the course of a decade. But the increasingly vocal resistance of American pilots and their crews and their growing reluctance to continue the destruction and killing of innocent people helped to influence the congressional debate.

'I'm not going to fly any more missions'

Charlie Clements

I grew up on military bases because my father was in the Air Force, and I suppose I was groomed from the time I was a little boy to go into the Air Force. My brother went to the Air Force Academy and I followed. At the Academy, we were instilled with a tremendous sense of duty and discipline, and of honor and ethics—a theme that one dealt with almost every day there, because one could take a pencil from somebody else and if you didn't return it, that was considered an honor violation and you would have to turn yourself in and leave the Academy. It was a black-and-white world. I think it was that sense of honor that probably led me to my refusal to fly anymore in Vietnam.

Charlie Clements, 1988.
Source: Photo by William Short.

I entered pilot training with the clear understanding that I didn't want to kill anybody, but I can't tell you why I felt that way. I trained in a C-130, then went to Vietnam and slowly began to see things differently. I began to have a real revulsion about what was going on, but I never thought about quitting.

I flew a secret mission to Cambodia, and I remember looking out of the plane and seeing vast areas that looked like the moon. Only one thing did that: B-52s. I realized we were conducting massive bombing operations there. We began ferrying troops from Saigon to Parrot's Beak, positioning troops for an invasion. I was furious. I had a cold, so I declared myself unfit to fly.

I went off to California for a few days and went to an antiwar rally at San Francisco State with a friend. I felt, This is it; I'm not going to go back., I'm not going to fly any more missions. Somehow the organizers got me to speak and I just told people, "I'm a lieutenant in the Air Force and I'm not going to fly anymore. I've seen a lot of terrible things and I'm saying *no*."

I went back to Vietnam and asked for a transfer to a unit that didn't have anything to do with Vietnam. Some months later, I got a call to go to San Antonio, where I saw this Air Force psychiatrist. He said, "Don't worry, Clements, we'll have you back in Saigon in a week; you're in the old three-year slump." I said, "You're pretty fucked-up if you think I'm going back." I talked about the Phoenix Program, about secret bases in Laos, about flying planeloads of money down there for this black-marketing scam, about secret missions into Cambodia, and coups and invasions, and I think he thought I was totally whacked.

He gave me an envelope and sent me across town to someplace. I went across town, gave them this envelope, and they gave me a pair of pajamas. I had gone in the back door of a psychiatric ward and there I was! I couldn't make any telephone calls, I couldn't have any visitors, and I was given medications. If I didn't take the medication, I was told I would be strapped down and injected. I didn't know if I was crazy or not, but I was beginning to think so, because the nurses and doctors were intelligent, educated people, and they were treating me like I was one of the other patients. Then the major from across town came and said that if I would agree to go back to Saigon, they would drop all this psychiatric stuff. That was a turning point for me, because I knew if I was crazy, I was crazy because I chose to be. Soon after, a friend of mine kind of broke into the ward. We were supposed to have dinner the night I had disappeared, and he finally found me.

Interviewed 1988 by Willa Seidenberg and William Short

The Next Generation Resists

Iraq and Afghanistan Wars Reawaken Military Protest

David Cortright

History doesn't repeat itself, exactly, but there are recurring patterns and cycles of protest. Like the GIs of the Vietnam era, many of the soldiers who served in Iraq and Afghanistan spoke out against war. In the years 2003–2011, dozens of antiwar organizations emerged among recent veterans, military family members, and active-duty soldiers, some of which are still active today. This military antiwar movement was smaller than the Vietnam-era resistance, as was the war itself and the broader antiwar movement, but soldiers and veterans played an important role in mobilizing opposition to war. They also generated pressure for improving military benefits and healing the physical and emotional wounds of returning veterans.

One of the most influential organizations within this movement was Iraq Veterans Against the War (IVAW), patterned after its Vietnam-era namesake, Vietnam Veterans Against the War. IVAW was never a large organization, with less than a thousand members and eight chapters at its peak in early 2008, but it became the public face of dissent within a military increasingly plagued by poor morale.[1] The consequences of fighting seemingly endless wars of occupation and serving multiple deployments led many troops to question their mission. Army surveys of junior enlistees during the war consistently found low morale among soldiers in Iraq and Afghanistan. A 2006 Zogby International poll among troops in Iraq found 72 percent agreeing that U.S. troops should be pulled out within one year, with 29 percent of those urging immediate withdrawal.[2]

Unlike GIs of the Vietnam era, soldiers opposed to the Iraq and Afghanistan wars did not publish underground newspapers. They expressed their grievances through blogs and e-mails. Iraq and Afghanistan were the first social media wars, and many troops used their access to the Internet to send

Participants of the Winter Soldier hearing sponsored by Iraq Veterans Against the War, in March 2008 in Silver Spring, Maryland. The hearing included testimony by some two hundred Iraq and Afghanistan war veterans, including accounts of atrocities committed by U.S. forces. The hearing was inspired by the Winter Soldier Investigation sponsored by Vietnam Veterans Against the War in 1971. Source: Photo copyright by Mathieu Grandjean.

antiwar messages to family, friends, and hometown newspapers. IVAW member Garett Reppenhagen helped to start the "Fight to Survive" blog while serving as a sniper in Iraq in 2004. The blog was intended as "the mouthpiece for a group of soldiers who are fighting in a war they oppose for a president they didn't elect while the petrochemical complex turns the blood of their fallen comrades into oil."[3]

The most significant action organized by IVAW was the Winter Soldier hearing. The goal was to create a kind of truth commission that would cut through the propaganda of military and political leaders to tell Americans what was actually happening in Iraq and Afghanistan. In selecting the appellation Winter Soldier, IVAW reached back to the war-crimes hearings organized by VVAW in 1971. The reference to "winter soldier" comes from Thomas Paine's 1776 patriotic tribute to the Revolutionary War soldiers who stood by their country not just in summer but in the darkest months of winter. Antiwar veterans from both wars sought to embrace this spirit of patriotism and were channeling Dr. Martin Luther King, Jr.'s declaration, "I oppose the Vietnam War because I love America."[4] True patriots, the veterans asserted, speak out against the abuses of power that lead to unjust war. They sought to use their distinctive military identity to reframe the meaning of patriotism, to take back the flag from militarism and assert it as a symbol of antiwar dissent.

About two hundred recent veterans participated in the March 2008 Winter Soldier hearing, including a few active-duty troops. Approximately fifty gave testimony. Over three days of often emotional, poignant testimony at a labor center near Washington, D.C., the veterans told stories of their deployments in Iraq and Afghanistan, addressing themes such as disregard for the rules of engagement, dehumanization of the enemy, the breakdown of the military, sexual abuse, and profiteering by military contractors.

To ensure the accuracy of the presentations, IVAW leaders carefully validated each soldier's military service record. They verified their stories by cross-referencing incidents with military records and media reports and by checking with other soldiers or Marines who were present at the locations and dates mentioned. This guaranteed that the evidence presented at the 2008 Winter Soldier hearing was solidly documented. Pro-war groups organized a small protest outside the event and tried to "swift-boat" the IVAW members, but they were unsuccessful.

No incidents of major mass atrocities were revealed during the hearing, but there were plenty of stories of racism and dehumanization of Iraqis, the killing of civilians, the torture and abuse of prisoners, sexual abuse against women, the breakdown of military morale and discipline, and the lack of adequate health services for wounded and traumatized veterans when they returned home.[5]

The soldiers spoke of the terror and futility of conducting nighttime house raids in Iraq and Afghanistan. In the typical incident, a squad of heavily armed U.S. soldiers would arrive unannounced and uninvited to a home. They would burst in, weapons drawn, and awaken the entire household to conduct a search (often damaging property) for weapons and supposed terrorists. They would separate the women and children and forcefully detain and take away military-age men and boys. In many cases, the soldiers testified, they went to the wrong house and detained the wrong persons.

House raids needlessly exposed troops to the danger of attack and generated hatred and enmity from the civilian populations they were supposedly sent to help. The soldiers who had to carry out these raids suffered psychologically along with the families they violated and abused. Participation in such missions wore on their consciences, generating what experts call "moral injury," the emotional cost of seeing or committing acts of moral transgression.[6]

The Winter Soldier hearing received considerable publicity. Pacifica Radio led the coverage, and the indomitable Amy Goodman from *Democracy Now!* reported live from the event. CBS, NPR, Fox, and other networks were also there. *The Washington Post, Newsday, The Boston Globe,* and other papers covered the event, and stories appeared in *Stars and Stripes* and in *Army Times, Navy Times* and other major military publications.

Antiwar dissent was not supposed to happen in an all-volunteer military. The Nixon administration created a volunteer Army in the early 1970s to undercut civilian draft resistance and the antiwar movement, and to prevent a repeat of the GI revolt that eroded military effectiveness during the Vietnam era.[7] It was assumed that soldiers who volunteer would be less likely to dissent and more willing to follow orders. But soldiers who serve in the military today do not trade away their consciences when they volunteer. They enlist not because they love war but, in most instances, because they need the employment and educational benefits recruiters offer. Like their counterparts in the Vietnam era, they have raised their voices to speak truth to power.

'We displayed a disturbing level of contempt towards the Iraqi people'

Kelly Dougherty

Kelly Dougherty.
Source: Photo and copyright by Gerrie Rouse.

When I was seventeen in 1996, I joined the Colorado Army National Guard as a way to pay for college. My best friend and I enlisted together as medics but were attached to a military police [MP] company, and eventually we were trained as MPs. I opposed the invasion of Iraq before the war started. When I received my notice of deployment, I didn't want to go, but refusing seemed impossible and I felt obligated to my fellow soldiers.

I entered Iraq a few weeks after the initial invasion and was unprepared for the poverty and destruction I saw. A culture of chauvinism and dehumanization was pervasive in the military, and we displayed a disturbing level of contempt towards the Iraqi people. We thought they should be grateful to us for "liberating" them, but we also despised them. We were under an enormous amount of stress and we often focused our anger, fear, and frustration onto the Iraqi people.

When we imagine war, we often think of soldiers and great battles. In reality, the violence is more pervasive, less heroic, and mainly targets innocent people. One day, my MP team was called to the scene of an accident. A young boy had been herding donkeys across the highway and was struck and killed by a U.S. Army convoy. That little boy didn't die in a battle, but he was still a casualty of war—and people like him were being hurt, killed, displaced, and terrorized every day because of the U.S. occupation.

My unit's mission was to provide convoy security to corporations. When one of their semi trucks would break down, we would secure the truck until it could be recovered. But almost every time, after hours of tense conflict with crowds of civilians, we'd receive a call to abandon the truck after destroying its engine and burning its contents. We frequently set tankers of diesel on fire, and one time we burned a truck with pallets of food inside. Sitting in a Humvee turret [and] pointing an automatic machine gun at bewildered kids and men while we burned food didn't quite match the image of heroism that military mythology seeks to evoke.

For me, there was also the stress of living within the military's abusive and misogynistic culture. I could never feel safe, even when I returned to my base. We were warned of men attacking women in the showers and while they were running. Men in my unit spoke disparagingly about women constantly. Women were singled out for harassment because they were "too slutty" or suspected of being lesbians. I had to work closely with men who told me that women shouldn't be in the military. One man in particular was especially hostile and threatening toward me. While I was in Iraq, I decided I needed to do more to oppose the war, but I had no idea where to start.

After I got home in 2004, I went to the Veterans For Peace (VFP) convention in Boston with my dad. There I met other Iraq veterans; Mike Hoffman, Alex Ryabov, Jimmy Massey, Tim Goodrich, and Diana Morrison were the first vets I'd met who openly opposed the war. They invited me to be involved in an organization they were starting for post-9/11 veterans who wanted to bring the troops home. On the final day of the convention, we announced the formation of Iraq Veterans Against the War (IVAW).

When I returned home to Colorado Springs, I began meeting people, speaking publicly, and recruiting new IVAW members. I helped start the first IVAW chapter, was elected to the board, and worked as the executive director. I've been fortunate to be part of a community of radical, loving, creative, and amazing veterans. I believe that veterans have incredible power to create change by using our experience and perspective to challenge the narratives that perpetuate the violence and injustice of war and militarism.

Jonathan Hutto. Source: Photo and copyrightby Gerrie Rouse.

'My mother educated me on the struggle for justice'

Jonathan Hutto

When someone asks me how I became a public advocate for peace, I respond that I was born into it. I grew up in Atlanta, a city once known as the cradle of the Old South that became the crucible of the New South. My mother educated me on the struggle for justice and told stories of a loving and cohesive black community in the midst of a hateful white power structure. One story she told was of a college classmate named George who was drafted for Vietnam. Mom received regular letters from him, including a picture of him with his rifle, and then suddenly the letters stopped, and she never heard from him again. To this day, she believes that George was killed in Vietnam.

My mom was in Ebenezer Baptist Church in 1967 when the Reverend Dr. Martin Luther King, Jr. first spoke publicly against the Vietnam War. She also vividly tells about hearing a fiery young Stokely Carmichael speak out against the war. Thirty years later, when I was president of the Howard University Student Association, I had the honor of hosting and introducing him by his chosen name, Kwame Ture. His speech that night was a watershed moment in my life. Kwame said that the struggle for justice is eternal. "Once you work for the people," he said, "the people will never forsake you." Kwame's dictum has become a lived experience for me.

After graduating from Howard, I took a job with the ACLU in Washington, D.C. A year later, I accepted a position in the Mid-Atlantic office of Amnesty International. I truly loved my work at Amnesty, which took me throughout the region, organizing for human rights. But nonprofit employment was not enough to sustain me, as I had become a full-time single dad and faced mountains of student debt. By chance, a Navy recruiter approached me in a coffee shop in Maryland. I resisted at first, but he told me about the Navy's tuition benefits and student loan repayment program. With no other alternative, I signed up.

After boot camp, I went to Navy apprentice school in Maryland to learn photography and journalism—and I was introduced to the "real" Navy. When I explained my life experiences and my motivation for joining the Navy, I described the military as an "affirmative action" employer. After that, my instructors homed in on me and I was written up for every minor infraction possible. I survived apprentice school and was assigned to the USS *Theodore Roosevelt*, which deployed off the coast of Iraq from September 2005 to March 2006.

During deployment, I became involved in antiracist struggles in my unit. In February 2006, some white petty officers displayed a hangman's noose in my face. I filed an equal-opportunity case against the perpetrators. Around this time, a former professor sent me a copy of *Soldiers in Revolt,* by David Cortright. This book gave me a road map for the anguish and frustration I felt serving in a war that I was ideologically opposed to, and educated me on a history I knew very little about. I was elated when Cortright accepted my invitation to come to Norfolk when the ship returned.

Cortright spoke to more than one hundred people at a local YMCA in June 2006. We then gathered at a local professor's home for an impromptu meeting with twelve active-duty service members, which sparked the launching of the Appeal for Redress to end the war in Iraq. In January 2007, we delivered over one thousand signed appeals to members of Congress in Washington. In October that year, we received the coveted Letelier-Moffit Human Rights Award from the Institute for Policy Studies. By then we had delivered more than two thousand appeals to members of Congress, calling for an end to U.S. wars of aggression and occupation.

I am a lifelong community organizer and human rights defender. I am eternally grateful for the sacrifices of GI movement veterans.

'Our healing is connected to the healing of those we harmed'

Camilo Mejía

When I first heard the news that my unit was deploying to the Middle East, I had nearly completed my eight years of service in the U.S. Army Infantry. It was the beginning of 2003 and my mind had begun to turn against war and militarism, which included the impending U.S. invasion of Iraq. Despite my growing antiwar feelings, however, I was compelled to remain in the military through the little-known "stop loss" law, which gave President Bush the ability to go to war without congressional approval, and to keep troops in the service beyond the end of their contracts.

Camilo Mejía.
Source: Photo by Ellen Davidson.

The illegality and impunity with which Bush and his administration forced the invasion and occupation of Iraq down everyone's throat were at the core of my issues with the war. But those issues were largely intellectual and abstract—the product of reading articles about 9-11, weapons of mass destruction, and stockpiles of chemical weapons. To me, these were justifications that never added up.

My issues against the war became real and hard to bear during my first mission in Iraq. It was April 2003, and the dry heat was extreme at our camp, an old Iraqi Air Force base in the desert town of Al Assad. Our area of operations there was an old jet bunker that served as an improvised detention camp, where we psychologically tortured detainees in order to "soften them up for interrogation." While the tactics we employed in our first mission were deplorable, including sensory deprivation and mock executions, they merely set the stage for more atrocious behavior on our part.

While stationed in Ar Ramadi, capital of the Al Anbar Province, I began to question the soundness of our missions. My main concerns had to do with the mistreatment of Iraqis, which included arbitrary detentions, torture, and shootings of unarmed civilians. I mostly concentrated my criticism on tactics and strategy, or lack thereof. Our brass had made it clear that we were there to get awards and medals, which could only be won through combat.

The careerism of our officer corps drove the obsession with medals and awards and led to the commission of war crimes and the habitual murder of unarmed civilians. These people were killed in battles that should never have taken place in civilian areas, including mosques, schools, and public squares. My fellow squad leaders secretly shared the concerns I expressed, but the military's culture of silence and blind obedience left me alone with my objections.

When I returned to the States on a two-week furlough, safe from improvised explosive devices and sniper fire, and besieged by the morbid curiosity of those who glorify war, I decided I could no longer justify the harm we were inflicting on the country and people of Iraq. I decided to take a public antiwar stance, refusing to return to my unit in Ar Ramadi. My decision landed me in a military prison for nine months and prompted Amnesty International to declare me a prisoner of conscience.

Upon my release from prison, now fourteen years ago, I joined the military resistance to the so-called Global War on Terror. I became active with organizations like Citizen Soldier, Iraq Veterans Against the War, Military Families Speak Out, and Veterans For Peace, among others. Our efforts ultimately failed to end the U.S. war against Iraq, but our collective antiwar resistance expanded to include U.S. militarism and endless war, and is now grounded in the understanding that peace means a lot more than the absence of war. I, along with my brothers and sisters in the military resistance, have come to recognize that our healing is connected to the healing of those we harmed, and to the need to rebuild our world in a way that prevents future generations from having to join our movement.

Confronting the Legacies of War 13

A Message from Mme Nguyen Thi Binh

On November 4, 1968, Nguyen Thi Binh arrived in Paris as deputy head of the National Liberation Front's delegation to the Paris Conference on Vietnam. For years she had traveled internationally as a diplomat, consolidating support for Vietnam's independence and to pressure the United States government to stop the bombing and begin peace talks. It was during her diplomatic work in Paris that Mme. Binh met American antiwar activists, including Cora Weiss, soldiers who opposed the war. and others. In 1973, after five years of negotiations, the United States and Vietnam signed the Paris Peace Accords to end the war. Mme. Binh was a signatory.

More than twenty years earlier, she had been a student activist in Vietnam, opposing the reestablishment of French rule after World War II. It was a dangerous choice that landed her in Saigon's Chi Hoa prison for three years, until 1954. Her birth name was Nguyen Chau Sa. As a member of the underground, she took the alias Yen Sa, but after the establishment of the National Liberation Front in 1961, she began working for the Reunification Commission in Hanoi, concentrating on diplomacy. That is when she adopted the name she uses today, Nguyen Thi Binh.

Binh is the Vietnamese word for peace.

Dear American Veterans,

During the U.S. war in Vietnam from 1954–1975, in which millions of American soldiers took part, many of them opposed the war almost as soon as they went into the army. After they became veterans, they joined U.S. veteran organizations including Vietnam Veterans Against the War and later Veterans For Peace. They conducted many actions and activities aimed at stopping the war and restoring peace in Vietnam. This public and vocal opposition

Mme. Nguyen Thi Binh at the office of her Vietnam Foundation for Peace and Development, October 16, 2016.
Source: Photo by Ron Carver.

Nguyen Thi Binh signs the Paris Peace Accords on January 27, 1973, a crucial step toward ending America's war in Vietnam.

to the war contributed to the strong development of a peace movement among the American people who were demanding to end the war, one of the important factors that brought peace to Vietnam.

After 1975, U.S. veterans continued their activities to move beyond the past and to reconcile our two nations, to normalize relations and build friendly and cooperative relationships between our two peoples. Not content only to offer moral backing to Vietnam, American veteran organizations have also extended material support through humanitarian projects for Vietnam such as building schools and clinics. They have supported many projects to help Agent Orange victims like the Van Canh Friendship Village project; the unexploded mine- and bomb-clearing project run by Project RENEW and supported by Veterans For Peace, as well as a project that collects relics of the fallen Vietnamese soldiers to help find their remains which has been carried out by the Vietnam Veterans of America.

I highly appreciate the activities and efforts of U.S. veterans in the process of "shelving the past and looking to the future," promoting reconciliation and solidarity with Vietnam. I strongly hope that these activities will be further strengthened, contributing to peace, reconciliation, and friendship, and sustaining cooperation between the people of our two countries, Vietnam and the U.S.A.

Nguyen Thi Binh
Former Vice President of the Socialist Republic of Vietnam
President of the Vietnam Peace and Development Foundation
Hanoi, February 27, 2019

'I was confused about who I was as an American'

Chuck Searcy

Chuck Searcy stands by an ARVN bunker in 1967, Saigon. Child in foreground is selling newspapers. Source: Photo courtesy of Chuck Searcy.

After I dropped out of the University of Georgia in 1965, I was about to be drafted, so I enlisted in the Army in 1966, looking for a better deal and hoping to avoid the war. It didn't work. In June 1967, I was on a plane to Vietnam. I wasn't happy. But my father was a POW in World War II and all my uncles had been in the military, so it was my turn.

I was trained as a Military Intelligence analyst and assigned to the 519th MI Battalion in Saigon. We were support personnel for the Combined Intelligence Center, Vietnam, a kind of think tank, a windowless concrete building near the Tan Son Nhat air base.

We churned out classified reports on Vietcong and North Vietnamese; we also passed around Ho Chi Minh's speeches, the Vietnamese Declaration of Independence, the Geneva Agreements, everything we could find. Most of us turned against the war. We felt we were part of an institutional lie.

The 1968 Tet Offensive brought the war to Saigon. There was huge bombing and destruction, mainly from our airpower and artillery weapons. Swarms of refugees ebbed through neighborhoods of burned homes and charred debris around our compound on the Saigon River.

When I left in June 1968, I was confused about who I was as an American, I no longer trusted my government to tell the truth to the American people. I was angry and bitter.

I was transferred to U.S. Army Europe headquarters in Germany. I had a year left in the Army, a year to cool down, reflect on my Vietnam experience, and put it all in perspective. I got beyond my anger and confusion, sharpened my focus, and decided to return to the University of Georgia and get involved in the antiwar movement.

I settled into a class and study routine. One day, a young guy in a class who knew I was a Vietnam vet said there would be a peace demonstration the next night on campus, and the organizers wondered if I would speak. "You're the only Vietnam vet we've ever met," he explained. I wrote out some notes on a yellow pad and explained forthrightly the tragedy of the war for innocent Vietnamese people and also to American families; the lies we had been told. At the end of the speech, nine guys came out of nowhere, all Vietnam vets. None of us knew each other. The next morning we met and formed a chapter of Vietnam Veterans Against the War.

My parents saw me on TV protesting the war and they were upset, angry. We had terrible arguments. "You're not an American anymore," my father said. "What happened to you over there? Did they turn you into a Communist?"

My parents and I had no contact for two years. Then one day my father phoned and asked me to meet him for a cup of coffee. "Your mother and I have been talking," he said. "We've decided this war is a terrible thing. It's got to stop. We think you were right, and we were wrong. We'd like for you to come back home."

It was powerful moment, one I will never forget.

Remediation

Some American military veterans who served in Vietnam worked afterward to provide humanitarian assistance and redress the damage caused by the U.S. war. American and Vietnamese war veterans collaborated to facilitate searches for those missing in action. They worked to locate and neutralize unexploded munitions and provide support for those suffering the effects of Agent Orange. Their efforts helped to create the conditions for new diplomatic relations and a relationship of friendship between Vietnam and the United States.

'The moral thing for us to do'

Chuck Searcy

Many years after leaving the military and finishing school, after various jobs, two marriages, and many memories and reminders of Vietnam, an old army buddy was in Atlanta for a convention. He and I had dinner, and by the end we'd decided we were going back to Vietnam, as tourists.

In 1992, we traveled the whole country. The Vietnamese people were warm, welcoming, and forgiving. It was a journey of reconciliation and forgiveness. I decided I wanted to come back and help with the recovery that was still under way.

In 1995, the Vietnam Veterans of America Foundation asked me to launch a new orthopedic workshop at the Children's Hospital in Hanoi, funded by USAID. During that work with doctors and medical staff, I learned that more than 100,000 children and adults had been killed or injured by unexploded ordnance (UXO) since the fighting ended in 1975. Every week there was a new report in the newspaper or on TV of a farmer or another child being killed or injured.

Chuck Searcy, in Quang Tri Province, Vietnam, in October 2016. Searcy cofounded Project RENEW with Vietnamese colleagues.
Source: Photo by Ron Carver.

Other American veterans, international friends, even U.S. embassy staff and visiting congressional delegations began to ask, "Why aren't we Americans doing something to help end this problem? After all, most of the munitions were ours." (The United States dropped more than eight million tons of ordnance on Vietnam, more than three times the tonnage in all of World War II.)

Thanks to key members of the Congress, U.S. funds were eventually appropriated to support this effort. Out of this came Project RENEW, with which I'm still associated as "international adviser."

Project RENEW's Nguyen Thi Dieu Linh leads a staff of more than 150 people in mapping, identifying, and detonating unexploded ordnance (UXOs) in Quang Tri Province.
Source: Photo by Ron Carver.

Two staff members from Project RENEW systematically comb a field, dropping red flags wherever their metal detector finds UXOs. Project RENEW is largely funded by Norwegian People's Aid, with additional funding by the U.S. government. Source: Photo by Ron Carver.

Hundreds of thousands of small unexploded devices like this baseball-shaped bomb litter Vietnam's countryside, endangering people to this day. Source: Photo by Ron Carver.

Project RENEW staff members detonate an antipersonnel bomb, October 2016. Source: Photo by Nguyen Thi Hong Hanh.

Nguyen Thi Chat tends to her thirty-six-year-old daughter, a second-generation victim of Agent Orange. Her daughter, Nguyen Thi Hai, has never been able to walk, communicate, or function normally. While a soldier fighting for Vietnam's independence, Hai's father was repeatedly sprayed with Agent Orange by American warplanes. Source: Photo by Ron Carver.

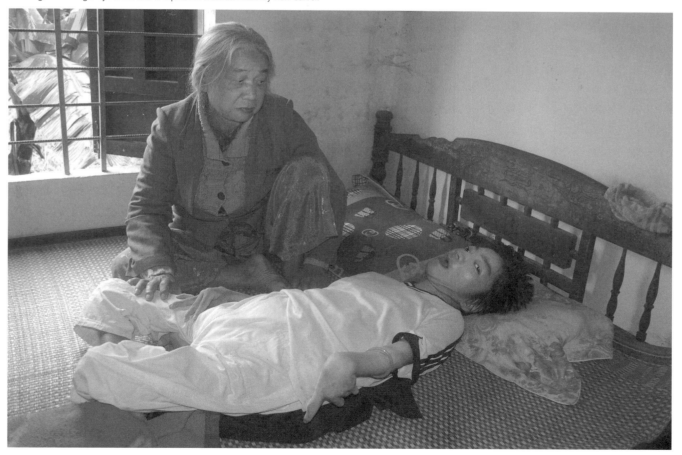

Tran Huu Loi is director of two Project RENEW workshops that serve people who were blinded by the postwar explosions of buried antipersonnel bombs. Source: Photo by Ron Carver.

Since 2001, RENEW staff and Norwegian People's Aid (NPA), our main partner, have worked with other NGOs and the provincial government of Quang Tri Province, site of the former DMZ that separated north and south during the war. We have destroyed more than 600,000 bombs. In the last two years, 2018 and 2017, there were *zero* deaths from UXO— the first years since the war ended in 1975 that not a single fatality occurred in the province.

We also deal with Agent Orange, helping families whose lives have been devastated by the toxic chemical dioxin that is the by-product of America's use of this deadly herbicide. U.S. veterans have begun to receive compensation, rightly so, for their illnesses related to Agent Orange; now, for the first time, the U.S. government is providing funds to support Vietnamese families living with severe disabilities, many of them assumed to be related to Agent Orange. The Unites States has also paid most of the cost of the dioxin cleanup effort at the Da Nang airport, and will soon begin the cleanup of the Bien Hoa air base near Ho Chi Minh City. It's forty years late, but better late than never.

Some people ask if I'm doing this out of guilt. No. I don't feel guilt. I feel *responsibility* as an American, as a Vietnam vet, for what we did here, and I

● **Do you think I can have a productive life?**

Ho Van Lai

Ho Van Lai and three friends were playing with the small bombs that must have worked their way up from under the surface of the soil. He was ten years old and living in Cua Viet township.

When Lai was released from the hospital, it took him a year to recover before he was able to attend a school for the visually impaired. He returned to the sixth grade after an absence of four years, finally graduating from high school.

Lai attended university for a year and a half, but his failing eyesight led him to drop out again. With help from Project RENEW's Prosthetics and Orthotic program, he is mobile and volunteers at the center.

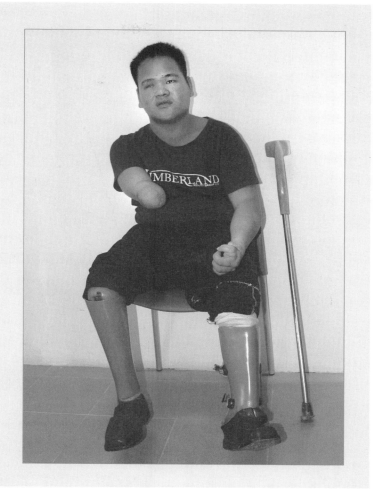

Ho Van Lai. Source: Photo by Ron Carver.

think the moral thing for us to do is to admit what we did and work with the Vietnamese to reduce and try to eliminate the lingering consequences. It's not about guilt. It's about doing the right thing.

Restoration Projects Include U.S. Veterans

With a vision to foster "people-to-people diplomacy," Fredy Champagne launched the Veterans–Viet Nam Restoration Project (VVRP) in 1988. The group reached out to the U.S. and Vietnamese governments and to veterans' organizations and became the first American NGO permitted to undertake a humanitarian service project in Vietnam following the war.

In 1989, Champagne and seventeen VVRP members traveled to Vung Tao and assisted Vietnamese workers to construct the Friendship Medical Clinic. Over the following twenty-five years, VVRP completed numerous other projects, including a second clinic, in Yen Vien, near Hanoi, and rebuilding schools in Thua Thien Province.

Champagne also organized and led the first "Peace Walk in Viet Nam," parading through Hanoi, Vinh, Da Nang, Nha Trang, and Saigon in 1991. He led the second Peace Walk just before the U.S. embargo was lifted in 1993.

Fredy Champagne, aka Fred Stafford Higdon, Jr., was born August 29, 1946.

'I had unfinished business with the Vietnamese people'

Fredy Champagne

I was nineteen years old and politically uneducated when I enlisted in July 1965. During basic training at Fort Gordon, in Georgia, we heard that Lyndon Johnson was sending the First Cavalry Division to Vietnam. We wondered, Where is this country called Vietnam?

Fredy Champagne in Vietnam, 1966.
Source: Photo courtesy of Fredy Champagne.

VVRP Peace Walks took place in 1991 and 1993. Source: Courtesy of Fredy Champagne.

I was deployed to Vietnam for a year starting in November 1965. My MOS was 11 Bravo, infantry rifleman, Spec. 4. I was stationed in Lai Khe, Song Be Province, northwest of Saigon.

We were told the enemy were the people with black pajamas and cone hats, but on operations in the bush, all the people were dressed like that. Farmers in the fields were being shot down from helicopter gunners. One day while on convoy duty, we crossed an intersection and there was a young dead

Members of Veterans–Viet Nam Restoration Project (VVRP) celebrated at the opening of the Friendship Medical Clinic in Vung Tau in 1989. Source: Photo courtesy of Fredy Champagne.

VC soldier, tied to a post with wire, and his head was split open by gunfire. This image haunts me still. Forever in my mind, this young soldier was a bucket of brains, with the top half of his skull gone. Sad but true.

I knew then that the war was unjust, and that the generals and politicians were lying to us about the war and its reasons to intervene in a sovereign country's affairs. I knew something was wrong, but I was not educated about the politics. I did not know at that time that the United States had stopped the 1957 elections.

Twenty-two years later, I felt the urge to return to Vietnam and see the country at peace. It seemed that young dead VC was calling me, reminding me I had unfinished business with the Vietnamese people. I felt the time was right for ending the U.S. trade embargo against the Vietnamese people; the embargo itself was a war crime. VVRP was the result.

Our motto was Wage Peace, of course. Our projects helped veterans, including myself, heal from the PTSD wounds of Vietnam, while working for reconciliation with the United States.

'I was about five at my first Agent Orange Awareness rally'

Heather Bowser

My father, Bill Morris, had two April Fools' Days in 1969, as he flew across the International Date Line toward home after his tour in Vietnam. He served with the Army's 506 Field Depot, First Logistical Command, at the Long Binh base in Dong Nai Province. His base was sprayed with dioxin-tainted herbicide nearly daily, unbeknownst to him or thousands of others. The base was close to Bien Hoa airport, where Operation Ranch Hand's sorties took off. He was poisoned there. That cruel April Fools' Day joke was on him, and his family.

Dad married my mother, his college sweetheart, nine days before leaving for Vietnam. He had left college a semester before graduation and he was

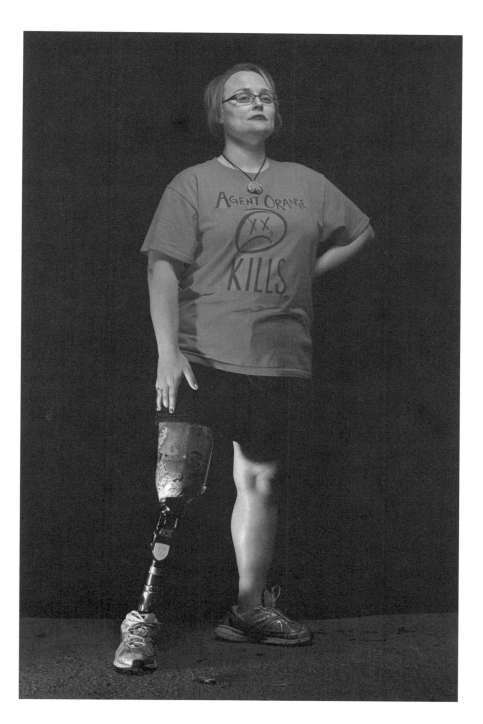

Heather Bowser.
Source: Photo by Mathieu Asselin.

aware that his decision would place him back into the draft. With his number coming close, he enlisted for three years, having been promised he would be kept stateside. Of course, that was a lie told to fulfill the government's need for bodies to fight its war.

After his tour, my parents wanted to put the war behind them. Their dreams for a large family changed after my mother suffered two miscarriages. In October 1972, my mother went into labor and I was born two months premature, missing several of my fingers, my big toe on my left foot, and my right leg below the knee. They had no idea what had caused my birth defects. My mother went on to have another miscarriage. Then my brother was born healthy in 1978.

Also in 1978, when a twenty-eight-year-old Vietnam veteran named Paul Reutersah was dying of stomach cancer, he announced on *The Today Show*, "I died in Vietnam, but I didn't even know it." That's how my parents found out about the chemical herbicide tainted with dioxin, Agent Orange, that had been sprayed in massive amounts via Operation Ranch Hand in Dong Nai Province.

Already, life was spiraling downward for my parents. My father wasn't dealing with his sense of guilt over my birth defects, nor with his wartime experiences. My mother was frustrated with my father's drinking and withdrawn behavior. She also blamed herself for losing three babies to miscarriage.

My parents did what many who find themselves activists do: They started looking for others with similar issues. They found them within a two-hour drive of our Ohio town. Others who had children with similar and even worse birth defects than mine. Other Vietnam veterans with cancer and "old man's" diseases, as my dad would say. I have pictures of myself when I was about five at my first Agent Orange Awareness rally. I saw pictures of children from Vietnam who also had devastating birth defects. My parents helped start the first Ohio chapter of a new group that was forming, Agent Orange International. Many Vietnam veterans and their families got involved, and we were gaining strength.

Then it happened.

Dad went to work one day in the steel mill and felt ill. He was rushed to the hospital, where he learned that five of the arteries feeding his heart were blocked. He needed immediate bypass surgery, at thirty-eight years old.

It was 1986 and in no way was the Veterans Administration admitting that Agent Orange had caused any ailments. My father survived the surgery, but financially it devastated my parents for decades. It was a terrifying time as a child. Dad went on to develop diabetes at forty, he had a stroke at forty-eight, and at fifty, he died of a massive heart attack—all while the VA denied his exposure. It's hard to be an activist when you are fighting for your life and income. In 1998, I lost my father to a war he physically left in 1969.

I often start conversations with men in "Vietnam Veteran" ball caps. At first, they think I'm going to give them the canned "Thank you for your ser-

> **My parents helped start the Ohio chapter of Agent Orange International.**

vice" spiel. I ask them what branch of service they belong to and where were they stationed. If they were in the Army, I ask what their MOS was.[1] My knowledge of military terminology helps peel the layers quite quickly. I see their vulnerability as they answer. They are cautious and they question why I know so much.

I know so much because I've lived this since I was born. I tell them my dad passed twenty-plus years ago because of his exposure, I was born with birth defects because of Agent Orange, and I've traveled to Vietnam four times to meet children who are still being born like me, due to residual dioxin in their environment. Usually, it's nearly all these vets can take. The survivor's guilt many carry is just too much. But it's never been their fault.

My activism has taken me around the world, but it hasn't yet persuaded the U.S. government to take responsibility for what it did to those affected by Agent Orange. I feel this is my biggest failure, because if anyone was born to do this, it is me.

It is not enough to have awareness; we must create change. At times, it seems like a fool's journey, but that's why I keep going.

There Is So Much We Can Do Together

Tran Xuan Thao

I was showing a group of Americans our newly renovated ground-floor exhibit just after I returned from visiting my family in our hometown. They asked me, as many visitors do, why Vietnamese people don't hate Americans. "After all we did," an older American man said. "We dropped more bombs on Vietnam than on both fronts during World War Two."

"And chemical weapons, and the My Lai Massacre, and God knows what else," his wife added.

"We lost fifty-three thousand soldiers," a college senior from Toledo, Ohio, exclaimed. "But you lost three million men, women, and children."

Sometimes our visitors toss out their own theories. "Perhaps it's your Buddhist religion," some speculate. "You just forgive and forget."

"Maybe it's because seventy percent of the population was born after the war. "

I was just a small girl, seven years old, when the war ended. And both of my parents survived. Yet the ravages of the American war scored us deeply and in many ways. I remember my mother, terrified by the sight and sound of American warplanes flying overhead, imploring me to grab hold of a tree to protect myself from falling down.

Tran Xuan Thao, Ph.D., director of the War Remnants Museum, Ho Chi Minh City.
Source: Photo by Ron Carver.

My mother tells me stories of being evacuated from our village to flee approaching American troops. She recounts a close call when I was a baby and she set me down to help my father pull his boat over an earthen dam. Only when she lifted me off the ground did she discover that she had set me down very near an explosive device.

When the American platoons would sweep through our villages they often confiscated our chickens and food. One time, they offered to trade their food for ours, leaving us some American dried rice that you don't need to cook. You just add water. That was my first taste of American food, and I loved it.

Phan Van Xoan, my mother's brother, left our village in 1954 to move to the North. For years his job was to protect Ho Chi Minh. During the peace talks, he was stationed in Paris, protecting Vietnam's delegation. My uncle Xoan was a general when he returned to our village after the war, in 1976. That is when he met his twenty-one-year-old daughter for the first time. She was in my aunt's womb when he left to serve our country.

Today, Vietnam has recovered in many ways and moved on from the war. Yet we are still uncovering antipersonnel bombs in some of the rural areas. And we are working hard to help second- and third-generation victims of Agent Orange poisoning.

All is not bleak. We invite you to come and see for yourself. Our economy is growing and so are our cities, with soaring tall buildings. Our beaches are as beautiful as any in the world. Our terraced mountains, teeming with excellent coffee, are as stunning as they are productive. Come and see.

Old Hanoi retains the beauty of its French architecture and the tastes of fine French cuisine. Your favorite chefs, including Anthony Bourdain, heap

War Remnants Museum.
Source: Photo by Ron Carver.

praise on both our tasty street food and our fancier five-star restaurants. You will find an abundance of fresh fish throughout Vietnam, as no place is far from the sea. We have excellent vegetarian restaurants and delicious fresh vegetables of all sorts everywhere you go. Our pho is so good, we eat it for breakfast!

Come and visit us and our wonderful museums. The War Remnants Museum, where I am director, was rated one of the top twenty in the world in a Trip Advisor poll.

That brings me back to one of the most common misconceptions by Americans who are surprised by the warm reception they receive.

Our people generously forgive and embrace our visitors. At the same time, we don't forget. You will see this when you visit my museum. We have two missions. One is to remember the hardships and the sacrifices of our fathers and mothers, and those who still suffer from the legacies of war. Our other mission is to honor the citizens of the world who supported our struggles for liberation, independence, and unification.

The first thing you see when you enter my museum is an exhibit dedicated to those international allies. We display banners, posters, books, and peace pamphlets. We also have portraits of specific, special people we consider heroes. We have long had a photograph of the Quaker pacifist Norman Morrison, from Baltimore, Maryland, whose self-immolation made the world take notice of our own suffering.

High on a wall you will see a portrait of the American war veteran Chuck Searcy—the same portrait that appears in this book. He first came to Saigon as a warrior. He returned in 1995 with a relief program and again in 2001 to begin a project to clear leftover land mines.

You will also see that we now have a permanent installation of the "Waging Peace" exhibit, which we commissioned in 2016 to tell the story of the U.S. soldiers and veterans who opposed America's war in Vietnam. In this exhibit you will find the photos and stories of America's early resisters, Richard Steinke, the Fort Hood Three, and Howard Levy.

Even in the darkest days of the war we heard stories of these people, who we considered brave souls. Our radio broadcasts and our diplomats returning from visits throughout the world told us about the soldiers who said, "No more war," and the veterans who told the truth. We heard about them and Jane Fonda and Cora Weiss, Tom Hayden, Martin Luther King, Muhammad Ali, and your baby doctor, Benjamin Spock. We even have a copy of *Dr. Spock on Vietnam* in our collection of books advocating peace.

This, I believe, is the answer to the question so often posed to me by American visitors who are surprised at the warmth displayed by Vietnamese people they meet. We know that for many years, so many Americans defied and resisted their government's war. And for all these years we have been able to differentiate the actions of your government from the love and solidarity of your people. We don't forget the horrors of war, but we forgive in order to move on. There is so much we can do together.

Behind the Scenes 14

Funding the Movement:
The U.S. Servicemen's Fund

Paul Lauter

In June of 1971, I was out of a job. Although my courses at the University of Maryland, Baltimore County, including Revolutionary Literature, had gone quite well, the dean didn't see it that way. Clearly, he didn't appreciate a teacher who conspired with students to oppose the war, or a man who agitated for women's studies. And so I was gone at the end of my two-year contract. But opportunity emerged from adversity. A movement friend proposed that I take the reins of the United States Servicemen's Fund (USSF), an organization founded by Robert Zevin, Fred Gardner, and other antiwar campaigners to support GI peace activity. Though I wasn't a veteran, I was deeply committed to ending the war and had raised money for antiwar projects. I became national director of USSF.

Zevin, an economics professor at Columbia University, had been instrumental in organizing Resist, created to support draft resisters, as well as to promote civilian opposition to the draft laws, and antiwar activity among GIs. He also served as a wealth-management adviser to some well-to-do peaceniks. It was a short step from Resist to USSF.

USSF's charter committed it to helping provide GIs with places of amusement and relaxation, like coffeehouses; to staging entertainments; and to supporting self-expression in the form of underground newspapers. It did all three. Wisely, Zevin had obtained IRS approval to make the organization nonprofit, allowing USSF to raise funds, which accelerated and expanded the GI movement. In fact, some people who supported the antiwar movement were nervous about fomenting peace action among GIs. Of course, the more popular GI coffeehouses became and the more GI newspapers spread antiwar ideas, the more they were hated—and feared—by military authorities and local pro-war bigwigs.

Actors Donald Sutherland and Jane Fonda perform at their FTA show in Okinawa in 1972. The show toured throughout Asia to entertain troops. Source: Photo courtesy of Displaced Films.

Facing page: A poster for the FTA show. Source: Courtesy Displaced Films.

I moved the USSF headquarters from Zevin's house in Riverdale to an inexpensive office on Greenwich Avenue, near subway stops in New York's West Village. It overlooked the schoolyard behind the building where the writer Grace Paley, an extraordinarily supportive person, and a dear friend, had her apartment. Down the street was a branch of Sutter's bakery, my favorite. If I can't live in the Village, I thought, at least I can work there.

That's when I met Dr. Howard Levy, the young Army captain who had just served a twenty-six-month term in Leavenworth prison for refusing to train Green Berets in elementary dermatology. Howard played a key role in USSF, both as an icon of military resistance[1] and as a source of original ideas about what the organization should undertake. For example, he proposed a kind of antiwar, pro-GI, Bob Hope–style spectacle, which would come to be called the "FTA Show." Implemented by Jane Fonda, Donald Sutherland, Len Chandler, Holly Near, and others, it became one of USSF's main attractions, and drew enormous audiences of GIs, both within the United States. and in Asia.

The more successful USSF and the GI movement became, the heavier the hand of government repression. We weren't surprised when local pro-war politicians and police chiefs tried to prevent coffeehouses from functioning—from denying them operating permits to keeping them from using local facilities. Nor were we shocked when local vigilantes broke coffeehouse windows and set the buildings afire. President Nixon and his accomplices made other devious maneuvers—for example, they tried to get the Internal Revenue Service to take away USSF's tax-exempt status. Faced with a lawsuit filed by the Center for Constitutional Rights (CCR), the IRS dropped that plan—though it did continue to audit the returns of people like me who were affiliated with USSF.

The Nixon people also attacked the fund-raising base for antiwar organizations. At some point in 1970, the USSF mailing list was stolen from its Cambridge office; later, via the Cambridge "Red Squad," these documents, obtained through illegal search and seizure, surfaced in the hands of the House of Representatives Committee on Internal Security, chaired by Richard Ichord. Senator Eastland's Subcommittee on Internal Security also moved to subpoena USSF's bank records. CCR attempted to prevent this action. But a few days after the war ended, in 1975, the majority of the U.S. Supreme Court held that the speech and debate clause of the Constitution barred the court from considering whether the subpoena violated the First Amendment rights of USSF and its members (Justice Douglas dissented). Effectively, the Eastland committee could go ahead with its subpoena.

From the government's point of view, they had to fight the war not only in the jungles of Vietnam, Laos, and Cambodia but on the campuses, in the courtrooms, and on the streets of America. They did so, with malice toward all and charity to none of us who placed organizations like USSF in the path of their destruction.

Origins of the GI Press Collection of the Wisconsin Historical Society

Doris Friedensohn

In the summer of 1994, James Lewes spent two months photocopying GI newspapers for a dissertation, "Protest and Survive: The GI Underground Press in the Vietnam War." [2] It was an eye-opening project, deserving a large audience. After all, most Americans identified antiwar activities with students and churchmen, artists, intellectuals, hippies, and (some) moms pushing strollers—but not with GIs.

Lewes became hooked on the materials and their endlessly surprising revelations. In fact, "Protest and Survive" and the issues raised and addressed in hundreds of GI publications dominated Lewes's life for the next twenty-five years. He returned to the archives from which his dissertation emerged in 2004 to digitize these papers, now considerably deteriorated, for the antiwar film, *Sir! No Sir!*, produced by David Zeiger of Displaced Films.

David Zeiger wrote, directed, and produced *Sir! No Sir!*, a 2005 feature-length documentary that was the first cinematic exploration of the Vietnam-era, GI antiwar movement. Zeiger's research and archive for the film, which helped to inspire this book, can be found at www.displacedfilms.com.

Later, Zeiger challenged him to stay with his skills in photographing and digitizing documents, especially newspapers. Lewes set out to locate the remaining GI newspapers, preserve them in digital form, and find a way to make them available online. He imagined a text-searchable format and a downloading process that would reproduce the papers in the size they were originally published.

It would take patience, cunning, fundraising ability, and perseverance to identify all the newspapers produced by the GI movement, but Lewes, fortunately, had the right temperament for the task. He began with his own listing of GI papers from "Protest and Survive." He added papers listed in David Cortright's *Soldiers in Revolt* and Jim Danky's microfilm collection, Miscellaneous Vietnam Era GI Underground Papers, published by the Wisconsin Historical Society; that gave him three hundred titles as a start. Lewes also searched the online catalogues of the Deering Library and the Swarthmore College Peace Collection, which were known to be repositories of GI materials. Next, with access to the WorldCat database, he found additional titles at the Spencer Library of the University of Kansas and the Walter Reuther Archive at Wayne State University.

To gain permission to digitize the holdings, Lewes needed patience, diplomacy, and even a touch of guile. With very limited funds, he began with institutions near his home in Philadelphia. After raising funds, he spent time in Madison, Detroit, Ann Arbor, Oakland, and Seattle, traveling with a digital scanner at his side and a laptop slung over his shoulder. Lewes also identified a number of private collections, and his relationship with Reveal Digital opened the door to the collections of the Deering and Spencer libraries. Still, it was a limited and lonely one-man operation.

In March 2013, Lewes was rewarded for his steadiness and commitment when the Wisconsin Historical Society offered to partner with his project. Lewes would provide the Historical Society with all digital images created, including material from its collection. The Historical Society would create and maintain a Web-based, open access, text-searchable database. It would also provide digital scans of fifteen reels of microfilm.

In 2013, Lewes moved to Amsterdam. There, at the International Institute of Social History, he began cataloging periodicals in a collection integrating the records of GI movement supporters Dieter Brunn, David Harris, and Max Watts. These materials transformed the project as it grew from 200 to 748 newspapers and newsletters and added hundreds of mailings, posters, flyers, and miscellaneous communications.

It was an incredible leap forward. Some 750 groups in twenty-one countries in Asia, Africa, Europe, and North America were sources of materials. Among the materials were three (out of four) GI papers produced by and for female GIs; the only paper known to have been published by First Nation GIs; and the only paper to have been published by GIs in South Vietnam. Lewes also came upon newspapers and pamphlets produced for and by the civil rights, peace, and women's movements in the United States and Europe, and publications by countercultural organizations that flourished at the same time. As the nonmilitary materials make clear, the GI movement did not exist in a social or political void. Antiwar activists and those fighting for social justice not only shared information and tactics but evolved together. Lewes's comprehensive archive tells this little-known story.

'How I became an antiwar photographer'

Alan Pogue

I was drafted and I volunteered for medic training. I read philosophy and theology in the chapel at Fort Carson in my off time, and I was reading *The Making of a Mind,* the World War I letters of French priest, theologian, and paleontologist Teilhard de Chardin, when along came Chaplain Donald Shea. He saw what I was reading and invited me to be his assistant. He traded a very large statue of Saint Patrick to the division surgeon in return for the surgeon's letting my MOS be changed to chaplain's assistant. The Catholic mafia at work.

Chaplain Shea volunteered for the Special Forces. I said I'd join him, jump out of planes and all, but then I was told I'd have to stay longer in the Army to pay them for my training. Shea went to Germany—my mistake. The next chaplains I drew were time-serving duds, so I volunteered for Vietnam as a chaplain's assistant. The priest I got in Chu Lai, Americal Division, was an orphan who had become a Benedictine. Being surrounded by orphans drove him quite crazy. He was also making passes at me. I could ignore the passes, but then he wouldn't speak to me.

I volunteered to be a combat medic with the 198th Light Infantry. After gathering my medic gear, I was flown out by myself and dropped with Company D. That night, our ambush patrol killed two teenaged girls. That was my "Hello Vietnam," and it only got worse—the end of illusions about Camelot and all that. Our foreign policy was murder. I was enlightened in the most negative fashion. I treated the Vietnamese as often as I could but was under no illusion that this rescued me from our collective guilt. Only the U.S. military's not being there would be helpful.

My mother had given me a Kodak Instamatic and asked that I send pictures home, since I'd most likely not write. The helicopter pilots were kind enough to take my film along with my medical supply orders and bring my prints back to me.

My interest in photography grew. On R&R in Tokyo, my mission was to buy a Nikon camera outfit, and I did so at the Naval Exchange. My other aim

During Alan Pogue's deployment in Vietnam as a medic, he helped Vietnamese civilians when he could. "The man I am working on had a series of boils on his back. I worked on them for the two days we were in the area. He needed to be at a clinic or in a hospital. I was always frustrated by how little I could do." Source: Photo courtesy Alan Pogue.

was to meet the father of Aikido, Morihei Ueshiba, and I did meet him at the Aikido Hombu (headquarters).

I spent five months being shot at while trying to save others from bleeding to death. During slack time, I read Thomas Merton and all of D. T. Suzuki's works in English. I became an atheist in a foxhole. There is no god in Buddhism.

I followed Suzuki's example and remained unaligned—no joining of any particular branch. I also read Saint Augustine's *Confessions* in a B-52 bomb crater I used as my field office. The tenets of the Church rang hollow; the words without content. Dumb luck kept me alive through the Tet Offensive, trip wires, machine-gun fire, mortars.

My dead friends and the deaths of so many Vietnamese weigh on me. Moral injury is corrosive. They died because of the enormous greed of my political leaders and, at least, the cluelessness of my so-called moral leaders. Other self-styled moral leaders were cheerleaders, coconspirators, for the greedy politicians.

At least we may inform others of the truth, that all wars are generated by greed that cancels out humanity. War is a racket, clothed in a crude appeal to patriotism, which becomes only racism and all forms of hatred of "the other," who are evil.

Taking Portraits and Oral Histories

William Short and Willa Seidenberg

The photographs and oral histories we contributed to this book were taken over the course of five years, from 1986 to 1991.[3]

When we arrived for interviews, lugging along tape recorders and a portable photographic studio, our only prior contact with the veteran was often just a short telephone conversation, and our knowledge of the veteran's experience sketchy. Yet each veteran willingly shared intimate, often painful details of his or her life with us. We approached every interview with a certain amount of apprehension, often fearing their story would strike an emotional chord in us. Indeed, many of the interviews were draining, yet remarkably moving. There were times when we could no longer bear to hear or think about Vietnam. But we always found ourselves enthusiastically recounting the story we had just heard and feeling a renewed inspiration from the strength of the veteran's words and convictions.

We tried to make the two- to four-hour interviews as relaxed as possible. Even though we had specific questions for all the veterans about their lives and their active resistance to the war, we wanted them to feel free to roam through memories at their own pace. We were interested in drawing forth their own stories as they remembered them, as they would wish for them to be passed on to another generation. In the process of editing the taped interviews, we often consulted with the veterans to assure that the statements accompanying their photographic portraits remained true to the essence of the interview. Thus, we sought to imbue our work with a collaborative spirit, a mutually contractual process, of which the veterans were an integral part. The same approach was used in creating the photographic portraits, which were taken at the end of each interview. We asked each veteran to bring some objects of personal value or significance to the portrait session. These objects were presented as an offering of who they were, or who they had become. Some felt they had nothing to offer but themselves, and that, after all, was the most valuable thing they could give.

Afterword

Recovering the Legacy of GI Dissent

Christian G. Appy

Waging Peace recovers the dramatic and inspiring story of the greatest movement of antiwar GIs and veterans in United States history. These men and women engaged in almost every imaginable form of dissent and defied a vast range of regulations and orders. They wore peace symbols on their uniforms, raised close-fisted power salutes, formed radical book clubs, visited antiwar coffeehouses, and circulated petitions; they organized peace demonstrations, gave speeches, lobbied Congress, performed guerrilla theater, and threw away their military medals; they published antiwar newspapers, fought for higher pay and First Amendment rights, and participated in marches, boycotts, hunger strikes, and occupations; they filed for conscientious objector status, went AWOL, and deserted. And they refused to fight.

Antiwar troops opposed the Vietnam War in countless ways, both individually and collectively. Their history and legacy are all the more remarkable when we consider an obvious but crucial fact: The military is an authoritarian institution with a myriad of methods to instill obedience and punish dissent—systematic indoctrination, punitive duty or reassignment, brutal forced labor or exercise, reprimands, demotions, courts-martial, imprisonment, and dishonorable discharges (to name just the most obvious).

Then there were the unofficial forms of control and discipline. Let one example serve. On October 10, 1969, *Life* magazine published a searing account of abuse and torture at the Camp Pendleton, California, Marine Corps brig, where some nine hundred men were imprisoned (75 percent of them for being absent without leave). Prisoners deemed disobedient were routinely "kicked, beaten, stomped, clubbed, and karate-chopped." Guards sometimes handcuffed men to the ceiling and left them hanging, or "trussed them in straitjackets," or "hog-tied" them "with straps and leg irons so that they can neither stand, sit nor lie down but must remain for hours in an agonizing crouch."

The legacies of dissent can still inform and inspire resistance in the present.

For all the potentially dire consequences of rebellion in the ranks, the GI movement exploded. By the early 1970s, there were probably more manifestations of antiwar activism within the military than on most college campuses. One study found that nearly half of all active-duty soldiers had participated in some form of disobedience or dissent. Many commanders in Vietnam had serious doubts that they could continue to field an effective fighting force. The nation was close to realizing what was once regarded as a hopelessly dreamy bumper sticker: "Suppose they gave a war and no one came." As Vietnam war correspondent Judith Coburn put it years later, "When I hear people say we could have won the war, I always think, Where were you going to get the soldiers?"

Most of the GI peace activists, like military personnel as a whole, were from working-class families. Whether they volunteered or were drafted, few had the options and advantages of their more privileged peers, who were generally able to avoid military service because of the many class biases of the Selective Service System (including draft deferments for full-time college students). The GI movement—an essentially working-class movement—played a significant role in expediting the U.S. military withdrawal from Vietnam and prompting civilian and military leaders to turn to an all-volunteer force. The GI movement also deserves credit for a dramatic increase in military pay from $134 per month for new enlisted men in January 1971 to $329 per month in January 1974.

Why, then, has this important story become an almost secret history? Why have so many of my students never heard about antiwar soldiers and veterans? The main answer is that in the decades after Vietnam, a pervasive negative stereotype of the antiwar movement emerged, fueled by the rightward shift in U.S politics marked by the election of Ronald Reagan as president in 1980. The most vibrant and diverse antiwar movement in U.S. history was increasingly caricatured as a band of craven, self-righteous, draft-dodging campus hippies who routinely vented their spleen on ordinary American soldiers returning from Vietnam. Stories began to emerge suggesting that *many* GIs and veterans were spat upon by antiwar protesters. There is no persuasive evidence to support this claim, but it became a powerful post-Vietnam myth that has effectively stigmatized and shamed the peace movement while also constructing a caricature of Vietnam veterans as patriotic victims.

Since the 1980s, many students have begun my courses on the Vietnam War convinced that the most shameful thing about the war was not the death and destruction the United States visited on Vietnam, or even the U.S. defeat, but the terrible way antiwar activists treated veterans.

With veterans so firmly cast in our national consciousness as the victims of peaceniks, the next logical step was to offer them automatic hero status. Since 9/11, the ritualized support for troops and veterans, far more symbolic than substantive, has become obsessive. "Thank you for your service" has become an American mantra and we are constantly reminded that we need to do more to demonstrate our gratitude. And so we have yellow ribbons, airport greeters, honor flights, benefit concerts, and "salutes to service," but no national debate about why our government continues to order troops to fight undeclared wars on false pretexts in distant countries where Americans are widely perceived as invaders; or why it persists with its failed policies long after a majority of the U.S. public has deemed the mission unnecessary, wasteful, and immoral. Nor has our "support" for troops been accompanied by any real effort to hear about their experiences and views.

If we did listen, we might find, as was true during the Vietnam War, that our nation's military personnel well understand the blatant contradictions between how our foreign policy is justified (always on the side of democracy, freedom, self-determination, and human rights), and its actual conduct and consequences (often on the side of repressive regimes and fought in ways that sow ever greater violence, misery, displacement, and chaos).

In Vietnam, American soldiers quickly realized that the United States wasn't supporting democracy or defending the South Vietnamese from foreign aggression. They knew that U.S. military tactics were destroying the land and people U.S. policy makers claimed to be protecting; they knew that the Communist-led southern insurgents—the Vietcong—and the regular troops from the North had deeper support among the people in the countryside than the U.S.-backed regime; and they knew that they faced an adversary whose fervent devotion to the cause of national liberation and reunification greatly exceeded their own sense of purpose.

In fact, most American soldiers were not strongly motivated by a political commitment to the defense of the U.S.-backed regime in Saigon. They often fought hard, but primarily out of a desire to save themselves and their buddies or because of the desire for revenge that combat almost invariably instills in combatants. Many American troops kept a personal calendar and marked off each day as it passed, as if their tour in Vietnam was a one-year prison sentence.

Despite the largely erased memory of the vibrant GI movement and the tarnished image of antiwar activism as a whole, the legacies of dissent can still inform and inspire resistance in the present. Like underground streams, the movements of the past continue to flow and can be tapped whenever history is treated with the critical respect it deserves. Consider the hopeful prediction made by one of the early military opponents of the Vietnam War, U.S. army doctor Howard Levy, who was sentenced to three years in prison for refusing to train a Special Forces (Green Beret) unit for duty in Vietnam. As his individual dissent blossomed into a collective rebellion, Levy said, "Future historians choosing to ignore the GI movement will find their reputation in tatters."

That forecast has yet to be realized. However, *Waging Peace* will encourage us to think more broadly about movements in the past and present that are ignored, marginalized, forgotten, or underestimated. For example, a recent study of twenty-first-century antiwar veterans and their families by Lisa Leitz points out that Iraq Veterans Against the War began to organize in 2004, just one year after the war began. It took considerably longer for opposition to develop against the Vietnam War. Moreover, IVAW was assisted and inspired by a number of former members of Vietnam Veterans Against the War. It is not too much to say that there is a "long GI and veterans' movement," sometimes dramatically visible, other times largely ignored, but enduring nonetheless.

There are also signs that progressive movements today are increasingly attentive to their commonalities with other groups at home and abroad. A new generation of activists is seeking to identify and explain how militarism, imperialism, nuclear weapons, environmental degradation, gross economic inequality, and dehumanization by race, religion, gender, and sexuality all reinforce and legitimize each other, and many have concluded that none can be effectively opposed without addressing them all. Yet all movements, however forward-looking, must draw meaning and inspiration from the struggles of the past. *Waging Peace* gives us back an important piece of that history.

Acknowledgments

First and foremost, we thank the members of the U.S. armed forces who took huge risks to oppose America's unjust war while they were still in uniform and subject to harassment, prosecution, and severe extrajudicial punishment.

This book is inspired by the exhibit "Waging Peace: U.S. Soldiers and Veterans who Opposed America's War in Vietnam." The exhibit was the idea of Huynh Ngoc Van, who was the director of Vietnam's War Remnant's Museum in 2016. Her successor, Dr. Tran Xuan Thao, and the staff of the museum worked with Ron Carver to make this tribute to peace-loving U.S. soldiers and veterans a reality.

We are grateful to Mme Nguyen Thi Binh for her decades of inspiration and leadership in the quest for peace.

The exhibit and book would not have been possible without the cooperation of Bui Van Nghi, secretary-general of the Vietnam USA Society; the Vietnam Union of Friendship Organizations; the Ho Chi Minh City People's Committee; the Ho Chi Minh City Union of Friendship Organizations; the Vietnam Foundation for Peace and Development; and Mme. Ton Nu Thi Ninh, president of the Ho Chi Minh City Foundation for Peace and Development. Nguyen Thi Hong Hanh and the Vietnam News Agency provided logistical support in Vietnam.

The exhibit and this book draw extensively from the Wisconsin Historical Society's GI Press Collection. This digitized searchable archive contains hundreds of GI antiwar newspapers. It includes over 88,000 searchable pages from more than 2,400 periodicals, pamphlets, and posters—original source materials that were created by or for members of the U.S. military during the American Vietnam War era. We encourage scholars and interested parties to browse this fascinating online resource. Access is free and open to the public via www.wisconsinhistory.org.

The GI Press Collection and the careful digitization of this material were the result of ten years of dedicated and indefatigable labor by Dr. James Lewes. All who have an interest in preserving the history of the GI antiwar movement owe a tremendous debt of gratitude to Lewes. We offer special thanks to the Wisconsin Historical Society for hosting the GI Press Collection and making this archive publicly available, and especially to archivist and administrator Matthew Blessing. We also thank curator and archivist Huub Sanders at the International Institute for Social History in Amsterdam, which houses one of the world's largest collections of GI antiwar papers and materials, the Brünn-Harris-Watts Papers.

We are grateful to the Sir! No Sir! GI Movement Archives; the Walter P. Reuther Library at Wayne State University, Detroit, Michigan; the Tamiment Library at New York University; the Swarthmore College Peace Collection; the Lasalle University Archive; the Stanford Libraries Department of Special Collections; the Pacific Northwest Antiwar and Radical History Project, University of Washington, Seattle; the Vietnam Center, Archive, and Museum of the Vietnam War at Texas Tech University; the National Archives at College Park, Maryland; and private collections maintained by former editors of the publications.

We are thankful to the staff and leadership of the Kroc Institute for International Peace Studies at the University of Notre Dame's Keough School of Global Affairs. We thank the Keough School's dean, Scott Appleby, and Kroc Institute directors Ruth Abbey and Asher Kaufman for their support of the production of the "Waging Peace" exhibit and its first showing in the United States; and for the May 2018 conference, "Voices of Conscience; Antiwar Opposition in the Military," which brought together ninety veterans, scholars and activists from around the world and helped to inspire further research on the history and impact of the GI movement and subsequent movements for peace within the military. We offer heartfelt thanks to the staff of the Kroc Institute who supported the conference, the exhibit, and this book, including Ellie Berruecos-Reed, Hannah Heinzekehr, Kristi Flaherty, Lisa Gallagher, Elena Bowman, Erin Corcoran, Caitlyn Paulsen, and Laurel Stone. Our thanks to Mark Robison, librarian at the University of Notre Dame's Hesburgh Library.

The "Waging Peace" exhibit, this book, and the GI movement itself owe tremendous thanks to Robert Zevin, the key founder, in 1968, of the United States Servicemen's Fund. USSF was the single largest funder of the GI coffeehouses and the newspapers that promoted the movement's story in real time.

Thanks to Armen Nercessian, Laurence Pulgram, and Mitchell Zimmerman of Fenwick West, who provided guidance on matters of copyright and intellectual property law. Others who worked diligently to produce this book include Leslie D. Bartlett, Nancy Coleman, and Gary Smith. Special thanks to Bruce Beyer, Ilene Carver, Virginia Chalmers, Gary Huck, Jeff Jones, Donna Kirchheimer, Peter Kirchheimer, Paul Lauter, Howard Levy, Sandy Hochman Levy, Amy Merrill, Carolyn Mugar, Willa Seidenberg, Chuck Searcy, William Short, Tom Wilber, Bonnie Willdorf, and David Zeiger. Very special thanks to Karen Jacob, who helped to mount the exhibit and provided loving support and inspiration to her spouse, David Cortright, throughout this work.

We thank New Village Press editor Ignacio Choi, copyeditor Carol Edwards, and designer Leigh McLellan for making this book better.

Finally, our gratitude to Lynne Elizabeth, the director of New Village Press, for her suggestion that we create this book. Lynne brought steadiness, vision and optimism throughout the complex process of bringing to life these stories in *Waging Peace in Vietnam*.

Voices and Contributors

Trent Angers is the founder of Acadian House Publishing in Lafayette, Louisiana. He is the author of *The Forgotten Hero of My Lai: The Hugh Thompson Story.*

Christian G. Appy is a professor of history at the University of Massachusetts, Amherst. He is the author of several books, including *American Reckoning: The Vietnam War and Our National Identity* (Viking, 2015) and *Working-Class War: American Combat Soldiers and Vietnam* (University of North Carolina Press, 1993).

Jan Barry is a poet and author whose books include *Earth Songs* (iUniverse, 2003), *Life After War & Other Poems* (Combat Paper Press, 2012) and (coeditor) *Winning Hearts and Minds: War Poems by Vietnam Veterans* (McGraw-Hill, 1972). A U.S. Army veteran of Vietnam, he coordinates Warrior Writers workshops and programs for veterans and family members in New Jersey.

Nguyen Thi Binh was appointed foreign minister of the Provisional Revolutionary Government of South Vietnam in 1969 and played a major role in negotiating the Paris Peace Accords. She was later minister of education of the Socialist Republic of Vietnam and vice president of Vietnam's National Assembly from 1992 to 2002.

Dave Blalock enlisted in the Army and served from 1968 to 1971; he served in Vietnam in 1969. Stateside, he was active in the GI movement at Fort McClellan, Alabama, and helped produce the GI newspaper *Left Face.*

Heather A. Bowser, MSED, LPCC, is an activist, artist, and mental health therapist. Heather founded Children of Vietnam Veterans Health Alliance (COVVHA), an organization dedicated to finding answers, resources, and ultimately justice for all secondary exposures to military herbicides known as Agent Orange.

Richard Boyle (1942–2016) was a writer, newspaper editor, political activist, journalist, and photographer who went to Vietnam as a freelancer and was a contributor to *Overseas Weekly.* He was at Firebase Pace in October 1971, where he witnessed a mutiny while the base was under siege. He is the author of *Flower of the Dragon* (Ramparts Press, 1972), which covers these events, and cowrote the screenplay for the film *Salvador* with Oliver Stone.

Ron Carver protested the war from 1965 until the American ground troops, sailors, and airmen returned home in 1975. He supported the GI movement, working full-time for two years at coffeehouses adjacent to Fort Dix, New Jersey, and Fort McClellan, Alabama. His first visit to Vietnam, in 2016, led to the publication of this book.

Fredy Champagne was active with Veterans for Peace for twenty-four years. In 1988, as executive director of the Veterans' Viet Nam Restoration Project, he organized teams of veterans to return to Vietnam to join with Vietnamese in building schools, medical clinics, and hospitals.

Robert Chenoweth was a POW in Vietnam from 1968 to 1973. He retired after a career as a museum curator with the National Park Service and now lives in Moscow, Idaho.

Charlie Clements served as a C-130 Air Force pilot in Southeast Asia until the invasion of Cambodia, when he refused to fly further missions. His story is documented in the Academy Award–winning film *Witness to War*.

Gerry Condon enlisted in the Army in 1967 and became a Green Beret. He refused to go to Vietnam and deserted to Canada and then Sweden in 1969. He returned to the United States in 1975 and was active in the defense of two Persian Gulf resisters.

David Cortright was active in the GI movement. He is the author or editor of twenty books and is a professor of peace studies and director of policy studies and the Peace Accords Matrix at the University of Notre Dame's Kroc Institute for International Peace Studies.

Paul Cox is cofounder of Veterans for Peace Chapter 69 in San Francisco. He works with the Vietnam Agent Orange Relief and Responsibility Campaign, seeking legislation to address the ongoing legacy of herbicide use during the Vietnam War.

Skip Delano enlisted in the Army and served from 1967 to 1970; he served one year in Vietnam. He cofounded *Left Face* at Fort McClellan, Alabama, and has remained active, lecturing in high schools and universities about the GI movement.

Carl Dix served in the Army from 1968 to 1972. He was one of the Fort Lewis Six, refused to go to Vietnam, and spent eighteen months in Leavenworth federal prison.

Barbara Doherty was, during the Vietnam War era, a member of Alameda People for Peace, a multi-generational antiwar community organization. Doherty is a longtime writer and editor for labor unions and nonprofit organizations and lives in the Washington, DC, area.

Kelly Dougherty joined the Colorado Army National Guard in 1996. She enlisted as a medic but was deployed as a member of the Military Police to

Hungary and Croatia and then to Kuwait and Iraq in 2003–2004. She was a cofounder and executive director of Iraq Veterans Against the War.

Donald Duncan (1930–2009) was drafted into the Army in 1954 and served until 1964. He served one and a half years in Vietnam with the Green Berets and resigned in opposition to the war. As an outspoken antiwar advocate, he authored *The New Legions*, a book critical of the military and U.S. policies.

W. D. Ehrhart is a Marine Corps veteran of the Vietnam War and a life member of Vietnam Veterans Against the War. His most recent book is *Thank You for Your Service: Collected Poems*, (McFarland & Company, 2019).

Carolyn Eisenberg is a professor of American foreign policy and U.S. history at Hofstra University. She is the author of a forthcoming book, *Never Lose: Nixon, Kissinger and the Illusion of National Security* (W. W. Norton).

David Fenton is the Chairman of Fenton Communications, which represented Nelson Mandela and the African National Congress and provided support for the rise of MoveOn.org, organic food sales, Yoko Ono's campaign against fracking in New York State, Al Gore's climate change work with the United Nations, and many other campaigns.

Clarence Fitch enlisted in the Marine Corps and served from 1966 to 1969; he served in Vietnam in 1968. While still on active duty, he became involved in GI organizing efforts, especially fighting for the rights of black servicemen.

Jane Fonda is an award-winning actress and a prominent advocate for peace, human rights, women and girls, and the environment. She was a leading voice in the Vietnam antiwar movement and visited coffeehouses, rallied support, and raised funds for the GI movement.

Doris Friedensohn is professor emerita of Women's Studies at New Jersey City University. Twice a Fulbright professor, her books and articles deal with innovative teaching, American diversity, eating and everyday life in the United States, and foreign travel. Her most recent publication is *Airports Are for Waiting and Other Traveler's Tales* (Full Court Press, 2019).

Mathieu Grandjean photographed the Winter Soldier event in 2008 for a long-term photo project called *Backdraft: What It Means to Support the Troops.* (See https://vimeo.com/channels/backdraft.)

Ron Haeberle was drafted into the U.S. Army in March 1966 and honorably discharged in April 1968. He continued as a photographer for work and as a hobby after his discharge. He has traveled over 2,500 miles on a bicycle throughout Southeast Asia.

Diana Mara Henry began her career in photojournalism as photo editor of the *Harvard Crimson*, 1967–1969. She has specialized in interpreting social issues and events and covered many political campaigns, as well as Vietnam Veterans Against the War. Her work has appeared in numerous publications. Named special collections of her photographs are housed at Harvard's Schlesinger Library and at UMass-Amherst's W. E. B. Du Bois Library. (See www.diana marahenry.com.)

Adam Hochschild is a former Army Reservist and activist against the Vietnam War. He is the author of nine books, including *King Leopold's Ghost* (Mariner Books, 1998), *Bury the Chains* (Houghton Mifflin Harcourt, 2005), and *To End All Wars* (Mariner Books, 2011).

Gary Huck has been a political cartoonist for four decades. He has published seven collections of cartoons with the cartoonist Mike Konopacki. Their original cartoons are archived at the Tamiment Library, New York University.

Tom Hurwitz, ASC, has been an award-winning cinematographer and director for the last forty-five years. He was one of the leaders of the Columbia student rebellion in 1968.

Jonathan W. Hutto, Sr., was an undergraduate student leader at Howard University. He served in the U.S. Navy and was a founder of the Appeal for Redress in 2007. He is the author of *Anti-War Soldier: How to Dissent Within the Ranks of the Military* (Nation Books, 2008). He is an active member of Veterans For Peace.

Terry Irvin was drafted into the Army and served from 1970 to 1971. He worked with the GI Alliance and the *Lewis-McChord Free Press* at Fort Lewis, Washington. He was arrested for distributing the Declaration of Independence on base on the Fourth of July.

James "JJ" Johnson was a member of the Fort Hood Three, the first soldiers to publicly refuse to serve in Vietnam. For their refusal in 1966, the three—African American, Latino, and white—each served twenty-eight months in the Fort Leavenworth federal prison. Johnson later worked for many years as a labor journalist and communications official for several major unions in New York, including 1199SEIU, the nation's largest health-care union.

John Kent is a 1968 graduate of the U.S. Naval Academy. After graduation, he was trained as a jet fighter pilot, but he refused to go to Vietnam. He helped to organize the San Diego Chapter of the Concerned Officers Movement and worked with Vietnam Veterans Against the War.

John Kerry enlisted in the Naval Reserve in 1966 and was awarded combat medals for his four months of service in Vietnam in 1968–1969. Upon returning to the United States, he joined Vietnam Veterans Against the War and became a national spokesman. His testimony in 1971 in the Fulbright hearings before the Senate Foreign Relations Committee linked war crimes to U.S. policies in Vietnam and brought attention to the GI movement. The day after his testimony, Kerry was part of the VVAW demonstration, where almost one thousand veterans tossed their medals and ribbons in front of the U.S. Capitol. Prior to normalization of U.S.-Vietnam relations in 1995, the then

Senator Kerry was instrumental in passing a bipartisan resolution to lift the trade embargo that had been in effect since the war's end.

Yusef Komunyakaa is the recipient of the 1994 Pulitzer Prize for poetry. His poem "Fragging" is from the collection, *Dien Cai Dau*, published in 1988 by Wesleyan University Press. Komunyakaa is the author of sixteen collections of poetry and is a professor in the Creative Writing Program at New York University.

Paul Lauter is the A.K. & G.M. Smith Professor Emeritus at Trinity College (Hartford, CT). He was national director of the United States Servicemen's Fund in the 1970s.

Francis Lenski is a Phi Beta Kappa graduate of the University of Notre Dame. He was a leader of GIs for Peace at Fort Bliss, Texas, and was discharged from the Army as a conscientious objector in 1970. He worked as a governmental attorney for over twenty years.

Howard Levy, MD, was court-martialed in 1967 and received a three-year sentence. He has practiced dermatology in the South Bronx at Lincoln Hospital for fifty years and has been active in many peace and civil rights movements.

Gerald McCarthy served with the First Marines and the First Combat Engineer Battalion in Vietnam in 1966–1967. After one tour, McCarthy deserted the military and did time in civilian jail and military prison. His early work, collected in *War Story* (Crossing Press, 1977), is a meditation on his experiences in Vietnam. He is a professor of English at St. Thomas Aquinas College in New York.

Keith Mather was drafted into the Army in 1967. He went AWOL and participated in the "Nine for Peace" and Presidio 27 sit-down strike by prisoners. After escaping the stockade and deserting to Canada, he returned to the United States in 1980 and was arrested in 1984, court-martialed, and imprisoned for more than four months. He was dishonorably discharged from the Army in 1985.

Camilo Mejía served in the Army for nearly nine years. He was the first known soldier in Iraq to refuse to fight, and he filed as a conscientious objector. Mejía was convicted of desertion and sentenced to a year in prison, prompting Amnesty International to declare him a prisoner of conscience.

Judy Olasov is a native of South Carolina. She worked in or with coffeehouses and projects in Fort Jackson, South Carolina; Fort Leonard Wood, Missouri; Fort Lewis and McChord Air Base, Washington; Alameda Naval Air Station, California; and national coffeehouse support from San Francisco. She still considers herself a member of the GI movement.

David Parsons is a professor and writer whose work focuses on the political, social, and cultural history of twentieth-century America. He served as an adviser for the New York Historical Society exhibition on the Vietnam War. He is the author of *Dangerous Grounds: Antiwar Coffeehouses and Military Dissent in the Vietnam Era* (University of North Carolina Press, 2017).

Greg Payton was drafted into the Army and served from 1967 to 1969. He received three courts-martial for a variety of charges and was involved in the 1968 prison riot at Long Binh Jail in South Vietnam. He returned to Vietnam in 1988 and traveled to South Africa in 1990 on behalf of Vietnam Veterans Against the War.

Alan Pogue was a combat medic in Chu Lai, Vietnam, in 1967. He is affiliated with the Texas Center for Documentary Photography. His work has appeared in *Newsweek, Southern Exposure, Texas Monthly, The Boston Globe,* and a variety of other publications.

Steve Rees was active in the antiwar movement with Students for a Democratic Society at UC Santa Cruz. After that he worked with the Movement for a Democratic Military in San Francisco and photographed active-duty dissenters and civilian supporters for the antiwar GI newspaper *Up Against the Bulkhead.* His photographs of the Sixties have appeared in films, history museums, libraries, books, and magazines.

Tom Roberts enlisted in the Army and served from 1967 to 1970; he served with Psychological Operations in Vietnam in 1967–1968. He cofounded the *aboveground* newspaper at Fort Carson, Colorado.

Susan Schnall was a Navy nurse who led the GI antiwar march in San Francisco in October 1968. She is an assistant adjunct professor at New York University's School of Professional Studies, Healthcare Management, and serves as the president of the New York City Veterans For Peace. She has organized scientific panels about Agent Orange at the American Public Health Association's annual meetings.

Chuck Searcy served with the 519th Military Intelligence Battalion in Saigon and later joined Vietnam Veterans Against the War. In 2001, he became a representative of the Vietnam Veterans Memorial Fund and helped launch Project RENEW in Quang Tri Province to clean up unexploded ordnance and provide medical assistance, rehabilitation, and income generation for victims.

Willa Seidenberg teaches radio journalism at the University of Southern California's Annenberg School for Communication and Journalism. She founded Annenberg Radio News and Intersections South LA, a community Web site for the South Los Angeles community. She is the coauthor, with William Short, of the book *A Matter of Conscience: GI Resistance During the Vietnam War* (Addison Gallery of American Art, 1992).

Derek Seidman is a researcher and historian based in Buffalo, New York. He has a Ph.D. in history from Brown University.

William Short served in combat in Vietnam and was a GI antiwar resister. He teaches photography at Moorpark College, in California. He was an artist in residence at the Addison Gallery of American Art in Andover Massachusetts. He is the coauthor, with Willa Seidenberg, of the book, *A Matter of Conscience: GI Resistance During the Vietnam War* (Addison Gallery of American Art, 1992).

Andy Stapp enlisted in the Army for the purpose of antiwar organizing from within from 1966 to 1968. He was court-martialed three times for antiwar activities. He founded the American Servicemen's Union and published *The Bond* newspaper.

Lamont B. Steptoe, a Vietnam veteran, is a poet, photographer, and publisher. He is the author of eight books of poetry, including *Mad Minute* (Whirlwind Press, 1993) *Uncle's South Sea China Blue Nightmare* (Plan B Press, 2003), and *Dusty Road* (Whirlwind Press, 1995).

Curt Stocker enlisted in the Army and served from 1967 to 1970; he served in Psychological Operations in Vietnam. He cofounded *aboveground* newspaper at Fort Carson, Colorado.

Dennis Stout enlisted in the Army and served from 1966 to 1969; he was decorated for his Vietnam service 1966–1967. While in Vietnam, he tried to report fourteen war crimes and received a personal threat against his life. Upon discharge, he went public with war crimes allegations and was again threatened.

Michael Sutherland (formerly Lindner) signed up for the Navy in the summer of 1966 and left for boot camp on January 2, 1967. He boarded the USS *Intrepid* that spring and jumped ship in Yokosuka, Japan, on October 23. He traveled by boat to Nakhodka, Russia, and arrived in Sweden just after Christmas. There he attended various schools and worked different jobs, mainly in construction. Mike still lives in Sweden with his wife, two children, and three grandchildren.

Tran Xuan Thao received her Ph.D. from Ho Chi Minh City University of Social Sciences and Humanities. Dr. Thao is the director of Vietnam's War Remnants Museum. Previously she was assistant director of the Southern Women's Museum in Ho Chi Minh City and director of the Ton Duc Thang Museum.

Hugh Thompson (1943–2005) retired as an Army major in 1983 after twenty-two years in the military (he had previously served in the Navy). On March 16, 1968, he and crewmates Larry Colburn and Glenn Andreotta landed their helicopter to rescue civilians—holding fellow U.S. soldiers at bay with their weapons—as the My Lai massacre was in progress. He remained in the military, testified before congressional and other inquiries, and received death threats for his action to stop the massacre. In 1998, Thompson, Colburn, and (posthumously) Andreotta were awarded the Soldier's Medal for heroism not involving conflict with the enemy.

John Tuma enlisted in the Army and served from 1969 to 1972. He was trained in Vietnamese and served as an interrogator in Vietnam in 1971. He refused to torture Viet Cong prisoners.

Michael Uhl served in Vietnam as an intelligence officer with the Eleventh Infantry. He cofounded the Safe Return Amnesty Committee, and Citizen Soldier, a GI/veterans advocacy organization. He coauthored *G.I Guinea Pigs: How the Pentagon Exposed Our Troops to Dangers More Deadly Than War* (Playboy Press, 1980) and has written *The War I Survived Was Vietnam* (McFarland, 2016) and the war memoir *Vietnam Awakening: My Journey from Combat to the Citizens' Commission of Inquiry on U.S. War Crimes in Vietnam* (McFarland, 2007).

Bruce Weigl was awarded the Army Bronze Star for service in Vietnam. As Weigl states in his best-selling prose memoir, *The Circle of Hanh* (2000), "The paradox of my life as a writer is that the war ruined my life and in return gave me my voice." Weigl is the author of more than a dozen books of poetry, including *Song of Napalm* (1988) and *The Abundance of Nothing* (2012).

Cora Weiss has been a well-known peace activist since the early 1960s. She became a leader of Women Strike for Peace and also of the New Mobilization Committee to End the War in Vietnam. She cochaired the November 15,1969, "New Mobe" demonstration in Washington, D.C. She is the UN representative of the International Peace Bureau, which she served as president. She is president of the Hague Appeal for Peace, former director of the Riverside Church Disarmament Program, and a principal organizer of the largest nuclear disarmament rally in U.S. history, held in New York City's Central Park on June 12, 1982.

Tom Wilber has made dozens of trips to Vietnam, locating sites, recovering materials, and conducting interviews about U.S. detainees held in the Democratic Republic of Vietnam from 1964 until 1973, one of whom was his father. He assists the Hoả Lò Prison Museum with historical and educational exhibits.

Mike Wong was drafted into the Army and served from 1969 to 1975. He went AWOL and deserted to Canada, returning to the United States in 1975. He became a political activist and served as a draft and military counselor during the Persian Gulf War.

Linda J. Yarr is research professor of the Practice of International Affairs and director of Partnerships for International Strategies in Asia (PISA) at the Elliott School of International Affairs at George Washington University, Washington, D.C.

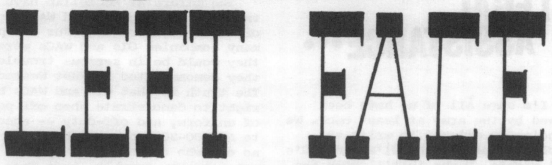

LEFT FACE

august-september 1971   written by and for gi's of ft. mc clellan

WESTY SIGN THE PEOPLE'S PEACE TREATY

LEGAL ASSISTANCE...

I'm sure all of us have been screwed by the army at least once. We are going to attempt to write an article monthly on the GI's and WAC's legal rights. Maybe that'll keep the lifers in line.

This month's article is devoted to guiding people just out of basic or A.I.T. who are becoming Permanent Party. Before your processing into a company is complete, feel it out. Get to know some of the people who have been in the company awhile. Ask them how the lifers are in that company, and if you have a chance of getting treated fairly. If the reactions are bad, you still have a chance of getting out of that company and into another. Look in the post newspapers for possible openings in an area that you'd be interested in. Talk to people at different processing points and ask about openings in other companies that can be open for you.

If you do happen to find an opening which you can fill, all you have to do is request to the commander or person in charge for the job. He willin turn cut orders for you, requesting that you be the one to fill the job.

This must be done before your complete processing is done. That's the most important thing.

If the company you have been assigned to seems favorable, take your full week for processing, even though you may be able to do it in two days. Have a few days vacation at the Army's expense and Good Luck to you unfortunate newcomers to the O.D. Circus.

If you have more questions and would like some free legal advice, call 238-8175.

The lifers at McClellan have an old trick of keeping GIs and WACs ignorant of their legal rights. For example, in many companies GIs and WACs were told they would be in serious trouble if they demonstrated against Westmoreland. The truth is that GIs and WACs have the right to demonstrate when off post, out of uniform, and off-duty -- according to AR 600-200, paragraph 46. In fact, no one who demonstrated against Westy got into any trouble. Left Face will assist you in prosecuting officers who try to restrict your right to demonstrate.

...AGAINST THE BRASS

WHOSE PAPER

Hello GI's and WAC's. We know we make mistakes in this paper so we need your criticisms and advice. Most important, we need your participation. This paper only means something if GI's and WAC's continue to write it. We want to be able to make this a better and bigger paper but we can't unless you help. We need people to write articles and draw cartoons and help lay out and distribute the paper. So if you are interested come to Left Face, 72 Pelham Heights, on Wednesday nights when we have open house. We'll be showing flicks and rapping. Or stop by any time. We work on the paper Monday nights. So please come by and help out.

GI's and WAC's United

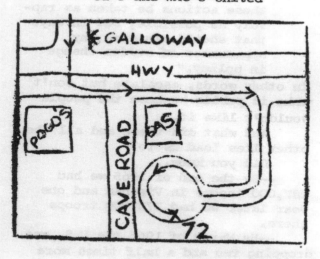

UP THE ORGANIZATION!

Fort McPherson, Georgia is the ideal place to be stationed unless you are a member of the TUSA Soldier show and CPT Peter Poncho is your OIC. Poncho, being a lifer from the word go, is an example of the children we have leading us.

As for the show itself, it is lead by a New York "director" Gal Gloss and his henchman E5 "Mr Mafia". They allow no one to become a privileged member of the unit unless they faithfully kiss ass. This is a real problem to the GI's and WAC's who refuse to kiss ass. Life is made very difficult for them by shit details, Article 15's, haircut regs and personal appearance. The living conditions are about the worst I have ever lived in. The GI's have a barracks to themselves and they don't have much shit except the details. But for the WAC's it is a different story. You live in an area large enough for 6 people but they put 20 and sometimes more girls into this area in double bunks with one locker and if you are lucky you get one drawer out of a dresser.

You learn that the Army only authorizes you 4 hours of sleep per night and no complaints should be made about the long hard hours of work. Plus the amount of time you spend sitting on your ass listening to either Poncho or Gloss or Mafia tell you what a privilege it is to be in the Show. One of Poncho's favorite expressions is "At Ease Cut Your Side Burns!" or for the WAC's "At Ease Pluck Your Eyebrows!"

So if you plan on going to the show, prepare for this shit because it is there.

FTA!!!

PENTAGON

This is for you people who don't know what the Pentagon Papers are. It's a complete official government study on Vietnam policy and U.S. involvement in Southeast Asia between the years 1950-1968 which was commissioned by Secretary of Defense Robert McNamara. It shows that the government has been lying to us for years about why we're in Vietnam and what we're doing there.

PAPERS

Here are just a few examples of what the documents from the Pentagon Papers reveal:

**In 1954 the U.S. backed Ngo Dinh Diem for President so they could get political power in South Vietnam. But by November 1963, Diem had become too independent in his policy so the CIA helped assassinate him. Boy, they sure lied to him didn't they? Just like they lied to the American people about what was going on.

**The government lied in early August 1964 about the Gulf of Tonkin incident, when the U.S. <u>claimed</u> that the U.S. destroyer Maddox was attacked by North Vietnamese PT boats. Less than 6 hours after the "attack", U.S. bombers bombed key targets in North Vietnam <u>which had been picked 4 months before</u>! Seventy-two hours later LBJ introduced the Tonkin resolution and got it passed by Congress, which didn't know that the resolution was also drafted <u>4 months before</u> the attack. Isn't it funny that all this was prepared in advance? Oh yes, the U.S. had already been secretly attacking North Vietnam for six months, hiding this aggression from the American people.

**The government lied, again, in April 1965. On April 1, LBJ sent into Vietnam 20,000 more troops and authorized a change in combat missions from defense to offense. One memo from a Presidential adviser says:

"The President desires that... these actions be taken as rapidly as possible, but in ways that should minimize any appearance of sudden change in policy."

In other words, escalate but don't make it public because the people wouldn't like it.

And what did these and all the other lies lead us to?

Did you know...

--By the end of 1965 we had 187,000 troops in Vietnam and one year later we had 375,000 troops there.

--By March of 1966 the U.S. was dropping two and a half times more of a bomb load on Vietnam per month than it did on Korea, and was flying as many missions into Laos as into North Vietnam. Also in 1966 the U.S. dropped <u>each week</u> a bomb tonnage equal to all the bombs dropped on Germany at the peak of World War II.

--Statistics also show that by 1966 U.S. GI's were killing two civilians for every South Vietnamese liberation fighter.

Well, what does this great government scandal mean to you? You, the GI whose life has been toyed with, should realize what the Pentagon Papers are all about. After all, you are the one who's dying in Vietnam. Not the men who are moving you around like chess pieces to suit them. What the hell, they sit in nice offices in Washington with air conditioning, drinking ice tea, while you're breaking your back to stay alive. Did you know that up to this week 45,411 GI's are dead and at least a million civilians?

So think about who's getting paid more and who risks less and you'll see you're just another chess piece to lose to them. Just think about it and maybe you'll fight for your Rights to live.

For copies of the Pentagon Papers write Left Face, P.O. Box 1595, Anniston, Alabama 36201.

vietnam

QUOTATIONS 1945•1970

"I would never send troops there."

Dwight D. Eisenhower
General, U.S. Army
New York City
June 8, 1952

" We have no plans at present to send combat troops to South Vietnam."

Robert S. McNamara
Secretary of defense
Nov 10, 1964

" The enemy has been defeated at every turn."

General William C. Westmoreland
Commander, U.S. Forces in Vietnam
Saigon, South Vietnam
June 9, 1968

" I can safely say that the end of the war is in sight."

Gen. Harkins
U.S. Commander,
South Vietnam,
Oct. 31, 1963

"He took the wraps off our secret weapon!"

" The United States...seeks no wider war."

Lyndon B. Johnson
President of the United States
Washington, D.C.
June 23, 1964

" The administration plans to prepare to move into North Vietnam."

Melvin R. Laird
Washington, D.C.
May 31, 1964

LIES LIES LIES !!

5

LIFER OF THE MONTH

the eagle (or is it a pig)

Lifer of the Month was no race at all this time. In fact, in winning this most deserved honor, you, Capt. Crawford, have truly distinquished yourself in the areas of Gross Incompetency, Immature Judgment, and Favoritism, to the highest degree.

Let it be known that when Billy became CO last July 2nd he chose a first Sgt. that has no mind of his own so he could run his company like a plantation. Billy, it won't work—your slaves are rising up angry.

In conclusion! Let it be said to you Billy (the child) Bad-Ass, Carry on; that someday, if the army is to survive, it must rid itself of the likes of you and give the power to the E.M.

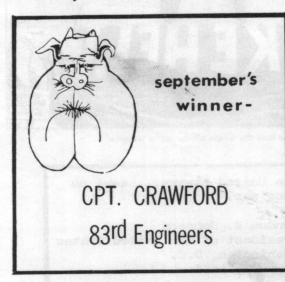

september's winner-

CPT. CRAWFORD
83rd Engineers

Junior Pig-of-the-Month:
    1/SGT Jesse Woodward

Runner-up Piggies:
    CPT Huggins
    SGM Hubbard
    1/SGT Causey

BETTER LUCK
NEXT TIME,
LIFERS!!

We ask you to help us find other suitable candidates. LEFT FACE has certain individuals on its staff whose job it is to investigate every nomination for LIFER OF THE MONTH. In this manner, we try to assure fairness in picking a monthly SUPER-LIFER.

Mail to:
LEFT FACE
P.O. Box 1595
Anniston, Ala. 36201

1. Candidate:_____
2. Company:_____
3. Qualifications:_____
_____

6

UNREST in the 83rd

Maybe you've heard about the hard times the guys have been having at the 83rd since the recent change in command. Crawford, the CO, has given 43 Article 15's since becoming CO in July (there are 180 guys in the company). Most of the charges are trumped up and the people getting charged have received outlandish punishments. As a result, transfers from EM's as well as NCO's have flooded the orderly room. Fear of blowing it has made many go AWOL.

Crawford seems to play with us as though we were toys. One NCO got busted, then went against his better judgment and accepted orders for Nam. Another NCO flipped out and went AWOL for good. There are six men AWOL as of now that haven't been dropped from roll.

Weren't we taught that the EM were the ultimate weapon? OK, if we are going to play this game of theirs let's play by the rules. More attention

is given to Mr. Keener's trucks than to EM problems. CPT Crawford, being the company commander, is responsible. It seems as though things are getting worse everyday. Crawford you started it, you stop it.

A few credits to Crawford's first command are: one burned motor pool, theft of numerous tools, numerous mess hall thefts, and a damaged day room. If the CID wants to find the guy responsible, the real criminal isn't in the barracks but in the Orderly Room.

burial blues

Burial Detail seems to be, in my opinion, the epitome of the Army's and U.S. Government's cover up of opression.
The working class of our nation are made to be the tools of war by laws made up by the ruling class. The government and the Army informs us of the honor to be on burial detail. This, I think, is a cheap misconception. I have heard story about drunken parties after a funeral. Even if a member of the detail did feel remorse it's still a bad joke. All this phony attention paid to a person who died, apparently for his country, who should have received attention before his death. If I were to die in this Army my family would never allow my body to be forced through the military

NEWS FLASH--83rd Eng.

The office of the motor pool was burned down by an arson. The whole office was ruined, all parts, books, and every paper except the 348 forms. The fire was one day before the big IG inspection. Did Warrant Officer Kinner burn down his own motor pool so he didn't have a chance to fail the inspection? Keep your eyes and ears open for more about unrest in the 83rd. FTA.

machine of nostalgia. I've been told it's my duty, I feel quite the contrary. It is my duty to let my ideas and feeling be known. I must not be a part of this gross and cruel ceremony.

JOHN   7

WORKING CLASS

AN INTERVIEW WITH JOHN & YOKO

What follows are excerpts of an interview of John Lennon and Yoko Ono by two reporters from the British underground paper Red Mole

YOUR LATEST RECORD AND YOUR RECENT PUBLIC STATEMENTS, ESPECIALLY THE INTERVIEWS IN ROLLING STONE, SUGGEST THAT YOUR VIEWS ARE BECOMING INCREASINGLY RADICAL AND POLITICAL. WHEN DID THIS START TO HAPPEN?

JOHN, I've always been politically minded, you know, and against the status quo. It's pretty basic when you're brought up, like I was, to hate and fear the police as a natural enemy and to despise the army as something that takes everybody away and leaves them dead somewhere. I mean, it's just a basic working class thing, though it begins to wear off when you get older, get a family and get swallowed up in the system.

In any case, I've never not been political, though religion tended to overshadow it in my acid days; that would be around '65 and '66. And that religion was directly the result of all that superstar shit--religion was an outlet for my repression. I thought, "Well, there's something else to life, isn't there? This isn't it, surely?"

I was always political in a way, you know. In the two books I wrote, even though they were written in a sort of Joycean gobbledygook, there's many knocks at religion and there is a play about a worker and a capitalist.

I've been satirizing the system since my childhood. I used to write magazines in school and hand them around. I was very conscious of class, they would say with a chip on my shoulder, because I knew what was happening to me and I knew about the class repression coming down on us--it was a fucking fact but in the hurricane Beatle world it got left out-- I got further from reality for a time.

WHAT DID YOU THINK WAS THE REASON FOR THE SUCCESS OF YOUR SORT OF MUSIC?

JOHN: Well, at the time it was thought that the workers had broken through, but I realize in retrospect that it's the same phony deal they give to blacks, it was just like they allowed blacks to be runners or boxers or entertainers. That's the choice they allow you--now the outlet is being a pop star, which is really what I'm saying in Working Class Hero.

As I told Rolling Stone, it's the same people who have the power, the class system didn't change one little bit. Of course there are a lot of people walking around with long hair now and some trendy middle class kids in pretty clothes. But nothing changed except that we all dressed up a bit, leaving the same bastards running everything.

OF COURSE, CLASS IS SOMETHING AMERICAN ROCK GROUPS HAVEN'T TACKLED YET

JOHN: Because they're all middle class and bourgeois and they don't want to show it. They're scared of workers actually, because the workers seem mainly right-wing in America, clinging on to their goods. But if these middle class groups realize what's happening, and what the class system has done, it's up to them to repatriate the people and to get out of all that bourgeois shit.

WHEN DID YOU START BREAKING OUT OF THE ROLE IMPOSED ON YOU AS A BEATLE?

JOHN: Even during the Beatle heyday I tried to go against it, so did George. We went to America's a few times and Epstein always tried to waffle on at us about saying nothing about Vietnam.

Then there came a time when George and I said, "Listen, when they ask next time, we're going to say that we don't like the war and we think they should get right out." That's what we did. At that time, this was a pretty radical thing to do, especially for the "Fab Four." It was the first opportunity I personally took to wave the flag a bit.

But you've gotta remember that I'd always felt represed. We were all so pressurized that there was

HERO

hardly any chance of expressing ourselves, especially in working at that rate, touring continually and always kept in a cocoon of myths and dreams. It's pretty hard when you are Caesar and everyone is saying how good you are and they are giving you all the goodies and the girls, it's pretty hard to break out of that to say, "well, I don't want to be kind, I want to be real."

So in its way the second political thing I did was to say "The Beatles are bigger than Jesus." That really broke the scene. I nearly got shot in America for that. It was a big trauma for all the kids that were following us.

Up to then there was this unspoken policy of not answering delicate questions, though I was always reading the papers, you know, the political bits. The continual awareness of what was going on made me feel ashamed I wasn't saying anything. I burst out because I could no longer play that game any more, it was just too much for me

Of course, going to America increased the build-up on me, especially as the war was going on there. In a way we'd turned out to be a Trojan Horse. The Fab Four moved right to the top and then sang about drugs and sex, and then I got more and more into the heavy stuff and that's when they started dropping us.

DO YOU THINK A LOT MORE YOUNG PEOPLE WILL BE GOING THROUGH THE SAME KIND OF CHANGES YOU DID?

JOHN: I think it shouldn't take much to get the youth here really going. You'd have to give them free rein to attack the local councils or to destroy the school authorities, like the students who break up the repression in the universities. It's already happening, though people have got to get together more.

And the women are very important too, we can't have a revolution that doesn't involve and liberate women. It's so subtle the way you're taught male superiority. It took me quite a long time to realize that my maleness was cutting off certain areas for Yoko. She's a red hot liberationist and was quick to show me where I was going wrong, even though it seemed to me that I was just acting naturally. That's why I'm always interested to know how people who claim to be radical treat women...It's ridiculous. How can you talk about power to the people unless you realize that people is both sexes.

YOKO: You can't love someone unless you are in an equal position with them. A lot of women have to cling to men out of fear or insecurity, and that's not love--basically that's why women hate men...

JOHN: and vice versa...

YOKO: So if you have a slave around the house, how can you expect to make a revolution outside it? The problem for women is that if we try to be free, then we naturally become lonely, because so many women are willing to become slaves and men usually prefer that. So you always have to take the chance: "Am I going to lose my man?" It's very sad.

"I felt an obligation . . . to write a song that people would sing in the pub or on a demonstration. That is why I would like to compose songs for the revolution now. . . ."

As soon as you're born they make you feel small
By giving you no time instead of it all
Till the pain is so big you feel nothing at all
A working class hero is something to be
A working class hero is something to be

They hurt you at home and they hit you at school
They hate you if you're clever and they despise a fool.
Till you're so fucking crazy you' can't follow their rules
A working class hero is something to be
A working class hero is something to be

When they've tortured and scared you for 20 odd years
Then they expect you to pick a career
When you can't really function you're so full of fear

There's room at the top they are telling you still
But first you must learn how to smile as you kill
If you want to be like the folks on the hill
A working class hero is something to be.

Yes a working class hero is something to be
If you want to be a hero well just follow me
If you want to be a hero well just follow me
A working class hero is something to be
A working class hero is something to be

Keep you doped with religion and sex and TV
And you think you're so clever and classless and free
But you're still fucking peasants as far as I can see
A working class hero is something to be
A working class hero is something to be

PEOPLE'S DEMONSTRATION

On July 30 and 31 General Westmoreland honored us with his presence at Fort McClellan. Prior to this the GI's and WAC's of this post were petitioning The People's Peace Treaty which was, and still is, to be submitted to congressman Dellums. After hearing that General Westmoreland was to visit our post, the GI's and WAC's felt that this would be a great opportunity to express our feelings on the issues of the war in Vietnam by submitting the petition of the Peoples Peace Treaty to him. The wives of GI's also feeling the same, petitioned to wives of other GI's and civilians.

We sent a letter to Col. McKean (Post Commander) signed by GI's and WAC's requesting permission to submitt all signed petitions of the People's Peace Treaty to the General, containing over 250 signatures. The day after Col. McKean received the letter we received a letter of reply which denied us of presenting the copies of the People's Peace Treaty to General Westmoreland.

While the Brass had their ass in gear getting ready for General Westmoreland, GI's and WAC's United felt that they could show their views toward the Army and the war by demonstrating during his visit here.

On Saturday morning, GI's and their wives put on a beautiful demonstration to show their beliefs and views. The demonstration started at Baltzell Gate at 7am. then moved to Galloway Gate during the ceromonies. The demonstration was a super sucess for the protestors. They got flipped off by pigs and lifers to show their mentality. Why not join the Peace movement instead of fucking the Vietnam civilization? Other happenings during the Peace Rally were attracting half the Anniston Pig Force, and upsetting the Military Pigs until they requested us to stop chanting because Westmoreland will hear us! The Post Pigs also escorted the Oxford Sun Editor away from the demonstrators because he was paying too much attention to us.

After the demonstration the GI's and their wives held a press conference to let the public know how they felt about the war, the murdering of the Vietnamese people, and the destruction of their farms, land, and life by chemical agents. The following statement was submitted by the wives of GI's so they could put what they feel before the public.

Women's Statement

As military wives and civilians we feel a strong urgency to end the war. During the past week we have been collecting signatures for the Peoples Peace Treaty. By personal contact with civilians we find that although some are afraid of signing a treaty of this kind, they feel we shouldn't be in Vietnam and are in favor of immediate withdrawal.

Most every family in the United States has a relative or friend involved in this war, a war in fact made by the United States government rather than the United States people or the people of Vietnam. We feel very deeply the tragedies that occur every day to our sisters in Vietnam. They live with war constantly, fighting both for their country and the lives of their men and children. We want this stopped now before more damage is done to us, the Vietnamese people and the world.

The following statement ex--presses views of the GI's involved in this action as well as thousands of other GI's both in the United States and Vietnam. It was read by a Vietnam Vet. stationed at Ft. Mc-Clellan.

GI's Statement

As members of the US Army we know what the war in Vietnam is about.

The People's peace Treaty was made up of students from the US, North and South Vietnam who wrote up the treaty, but but it was American Vietnam Vets who were the first to sign the treaty.

We want to end the slaughtering of the Vietnamese people. Those of us who have been to Nam know it is a slaughter. We are driving the Vietnamese out of their homes, killing their families, tearing up their land so that they cannot grow anything decent to eat, and we are destroying future generations with our chemical agents. We go through villages raping and stealing and killing. We call them gooks and throw them out of helicopters and we stuff our unit patches in their fatal wounds.

At the chemical school here at Ft. McClellan they teach us how to use defoliants. 50,000 tons of herbicides have been dropped on 43% of Vietnam's cultivated land and 42% of its forests during the war. They teach us to use Agent Orange which contains Thalidomide, which causes physicals deformities and

retardation in new-born children. Agent Blue, another defoliant, is composed of 54.29% arsenic. That's like going on a bad acid trip for the rest of your life!

We want to give the Vietnamese people a chance to govern themselves. They have been fighting to get rid of the Japanese and French for one hundred years. To them we are just another invading force seeking the riches of the land. Any veteran can tell you that all the time little Vietnamese kids come up to you and shout "Americans go home".

The war is wrong because it's a war against the Vietnamese people.. The American GI's do not know what they are fighting for in Vietnam. He goes to fight because he is ordered to go. The Vietnamese are fighting for their existance.

As GI's and WAC's signing The Peace Treaty we pledge to do whatever we can do to make peace with the people in Vietnam. More and more GI's in Vietnam are refusing to fight. Today at Ft. McClellan GI's and WAC's are uniting to shout, "Westy go home, end the war!

FUN & FLASHES

News Flash.
Ft. McClellan:

Cpt. Fred Berry deserves
a hand from the men at
HHC he is now in the pro-
cess of ending KP on
weekends. So lets give
this man a hand.
   RIGHT ON FRED!

News Flash
Ft. Lewis:

10 GI's arrested for
passing out subversive
literature which was
really the Decralation
of Independence. How
subversive can you get?
   RIGHT ON BROTHERS!!!

News Flash
Ft. McClellan:

Well GI's good news Col.
McKean got a hole in one
after all these years.
So what !!!
   RIGHT ON BILL.

News Flash
Ft. McClellan:

Hi GI's watch the Piggies
because they are enforcing
the new Hair Regulation.
   GO GET'em PIGS.

News Flash
Ft. McClellan:

LEFT FACE IS HERE AGAIN!!

Peace !

VOLAR GIs Battle MPs

Last June 27, the army sponsored a rock concert at Fort Ord, an experimental VOLAR base. The main attraction was Canned Heat.

Basic trainees were marched into the stadium, handed beers and commanded to sit in formation. GI's out of basic were allowed to sit on the lawn near the stage. MP's with walkie-talkies patrolled the bleachers and intelligence pigs ran around with their cameras.

Before Canned Heat began the music they gave a pro-war rap that ended with: "You shouldn't mind going to Vietnam. That's where the best grass is." The GI's booed and hissed, and soon fights broke out between GI's and MP's.

As Canned Heat played on, the fights went on, off and on. But when the MP's started pointing riot rifles and firing .45s into the air, GI's began to fight harder. Black soldiers were the first to be hauled off, but the GI's bombarded the MP's with beer cans and wine bottles, and stopped the pigs from making some arrests.

As soon as Canned Heat finished GI's poured out of the stadium and on to the streets, trashing a Greyhound bus and a bunch of army vehicles. The Drill Sergeant Training School was burned down and a classroom building was ransacked.

MP's struck back, breaking into snack bars and randomly beating up soldiers. They attacked a line of people in front of a base movie theater. Pretty soon all the on-base entertainment facilities were closed down and non-military people and cars were banned from the base.

OVER 100 GI'S WERE TREATED FOR INJURIES AT THE BASE HOSPITAL.

Several commanding officers are trying to get higher brass to reconsider the "benefits" of VOLAR. One of the first things they want to get rid of is beer.

Credit Union Rip-Off

MY thanks to the manager of the Fort McClellan Credit Union. After listening to the BULLSHITput out by him in training, I politely joined expecting to enjoy it's delightful benefits. Being a part time student at Jax State at times can be financially difficult so in order to purchase books i requested a loan. Might i add that I have no debt or bad credit. Anyway Iwas refused the loan on grounds that i was not 21, and therefore it was unlawful to lend to anyone under 21 (old enough to fight - young enough to get shit on). I reminded him that with a cosigner it was perfectly acceptable. He snapped back that it was against company policy and that it could not be arranged unless declared an emergency by the Red Cross.Why is he able to use GI's and their bread for personal benefit --Fucking Capitalist Pig. In other words , gimme your bread and shut up. Igot pissed and started raining hell which resulted in an immidiate offer to return my initial investment.

This is it man--wear your suit, drive your caddie and let the rest of us go to hell. Legal, yes. Fair, well that does not count.

THE REAL WAR = AS SEEN BY E.M.

TWO ACTIVE DUTY VETS STATIONED AT FORT McCLELLAN, ANSWERED THE FOLLOWING QUESTIONS ABOUT VIET NAM.

THEY CALL APON ALL FELLOW VETS TO DEMAND AN IMMEDIATE END TO THE WAR IN WHICH BOTH THE VIETNAMESE AND THEIR GI BROTHERS ARE BEING MAIMED AND KILLED. THEY ASK ALL GI'S WHO MAY BE GIVEN ORDERS TO NAM, TO READ THIS ARTICLE CARE-FULLY BEFORE DECIDING WHETHER OR NOT TO GO. BILL WAS IN VIET NAM FROM '70 TO 71 AS A GRUNT. BOB WAS THERE IN '67 AND '68 SERVING WITH BOTH INFRANTRY AND AVIATION UNITS.

WHAT DID YOU THINK YOU WERE GOING TO NAM FOR?

BOB-I had been told and believed that I was going to Nam to protect an oppressed people.

BILL-I didn't think about it much. Just wanted to do my time and get it over.

WHAT DO YOU THINK NOW?

BOB-I figure I was used to protect the interests of rich politicians big bussinessmen. Hell if I wasn't over there shooting up bullets and rockets how would Dow Chemical make its money.

BILL-Now I know that the bigwhigs in Washington used us in there power games. They sent us to try and crush the Vietnamese fight for freedom.

HOW DID MOST GI's TREAT THE VIET-NAMESE?

BOB-Pretty badly. Most of us had been taught that they were inferiors. The Army used the same racist prop-aganda that has been used against blacks in the States to make us look down on the Vietnamese and hate them. They wanted us to treat them like shit so we wouldn't know that the brass was the real enemy, and so the lifers could get over.

BILL-The Vietnamese people had every imaginable crime committed against them. The Army encouraged it.

WHAT S.O.P.s AND POLICIES DID YOUR UNIT HAVE REGARDING THE VIETNAMESE?

BILL-Well we had this gung ho Colonel who figured the way to become a gener-al was to increase the body count. He didn't care how many civilians, even kids, died, he didn't even care how many GIs died as long as he got a bigger body count.

Unit policy was to give 3 day passes to whoever killed the most people no matter who they were. Often we would grab some farmers in their fields and then the brass would fly out and give orders to kill them.

Our brigade mission was rice denial, that meant we were to take the peasants' food supplies away. If they had too much rice they were killed or sent to POW camps.

BOB-When we flew "fire fly" missions at night we had orders to kill any man woman, or child we saw. When we

VIET NAM
LOVE IT AND LEAVE

saw any body in free fire zones we were ordered to shoot to kill. After a while the guys stopped giving a damn and figured if the brass didn't give a damn, they didn't.

We did a lot of "resettlement" of Vietnamese. What that meant is we rounded up all the Vietnamese in a village and shipped them to barb-wire compounds. After they were out of their hooches we burned their homes in front of them.

WHAT DID THE VIETNAMESE FEEL ABOUT AMERICANS BEING IN VIETNAM?

BOB-It took me time to realize it but finally I realized they didn't want us in their country and were fighting us as a people to free themselves and get us out.

BILL-They seemed to feel we were hostile intruders and tried to rip off what they could from us.

HOW DID THE GIS YOU KNEW FEEL ABOUT THE WAR AND BEING IN 'NAM?

BILL-Most of the EM, didn't like having to be part of the war. We would see all this shit going on; people dying, civilians trying to stay alive and live the way they wanted to. We wondered what we were doing in 'Nam, destroying what the Vietnamese believed in and wanted. Hell, all they wanted was to be free. At least 85% of the guys, except the lifers, felt we didn't have any business there.

BOB-We saw that we were being made to destroy a whole culture. Even though we tried not to admit or think about it we knew we were fighting a beautiful and strong people, and that we we're the oppressors. We wanted to stop fighting and go home but couldn't.

HOW WAS THE MORALE IN YOUR UNITS?

BOB-Low. We wern't doing something we wanted to do. We we're doing what the brass said was right, but we knew it was wrong. We lived like shit and had to do the work while the godamn lifers got over and lived good.

BILL-It would have been lower but most of the lifers were afraid to mess with the guys, especially the dopers. Most everyone didn't give a shit after awhile. We only fired to protect ourselves except for the gugn ho, little shits and the lifers.

WHAT % OF GIS IN YOUR UNITS WE'RE INTO DOPE? WHY?

BOB-In my gun platoon almost 100% of the EM we're dopers. We did it to sleep at night and make 'Nam more bearable. It was the only thing we could do that we dug.

BILL-About 95% of my unit was into dope, about 50% we're on skag(heroin). We used it to escape 'Nam. We could feel beautiful and get away from the violence. We really were a brother-hood on dope, we could rap and get things off our minds instead of letting them grind on our brains.

WOULD YOU GO TO 'NAM AGAIN?

BOB- Not a chance. The only thing I ould fight for now is to free my self from the army and the system that made 'Nam happen. And to fight for the rights of oppressed people in this country and elsewhere.

BILL-No! GI's who havn't been to 'Nam should resist going, by every means possible. Vets should spread the real truth about 'Nam and demand an immediate end to the war. To go to 'Nam for money or cheap dope is bullshit, the only people making money are the big businesses and at least here you'll live to smoke your dope.

15

LEFT FACE
P.O. BOX 1595
ANNISTON, ALA. 36201

FREEDOM!

Abbreviations Used in This Book

ARVN	Army of the Republic of (South) Vietnam
CID	Criminal Investigation Command
CO	Commanding Officer
DMZ	Demilitarized Zone
DRV	Democratic Republic of Vietnam
IVAW	Iraq Veterans Against the War
MI	Military Intelligence
MOS	Military Occupational Specialty
MP	Military Police
NCO	Noncommissioned Officer
NGO	Nongovernmental Organization
NLF	National Liberation Front (of South Vietnam)
NVA	North Vietnamese Army
PX	Post Exchange
RTO	Radio Telephone Operator
RVN	Republic of (South) Vietnam
UXO	Unexploded Ordnance
VC	Vietcong, short for Việt Nam Cộng-sản, "Vietnamese communist", another term for the National Liberation Front of South Vietnam
VFP	Veterans For Peace
VVAW	Vietnam Veterans Against the War

Notes

Introduction

1. Robert Heinl, "The Collapse of the Armed Forces," *Armed Forces Journal*, June 7, 1971, 30.

2. Morris Janowitz, "Volunteer Armed Forces and Military Purpose," *Foreign Affairs*, April 1972, 428.

3. See the discussion of this distinction in David Cortright and Max Watts, *Left Face: Soldier Unions and Resistance Movements in Modern Armies* (Westport, CT: Greenwood Press, 1991), 19–22.

4. Howard C. Olson and R. William Rae, *Determination of the Potential for Dissidence in the U.S. Army*, Technical Paper RAC-TP-410 (McLean, VA: Research Analysis Corporation, March 1971); R. William Rae, Stephen B. Forman, and Howard C. Olson, *Future Impact of Dissident Elements Within the Army*, Technical Paper RAC-TP-441 (McLean, VA: Research Analysis Corporation, January 1972).

5. Richard Moser, *The New Winter Soldiers: G.I. and Veteran Dissent During the Vietnam Era* (New Brunswick, NJ: Rutgers University Press, 1996), 132.

6. Lawrence M. Baskir and William A. Strauss, *Chance and Circumstance: The Draft, the War, and the Vietnam Generation* (New York: Random House, 1978), 122.

7. All figures for desertion rates drawn from statistics provided to the author by the Office of the Assistant Secretary of Defense for Public Affairs, Magazine and Book Branch, 1973, as published in David Cortright, *Soldiers in Revolt: GI Resistance During the Vietnam War* (Chicago: Haymarket Books, 1975), 11–15.

8. Baskir and Strauss, *Chance and Circumstance*, 122.

9. Moser, *The New Winter Soldiers*, 80.

10. Ibid., 80.

11. Cortright, *Soldiers in Revolt*, 28–49.

12. Moser, *The New Winter Soldiers*, 132.

13. Shelby L. Stanton, *The Rise and Fall of an American Army: U.S. Ground Forces in Vietnam, 1965-1973* (Novato, CA: Presidio Press, 1985), 349.

14. "Investigation of Attempts to Subvert the United States Armed Services," *Hearings Before the Committee on Internal Security, House of Representatives*, 92nd Congress, 1st and 2nd sess., November 9, 10, 16, and 18, 1971 and May 2 and 3, 1972, 1972, II, 7051.

15. *Report by the Special Subcommittee on Disciplinary Problems in the U.S. Navy of the Committee on Armed Services, House of Representatives*, January 2, 1973, 92nd Congress, 2nd sess., 17670, 17684.

16. H. Bruce Franklin, *Crash Course: From the Good War to the Forever War* (New Brunswick, NJ: Rutgers University Press, 2018), 268–69.

17. "Air Force Takes 3 Officers Off Cambodia Runs," *New York Times*, June 6, 1973; "U.S. Judge Here Says Bombing of Cambodia Is 'Unauthorized,'" *New York Times*, July 26, 1973.

18. Michael Getler, *Washington Post*, May 31, 1973.

19. Stewart Alsop, *Newsweek*, December 7, 1970, 104.

20. "The War Within the War," *Time*, January 25, 1971, p. 44; "Army in Anguish," *Washington Post*, September 15, 1971

21. *San Francisco Examiner*, January 17, 1971.

22. Dale Van Atta, *With Honor: Melvin Laird in War, Peace, and Politics* (Madison: University of Wisconsin Press, 2008), 162.

Chapter 1

1. The author is grateful to Ron Carver for alerting her to the chronology of early efforts of resistance and peace mobilization among the military and civilians.

2. Robert D. McFadden, "Donald W. Duncan, 79, Ex-Green Beret and Early Critic of Vietnam War Is Dead," *New York Times, May 6, 2016.*

3. "The Fort Hood Three: The Case of the Three G.I.'s Who Said 'NO' to the War In Vietnam," pamphlet published by the Fort Hood Three Defense Committee, New York, New York, July 1966.

4. "Free Dr. Howard Levy," a march and rally flyer produced by the Fifth Avenue Peace Parade Committee, July 1967.

Chapter 2

1. This essay draws from some of my previous work on the GI underground press. See Derek Seidman, "Paper Soldiers: The Ally and the GI Underground Press During the Vietnam War," in *Protest on the Page: Essays on Print and the Culture of Dissent Since 1865,* ed. James L. Baughman, Jennifer Ratner-Rosenhagen, and James P. Danky (Madison, University of Wisconsin Press, 2015), 183–202; Derek Seidman, Archival Introduction to "The New Left and the Army: Let's Bridge the Gap!" Retrieved from www.viewpointmag.com.

2. David Cortright, *Soldiers in Revolt: GI Resistance during the Vietnam War* (Chicago: Haymarket Books, 2005), 55, 321.

3. James P. Danky, "The Oppositional Press," in *A History of the Book in America. Vol. 5, The Enduring Book: Print Culture in Postwar America,* ed. David Nord, Joan. S. Rubin, and Michael Schudson (Chapel Hill: University of North Carolina Press, 2009), 272–73.

4. Letter from A1C, Da Nang, *Vietnam GI*, June 1968, 2. Author's personal collection.

5. See "Lifer of the Month," *Left Face*, February 1971, 7. Accessed online at the Wisconsin Historical Society's digital GI Press Collection. *Left Face* was the GI paper published at Fort McClellan, Alabama.

6. See Skip Delano's essay in this volume.

7. See Seidman, "Paper Soldiers," in *Protest on the Page*, 183–202.

8. The Wisconsin Historical Society's digital GI Press Collection can be accessed online at http://content.wisconsinhistory.org/cdm/landingpage/collection/p15932coll8.

Chapter 3

1. David Cortright, *Soldiers in Revolt: GI Resistance During the Vietnam War* (Chicago: Haymarket Books, 1975), 12–13. Much of the material for this piece is also drawn from David Parsons, *Dangerous Grounds: Antiwar Coffeehouse and Military Dissent in the Vietnam Era* (Chapel Hill: University of North Carolina Press, 2017).

2. John Kifner, "Thousands of U.S. Troops Mobilized for Guard Duty at Democratic Convention," *New York Times,* August 25, 1968; J. Anthony Lukas, "Chicago is Prague," *New York Times*, August 25, 1968. See also Interview with Haywood T. "The Kid" Kirkland (Ari Sesu Merretazon) in Wallace Terry, *Bloods: An Oral History of the Vietnam War* (New York: Random House, 1984), 100. In the interview, one of several conversations Terry had with black GIs who refused riot duty at Chicago, Merretazon expresses a common sentiment: "I told them I'm not going there holding no weapon in front of my brothers and sisters"; "GI Black Panther Lists Motivation," *The Overseas Weekly–Pacific Edition*, May 3, 1969.

3. Fred Gardner, "Hollywood Confidential, Part I," *The Vietnam Generation Journal and Newsletter 3, no. 3 (November 1991). Available at http://www2.iath.virginia.edu/sixties/ HTML_docs/Texts/Narrative/Gardner_Hollywood_1.html.*

4. "The Covered Wagon," letter to *The New York Review of Books,* December 30, 1971. Available at https://www.nybooks.com/articles/1971/12/30/the-covered-wagon/. The letter was signed by a number of the USSF's most visible public supporters, including Noam Chomsky, Faye Dunaway, Jane Fonda, Dick Gregory, and Arthur Miller; "Visit From a Former P.O.W. George Smith," *Helping Hand*, no. 8 (February 1972). Available at http://displacedfilms.com /sir-no-sir-archive/archives_and_resources/library/articles/helping_hand_01.html; "Fort Dix Coffeehouse Bombing," USSF transcription of phone call from Leroy Townley. Townley was a member of the Fort Dix Coffeehouse collective and a witness to the incident; "Soldier Is Still Hospitalized After Bombing at Fort Dix," *New York Times,* February 17, 1970; Paul Eberle, "Dr. Levy on GI Repression," *Los Angeles Free Press,* May 15, 1970.

5. Nat Henderson, "Actress Barred from Ft. Hood," *Killeen Daily Herald*, May 12, 1970.

6. See Jerry Lembke, *The Spitting Image: Myth, Memory, and the Legacy of Vietnam (New* York: New York University Press, 1998).

Chapter 4

1. The Army, Air Force, Navy, Marines and Coast Guard all had Reserve components, and the Army and Air Force also had National Guard branches.

Chapter 6

1. FTA stood for the slogan Fun, Travel and Adventure, on Army recruitment posters; in GI slang, it stood for "Fuck the Army."

2. See Citizens Commission of Inquiry, eds. *The Dellums Committee Hearings on War Crimes in Vietnam* (New York: Vintage, 1972).

3. CCI was disbanded later that year. Jeremy Rifkin went on to organize the People's Bicentennial Commission, to promote a progressive alternative celebration of the nation's two hundredth anniversary in 1976. Tod Ensign and I formed the Safe Return Amnesty Committee and, until the Carter pardon in January 1977, campaigned for a full amnesty on behalf of those who evaded the draft and for GIs who, in unprecedented numbers, deserted the armed forces rather than support the war. An account of the work of Safe Return is available at www veteranscholar.com.

Chapter 7

1. Richard Moser, *The New Winter Soldiers: GI and Veteran Dissent During the Vietnam Era* (New Brunswick, NJ: Rutgers University Press, 1996), 80.

2. See also Robert K. Musil, "The Truth About Deserters," *The Nation*, April 16, 1973, 495–99.

3. William Short and Willa Seidenberg, with photographs by William Short, *A Matter of Conscience: GI Resistance During the Vietnam War* (Andover, MA: Addison Gallery of American Art), 16.

4. David Cortright, *Soldiers in Revolt: GI Resistance During the Vietnam War* (Chicago: Haymarket Books, 1975), 12.

Chapter 8

1. See the classic work by Wallace Terry, *Bloods, Black Veterans of the Vietnam War: An Oral History* (New York: Random House, 1984).

2. Moser, *The New Winter Soldiers: G.I. and Veteran Dissent During the Vietnam Era* (New Brunswick, NJ: Rutgers University Press, 1996), 51–52.

3. Joe Kolb, "Long Binh Jail Riot During the Vietnam War," *HistoryNet*, 6/12/2006, at http://www.historynet.com/long-binh-jail-riot-during-the-vietnam-war.htm.

4. Cecil Barr Currey, *Long Binh Jail: An Oral History of Vietnam's Most Notorious U.S. Military Prison* (Washington, DC: Potomac Books, 2001).

5. Flora Lewis, "The Rumble at Camp Lejeune," *The Atlantic*, January 1970, 35–41.

6. "Text of Camp Lejeune Committee's Report to Commanding General," *New York Times*, August 10, 1969.

7. Major Alan M. Osur, "Black-White Relations in the U.S. Military, 1940–1972," *Air University Review*, November-December 1981, at http://www.airpower.maxwell.af.mil/air chronicles/aureview/1981/nov-dec/osur.htm.

8.Senior Airman Nicole Leidholm, "Race Riots Shape Travis' History," Travis Air Force Base, news story, updated 11/8/2013, at https://www.travis.af.mil/News/Article/768141 /race-riots-shape-travis-history/.

9. A detailed account of the period before and during the *Kitty Hawk* uprising is provided in John Darrell Sherwood, *Black Sailor, White Navy: Racial Unrest in the Fleet During the Vietnam War Era* (New York: New York University Press, 2007), 55–102.

10. Quoted in Sherwood, *Black Sailor, White Navy,* 93.

11. Henry F. Leifermann, "A Sort of Mutiny: The Constellation Incident," *New York Times Magazine*, February 18, 1973, 21.

12. Sherwood, *Black Sailor, White Navy,* 157.

13. Details of the *Constellation* and *Kitty Hawk* incidents, and other episodes of enlisted resistance in the Navy are in *Report by the Special Subcommittee on Disciplinary Problems in the U.S. Navy of the Committee on Armed Services, House of Representatives,* 92nd Congress, 2nd sess., January 2, 1973, 17674–17679.

14. Sherwood, *Black Sailor, White Navy,* 163.

Chapter 9

1. *Congressional Record*, April 20, 1971, S 5116.

2. Congressional Quarterly, "Problems in the Ranks: Vietnam Disenchantment, Drug Addiction, Racism Contribute to Declining Morale," in *The Power of the Pentagon* (Washington DC: Congressional Quarterly, 1972), 22.

3. George Lepre, *Fragging: Why U.S. Soldiers Assaulted Their Officers in Vietnam* (Lubbock: Texas Tech University Press, 2011), 220.

4. Ibid., 220.

5. *Hearings Before the Defense Subcommittee of the Committee on Appropriations, House of Representatives,* 92nd Congress, 1st sess., May 17, June 10, 16, July 8, 14, August 5, September 16, 23, 1971 Part 9, 585.

6. Lepre, *Fragging*, 134–35.

7. Ibid., 136.

8. Ibid., 140.

9. Ibid., 23, 24.

10. Ibid., 24.

Chapter 10

1. Michael Maclear filmed an interview with Walter Eugene Wilber and Robert James Schweitzer in Hanoi on December 25, 1970. See Michael Maclear, "Hanoi Allows Interview with 2 P.O.W.'s," *New York Times*, December 28, 1973.

2. In more than twenty separate interviews I conducted in Hanoi and Haiphong from 2016 through 2018 with former Hoa Lo prison staff (including wardens, guards, the camp commander, the supply officer, and cooks), I received consistent reports that the food budget for a captured pilot was 60 percent greater than the food budget for a DRV Army officer, and that the pilots were provided medical treatment by the same doctors who treated Politburo members.

3. Seymour M. Hersh, "P.O.W. Who Made Antiwar Statements In Hanoi Recalls 'Pressure of Conscience,'" *New York Times*, April 2, 1973.

4. James P. Sterra, "P.O.W.'s Wife Says U.S. Killed Him," *New York Times*, June 29, 1973.

5. "The two (Miller and Wilber) retired with administrative letters of censure and *in lasting disgrace.*" (Italics added.) Stuart I. Rochester and Frederick Kiley, *Honor Bound: American Prisoners of War in Southeast Asia, 1961-1973* (Annapolis: Naval Institute Press, 2007), 568.

6. Trent Angers, *The Forgotten Hero of My Lai: The Hugh Thompson Story* (Lafayette, LA: Acadian House, 2014).

7. Seymour M. Hersh, *Reporter: A Memoir,* (New York: Knopf, 2018), 127–29.

8. Foreign Broadcast Information Service (CIA), "Captured U.S. Pilot Tells of Hope for Peace," CIA Files, reel 412, vol.29, November 1969, declassified November 24, 1981, 12, 28. Available at http://lcweb2.loc.gov/frd/pwmia/412/121834.pdf.

9. William Sloane Coffin, Jr., *Once to Every Man* (New York: Antheneum, 1977), 320.

10. David Cortright, *Soldiers In Revolt: GI Resistance During the Vietnam War (Chicago: Haymarket Books, 2005),* 35.

11. Howard Zinn, *A Peoples History of the United States: 1942 to the Present* (New York: HarperCollins, 1980), 494.

Chapter 11

1. North Vietnamese Army.

2. Leonard Guttridge, *Mutiny: A History of Naval Insurrection* (Annapolis, MD: Naval Institute Press, 1992), 255–56.

3. *Camp News,* August 15, 1972. *Camp News* was the underground newspaper for the Chicago Area Military Project. Available at http://content.wisconsinhistory.org/cdm /compoundobject/collection/p15932coll8/id/87007/rec/67.

4. *SOS News Los Angeles,* December 1972. Available at http://content.wisconsinhistory .org/cdm/compoundobject/collection/p15932coll8/id/8171/rec/4.

5. Earl Caldwell, "Kitty Hawk Back at Home Port; Sailors Describe Racial Conflict," *New York Times,* November 29,1972.

6. Guttridge, *Mutiny,* 268.

7. Everett Holles, "130 Refuse to Join Ship; Most Reassigned by Navy," *New York Times,* November 10, 1972.

8. "Navy Says Sailor Confessed He Set Blaze on Carrier," *New York Times,* November 28, 1972; "Seaman is Guilty in Carrier Blaze," *New York Times,* December 8, 1972.

9. H. Bruce Franklin, *Crash Course: From the Good War to the Forever War* (New Brunswick, NJ: Rutgers University Press, 2018), 266.

10. "Sailor is Freed by Navy Board in Trial on Sabotage of Carrier," *New York Times,* June 13, 1973; *Village Voice,* February 1, 1973.

11. Franklin, *Crash Course,* 266.

12. See Chapter Eight, as well as "The Stop Our Ship Resistance" essay in this chapter.

13. *Report by the Special Subcommittee on Disciplinary Problems in the U.S. Navy of the Committee on Armed Services, House of Representatives,* 92nd Congress, 2nd sess., January 2, 1973, 17674.

14. Max Hastings, *Vietnam: An Epic Tragedy,* 1945-1975. (New York: HarperCollins), 659–62.

15. "B-52 Pilot Who Refused Mission Calls War Not Worth the Killing," *New York Times,* January 12, 1973.

16. J. William Fulbright, Additional Letters from U.S. Airmen Involved in Cambodian Operations, *Congressional Record,* 93rd Congress, 1st sess., May 16, 1973, 15969–15970.

17. "Dear Senator … Letters from US. Flyers," *New York Times,* June 10, 1973.

18. William Shawcross, *Sideshow: Kissinger, Nixon, and the Destruction of Cambodia* (New York: Cooper Square Press), 291–94.

19. Although in a concession to President Nixon, Congress permitted the bombing of Cambodia to continue until August 15, 1973.

Chapter 12

1. See the excellent account of this movement and IVAW in Nan Levinson, *War Is Not a Game: The New Antiwar Soldiers and the Movement They Built* (New Brunswick, NJ: Rutgers University Press, 2014).

2. Nicholas D. Kristof, "The Soldiers Speak. Will President Bush Listen?" *New York Times*, February 28, 2006.

3. Quoted in Levinson, *War is Not a Game*, 128.

4. Martin Luther King, Jr., "Why I am Opposed to the War in Vietnam," sermon given at the Ebenezer Baptist Church, Atlanta, Georgia, April 16, 1967, in *A Call to Conscience: The Landmark Speeches of Dr. Martin Luther King, Jr.,* ed. Clayborne Carson and Kris Shepard (New York: Warner Books, 2001), 153.

5. A full account of the hearing and transcript of the soldier statements is available in Iraq Veterans Against the War and Aaron Glantz, *Winter Soldier Iraq and Afghanistan: Eyewitness Accounts of the Occupations* (Chicago: Haymarket Books, 2008).

6. Alice Lynd and Staughton Lynd, *Moral Injury and Nonviolent Resistance: Breaking the Cycle of Violence in the Military and Behind Bars* (Oakland, CA: PM Press, 2017).

7. I review the evidence on this in David Cortright, *Soldiers in Revolt: GI Resistance During the Vietnam War* (Chicago: Haymarket, 2005), 172–86.

Chapter 13

1. Military Occupational Specialty

Chapter 14

1. Howard Levy and the FTA show are featured in David Zeiger's film about the GI antiwar movement, *Sir! No Sir!* (Los Angeles: Displaced Films, 2005).

2. The dissertation was later published by Praeger Press. See James Lewes, *Protest and Survive: Underground GI Newspapers During the Vietnam War* (Westport, CT: Praeger Press, 2003).

3. William Short and Willa Seidenberg are coauthors of *A Matter of Conscience: GI Resistance During the Vietnam War* (Andover, MA: Addison Gallery of American Art, 1992).

Bibliography

Angers, Trent. *The Forgotten Hero of My Lai: The Hugh Thomson Story*. Lafayette, LA: Acadian Publishers, 2014.

Appy, Christian. *Working Class War: American Combat Soldiers and Vietnam*. Chapel Hill: University of North Carolina Press, 1993.

Boyle, Richard. *The Flower of the Dragon: The Breakdown of the U.S. Army in Vietnam*. San Francisco: Ramparts Press, 1972.

Citizens Commission of Inquiry, eds. *The Dellums Committee Hearing on War Crimes in Vietnam: An inquiry Into Command Responsibility in Southeast Asia*. New York: Vintage Books, 1972.

Cortright, David. *Soldiers in Revolt: GI Resistance During the Vietnam War*. Chicago: Haymarket Books, 1975.

Crowell, Joan. *Fort Dix Stockade: Our Prison Camp Next Door*. New York: Links, 1974.

Duncan, Donald. *The New Legions*. New York: Random House, 1967.

———. "The Whole Thing Was a Lie." *Ramparts*, February 1966, 12–24. Available at https://vietnamfulldisclosure.org/wp-content/uploads/2015/04/1966-02-Donald-W.-Duncan-The-Whole-Thing-Was-A-Lie-Ramparts.pdf.

Fonda, Jane. *My Life So Far*. New York: Random House, 2005.

Franklin, H. Bruce. *Crash Course: From the Good War to the Forever War*. New Brunswick, NJ: Rutgers University Press, 2018.

Gardner, Fred. *The Unlawful Concert: An Account of the Presidio Mutiny Case*. New York: Viking Press, 1970.

Heinl, Robert D., Jr. "The Collapse of the Armed Forces." *Armed Forces Journal*, June 7, 1971, 30–38.

Hutto, Jonathan W., Sr. *Antiwar Soldier: How to Dissent Within the Ranks of the Military*. New York: Nation Books, 2008.

Iraq Veterans Against the War, and Aaron Glantz. *Winter Soldier, Iraq and Afghanistan: Eyewitness Accounts of the Occupations*. Chicago: Haymarket Books, 2008.

Lembke, Jerry. *The Spitting Image: Myth, Memory, and the Legacy of Vietnam*. New York: New York University Press, 1998.

Lepre, George. *Fragging*. Lubbock: Texas Tech University Press, 2011.

Levinson, Nan. *War Is Not a Game: The New American Soldiers and the Movement They Built*. New Brunswick, NJ: Rutgers University Press, 2004.

Levy, Howard, and David Miller. *Going to Jail: The Political Prisoner*. New York: Grove Press, 1976.

Lewes, James. *Protest and Survive: Underground GI Newspapers During the Vietnam War*. Westport, CT: Praeger, 2003.

Mejía, Camilo. *The Road from Ar Ramadi: The Private Rebellion of Staff Sergeant Mejía*. New York: New Press, 2007.

Moser, Richard. *The New Winter Soldiers: GI and Veteran Dissent During the Vietnam Era*. New Brunswick, NJ: Rutgers University Press, 1996.

Musil, Robert K. "The Truth About Deserters." *The Nation*, April 16, 1973, 495–99.

Olson, Howard C., and R. William Rae. *Determination of the Potential for Dissidence in the US Army*. McLean, VA: Research Analysis Corp., 1971.

Parsons, David L. *Dangerous Grounds: Antiwar Coffeehouses and Military Dissent in the Vietnam Era*. Chapel Hill: University of North Carolina Press, 2017.

Rinaldi, Matthew. "The Olive-Drab Rebels: Military Organizing During the Vietnam Era." *Radical America* 8 (May–June 1974): 17–52.

Seidman, Derek. "Paper Soldiers: The Ally and the GI Underground Press During the Vietnam War." In *Protest on the Page: Essays on Print and the Culture of Dissent Since 1865*, edited by James L. Baughman, Jennifer Ratner-Rosenhagen, and James P. Danky, 183–202. Madison: University of Wisconsin Press, 2015.

———. "Vietnam and the Soldiers Revolt: The Politics of a Forgotten History." *Monthly Review* 68, no. 2 (June 2016): 45–57.

Sherwood, Darrell. *Black Sailor, White Navy: Racial Unrest in the Fleet During the Vietnam War Era*. New York: New York University Press, 2007.

Short, William, and Willa Seidenberg. *A Matter of Conscience: GI Resistance During the Vietnam War*. Andover, MA: Addison Gallery of American Art, 1992.

Strassfeld, Robert N. "Vietnam War on Trial: The Court-Martial of Dr. Howard B. Levy" (1994). Case Western University Law School, Faculty Publications, 551. Available at https://scholarlycommons.law.case.edu/faculty_publications/551.

Terry, Wallace, ed. *Bloods: An Oral History of the Vietnam War*. New York: Random House, 1984.

Uhl, Michael. *Vietnam Awakening: My Journey from Combat to the Citizens' Commission of Inquiry on U.S. War Crimes in Vietnam*. Jefferson, NC: McFarland, 2007.

Additional Resources

Appy, Christian. *Patriots: The Vietnam War Remembered from All Sides*. New York: Viking, 2003.

Bailey, Beth. *America's Army: Making the All-Volunteer Force*. Cambridge: Belknap Press of Harvard University Press, 2009.

Barnes, Peter. *Pawns: The Plight of the Citizen-Soldier*. New York: Knopf, 1972.

Baskir, Lawrence M., and William Strauss. *Chance and Circumstance: The Draft, the War, and the Vietnam Generation*. New York: Knopf, 1978.

Black, Samuel W. *Soul Soldiers: African Americans and the Vietnam Era*. Pittsburgh: Senator John Heinz Pittsburgh Regional History Center in association with the Smithsonian Institution, 2006.

Buzzanco, Robert. *Masters of War: Military Dissent and Politics in the Vietnam Era*. Cambridge: Cambridge University Press, 1996.

Cameron, Juan. "Our Gravest Military Problem Is Manpower." *Fortune*, April 1971, 60–63.

———. "The Armed Forces' Reluctant Retrenchment." *Fortune*, November 1970, 68.

Chapman, Jessica. *Cauldron of Resistance: Ngo Dinh Diem, The United States, and 1950s Southern Vietnam*. Ithaca, NY: Cornell University Press, 2013.

Cincinnatus. *Self-Destruction: The Disintegration and Decay of the United States Army During the Vietnam Era*. New York: W. W. Norton, 1981.

Cortright, David, and Max Watts. *Left Face: Soldier Unions and Resistance Movements in Modern Armies*. Westport, CT: Greenwood Press, 1991.

Currey, Cecil Barr. *Long Binh Jail: An Oral History of Vietnam's Most Notorious U.S. Military Prison*. Washington, DC: Potomac Books, 2001.

De Nike, Howard. *Mission (Un)Essential: Contemplations of a Civilian Court Lawyer in Military Court*. Berlin and San Francisco: Harald Kater Publishers, 2002.

Foley, Michael S. *Confronting the War Machine: Draft Resistance During the Vietnam War.* Chapel Hill: University of North Carolina Press, 2003.

Franklin, H. Bruce. *Vietnam and Other American Fantasies.* Amherst: University of Massachusetts Press, 2000.

Gabriel, Richard A., and Paul L. Savage. *Crisis in Command: Mismanagement in the Army.* New York: Hill and Wang, 1978.

Halstead, Fred. *GIs Speak Out Against the War: The Case of the Ft. Jackson 8.* New York: Pathfinder Press, 1970.

Heath, G. Louis, ed. *Mutiny Does Not Happen Lightly: The Literature of American Resistance to the Vietnam War.* Metuchen, NJ: Scarecrow Press, 1976.

Helmer, John. *Bringing the War Home: The American Soldier in Vietnam and After.* New York: Macmillan, 1974.

Hershberg, James. *Marigold: The Lost Chance for Peace in Vietnam.* Palo Alto: Stanford University Press/Wilson Center Press, 2012.

Hunt, Andrew E. *The Turning: A History of Vietnam Veterans Against the War.* New York: New York University Press, 1999.

Hunt, David. *Vietnam's Southern Revolution: From Peasant Insurrection to Total War.* Boston: University of Massachusetts Press, 2008.

Jamail, Dahr. *The Will to Resist: Soldiers Who Refuse to Fight in Iraq and Afghanistan.* Chicago: Haymarket Books, 2009.

Kirk, Donald. "Who Wants to Be the Last American Killed in Vietnam?" *New York Times Magazine*, September 19, 1971, 9. 59. 62. 66–69.

Lewis, Penny. *Hardhats, Hippies, and Hawks: The Vietnam Antiwar Movement as Myth and Memory.* Ithaca, NY: Cornell University Press, 2013.

Lifton, Robert Jay. *Home from the War: Vietnam Veterans; Neither Victims nor Executioners.* New York: Basic Books, 1973.

Linden, Eugene. "The Demoralization of an Army; Fragging and Other Withdrawal Symptoms." *Newsweek*, October 25, 1971, 67–68.

Logevall, Fredrik. *Embers of War: The Fall of an Empire and the Making of America's Vietnam.* New York: Random House, 2012.

Nicosia, Gerald. *Home to War: A History of the Vietnam Veterans' Movement.* New York: Three Rivers Press, 2001.

Nguyen, Lien-Hang. *Hanoi's War: An International History of the War for Peace in Vietnam.* Chapel Hill: University of North Carolina Press, 2012.

Prados, John. *The History of an Unwinnable War, 1945–1975.* Lawrence: University of Kansas Press, 2009.

Sherrill, Robert. *Military Justice Is to Justice as Military Music Is to Music.* New York: Harper & Row, 1970.

Small, Melvin, and William D. Hoover, eds. *Give Peace a Chance: Exploring the Vietnam Antiwar Movement.* Syracuse, NY: Syracuse University Press, 1992.

Smith, George E. *P.O.W. Two Years with the Vietcong.* San Francisco: Ramparts Press, 1971.

Stacewicz, Richard. *Winter Soldiers: An Oral History of the Vietnam Veterans Against the War.* New York: Twayne, 1997.

Stanton, Shelby. *The Rise and Fall of an American Army: U.S. Ground Forces in Vietnam, 1965–1973.* Novato, CA: Presidio Press, 1985

Stapp, Andy. *Up Against the Brass.* New York: Simon & Schuster, 1970.

Uhl, Michael. "My Lai." *Mekong Review,* February 2018, 3–6.

Uhl, Michael, and Tod Ensign. *GI Guinea Pigs: How the Pentagon Exposed Our Troops to Dangers More Deadly Than War.* New York: Playboy Press, 1980.

Weiner, Tom. *Called to Serve: Stories of Men and Women Confronted by the Vietnam War Draft.* Amherst and Florence, MA: Levellers Press, 2011.

Westheider, James E. *Brothers in Arms: The African American Experience in Vietnam.* Lanham, MD: Rowman and Littlefield, 2008.

Young, Marilyn B. *The Vietnam Wars 1945–1990.* New York: HarperCollins, 1991.

Zeiger, David. *History of the Oleo Strut Coffeehouse, 1968–1972.* Sir! No Sir! Digital Archive. Available at http://displacedfilms.com/sir-no-sir-archive/index.html

Zeiger, David, director. *Sir! No Sir!* Los Angeles: Displaced Films, 2005.

Zinn, Howard. *A People's History of the United States: 1492 to the Present.* New York: Harper-Collins, 1980.

Vietnam Poetry, Selected Works

Anderson, Doug. *The Moon Reflected Fire.* Farmington, ME: Alice James Books, 1994.

Balaban, John. *After Our War.* Pittsburgh: University of Pittsburgh Press, 1974.

———. *Locusts at the Edge of Summer: New & Selected Poems.* Port Townsend, WA: Copper Canyon, 1997.

Barry, Jan. *Earth Songs: New and Selected Poems.* Bloomington, IN: iUniverse, 2003.

Barry, Jan, Basil Paquet, and Larry Rottmann, eds. *Winning Hearts and Minds: War Poems by Vietnam Veterans.* New York: 1st Casualty Press, 1972.

Barry, Jan, and W. D. Ehrhart, eds. *Demilitarized Zones: Veterans After Vietnam.* Perkasie, PA: East River Anthology, 1976.

Bowen, Kevin, Nguyen Ba Chung, and Bruce Weigl, eds. *Mountain River: Vietnamese Poetry from the Wars.* Amherst: University of Massachusetts Press, 1998.

Brown, D. F. *Returning Fire.* San Francisco: San Francisco State University, 1984.

———. *Ghost of a Person Passing in Front of the Flag.* Houston: Bloomsday, 2018.

Casey, Michael. *Obscenities.* New Haven: Yale University Press, 1972.

Coleman, Horace. *Between a Rock and a Hard Place.* Kansas City: BkMk Press, 1977.

Connolly, David V. *Lost in America.* Silver Spring, MD: Viet Nam Generation/Burning Cities, 1994.

Ehrhart, W. D. *Beautiful Wreckage: New & Selected Poems.* Easthampton, MA: Adastra Press, 1999.

Ehrhart, W. D., ed. *Carrying the Darkness: The Poetry of the Vietnam War.* Lubbock: Texas Tech University Press, 1989.

———. *Unaccustomed Mercy: Soldier-Poets of the Vietnam War.* Lubbock: Texas Tech University Press, 1989.

Floyd, Bryan Alex. *The Long War Dead.* Sag Harbor, NY: Permanent Press, 1983.

Komunyakaa, Yusef. *Dien Cai Dau.* Middletown, CT: Wesleyan University Press, 1988.

McCarthy, Gerald. *War Story.* Berkeley: Crossing Press, 1977.

McDonald, Walter. *Caliban in Blue.* Lubbock: Texas Tech University Press, 1976.

Mahoney, Philip, ed. *From Both Sides Now: The Poetry of the Vietnam War and Its Aftermath.* New York: Scribner, 1998.

Ritterbusch, Dale. *Lessons Learned.* Silver Spring, MD: Viet Nam Generation/Burning Cities, 1995.

———. *Far from the Temple of Heaven.* Windsor, ONT: Black Moss Press, 2006.

Steptoe, Lamont B. *Uncle's South China Sea Blue Nightmare.* Alexandria, VA: Plan B Press, 1995.

Van Devanter, Lynda, and Joan Furey, eds. *Visions of War, Dreams of Peace: Writings of Women in the Vietnam War.* New York: Warner Books, 1991.

Weigl, Bruce. *Song of Napalm.* New York: Atlantic Monthly Press, 1991.

Index

Page references followed by *fig* indicate an illustration or photograph.